STUDIES IN ENGLISH LITERATURE

Volume XXIII

A QUANTITATIVE APPROACH

TO

THE STYLE OF

JONATHAN SWIFT

by

LOUIS TONKO MILIC
Columbia University

1967
MOUTON & CO.
THE HAGUE · PARIS

Printed in the Netherlands.

To the memory of my Father

ACKNOWLEDGMENTS

Professor James L. Clifford, as my chief sponsor and my guide in the Age of Swift and Johnson, has first title to my gratitude toward my elders. Professors Elliott Van Kirk Dobbie and Allen Walker Read both allowed my dissertation to interrupt their leaves of absence: for this I am grateful. To Professor Dobbie, I also express my thanks for his candor, his careful criticism and his warm sponsorship. To Professor Read, whose student I have been for fifteen years, I tender thanks for his inspiring example.

I am considerably indebted to Professor Colin L. Mallows both for his tireless advice on statistical problems and for his good grace. To Mr. Charles P. Hurd, the Registrar of the University, and Mr. Richard Gilmore, Manager of the Machine Service Division, I am grateful for the use of their valuable machines.

At the Watson Scientific Laboratories, I learned the use and value of electronic computers. To the International Business Machines Corporation, whose generosity made the installation available to the University, I offer my acknowledgments. To Dr. Kenneth King, the Director of the Laboratories, and to Mrs. Jayne Pisani, who taught me programming, I offer grateful thanks for their exceptional kindness.

I wish also to thank Professor Theodore R. Bashkow, of the School of Engineering, for putting the School's IBM 1620 computer and associated equipment at my disposal. To Mr. John N. Waddell, I am obligated, like many another researcher in the Columbia University Libraries, for his unfailing help. I must also thank Professor Inge D. Halpert for help in translating a German dissertation.

To my friend, Professor Harold E. Pagliaro, who drew all the graphs and has many other claims to my obligation – thanks multiplex. To Dr. P. L. Milic, I owe a great debt of thanks for advice and help given over a long period, including the original suggestion to use electronic machinery. To my mother, who typed the entire manuscript, a son's gratitude.

I am beholden to Mrs. Mira Merriman and Mrs. Virginia Glickstein for help in the final stages of the work. My affectionate thanks are gladly tendered to Miss Lilla M. Curley for considerable assistance with bibliography and proofreading. I am very grateful to my student, Mrs. Elizabeth MacAndrew, for extensive help with the Index.

More intangible assistance has come to me from my old friends, Professors Morroe Berger and James D. Merriman III, whom I thank for their invisible shares in this work.

To the Dean of Graduate Faculties, who gave me a grant of five hundred dollars for research expenses, I offer this belated thank you. I am glad to acknowledge the aid of the Committee on Publication of the Faculty of Philosophy, Columbia University.

Louis T. Milic

New York
April 10, 1966

TABLE OF CONTENTS

LIST OF TABLES

LIST OF FIGURES

INTRODUCTION

I have always loved Swift's work. The playfulness, the irony and ultimately the seriousness engaged me in that order. His toying with language, especially in the third book of *Gulliver's Travels* and in particular the language frame (so reminiscent of a computer programmed to "generate" English sentences), struck me as the perception of a man to whom the mysterious relation between symbol and thing was intuitively clear. The effectiveness of his own writing, the author's obvious ranking of grammatical propriety below the conveyance of meaning, reinforced my admiration for his intelligence. Then I became aware of his reputation as a purist and aware also of his occasional pronouncements about propriety and decorum in language. It seemed impossible to reconcile these formalistic tendencies with my earlier estimate of the man, though the idea of the master ironist pulling his reader's leg did not fail to occur to me. But there was no escaping the paradox: Swift the writer and Swift the rhetorician were two different persons.

To account for this division, I speculated that except for the superficial traits of composition the writer wrote without the approval of the rhetorician; almost in spite of him, wrote the way he would because he could not help it. In other words, I postulated the possibility of a writer's style as an unconscious reflection of his mind and personality. In the case of Swift, these influences were bound to be so forceful and constant that they would permeate all his writing more or less uniformly, except when the rhetorician was in the writer's seat, as in the *Proposal for Correcting . . . the English Tongue*. If this hypothesis was correct, the uniformity of the style might be detected by a close examination of those features over which the rhetorician had been unable to exert his influence, namely, the grammatical structure. It is not surprising that Swift consciously respected his own literary judgment. But it is surely curious that he thought of himself as Swift the rhetorician and equally strange that his contemporaries and a long line of commentators down to the present day have shared this mistaken opinion.

The regularity with which Swift's style has been accepted at his own valuation of praiseworthy writing moved me to wonder whether these critics, in commenting on his style, has said anything which could be observed and verified. I found almost nothing but adjectives: *clear, simple, direct, masculine, hard, round, salty, nervous, lucid,* and the like evasions. There was agreement that Swift's style was good but the agreement was uninformative and the criticism without interest. It seemed to me that these readers had formed partial responses to his work on the basis of passages that impressed them. I wondered whether it might not be possible to discard the picture of Swift the rhetorician and address myself to the writer's work exclusively. This I proposed to do on the basis of my assumption about the unconscious nature of a mature writer's style. The style, I suggest, contains a uniform and constant diffusion of his mind and personality, expressed through certain grammatical categories which may be measured objectively.

These categories are grammatical, rather than lexical, because the rhetorician has his eye on the diction and is always to be found issuing pronouncements about it or fussing with it after the writer has laid the words on the paper. An author's favorite expressions, in any case, are dear to him and after he has made them up, he is likely not only to use them but to persuade his friends to do likewise: Swift was very proud of his belittling prefix "hedge". The opportunity to use such favorites may not always occur, of course; the same is true of his vocabulary at large. This is in a large degree dictated by the context and the genre of composition. Any study of vocabulary, therefore, is likely to result in a predictable but useless variability. Grammatical categories are not affected in the same way. During his period of apprenticeship, a writer develops a certain variety of structures, strictly his own, which he continues to use and re-use with scarcely any change during the period of his mature writing. It is like his handwriting, unmistakably his but almost beyond his power to modify to any significant extent. In his grammar lies the key to his style, provided the proper categories for investigation can be developed.

That finding these should be easy is hardly to be expected. The writing process is still very mysterious; very little is known about it and it seems unlikely that the solution should be simple. But that at least a preliminary solution can be found seems to me inevitable. Such a solution would comprise an objective description of these submerged characteristics of the style in quantitative terms, precise enough to enable the student to identify the writer. Thus, I would expect to be able to separate Swift from Johnson and even from Addison.

The use of quantitative methods, supported by the use of an electronic computer, and with an apparatus of figures, tables and charts, raises an issue of some importance. For though it has become unnecessary to apologize for the quantitative approach – it has shown its usefulness even in fields to which it formerly was strange – the implication that the artist's work can be compassed in measurable quantities needs to be faced.

It is not my belief that everything of importance about a writer's performance can be identified, much less measured. I am even willing to admit that the measurable may turn out to be peripheral or secondary, though I would hope that this were not so. But I would say in my defense that the process of measuring is not autotelic: its ends are literary, bound to a fundamental interest in the writer and his work. And the mechanical process is always preceded by a knowledge of the text and accompanied by a devotion to its literary qualities. Moreover, in this method, before anything is counted or measured, the same critical intellectual process, the same sort of intuition, takes place, as in the usual literary study.

As my reader knows, measurement is nothing new in literary

work. Every responsible scholar who makes a statement about
the density of metaphor in Shakespeare or the number of military
characters in his plays, makes some kind of numerical estimate
about his material. Even a reference to likelihood, casually or
seriously made, implies a numerical probability. The substitution
of precise for approximate statements of quantity cannot be considered a very serious failing.

Nor should it be inferred that I have reduced the writer to the
status of a mere unconscious producer, with no control over his
mind's intention and effect. In an important sense Swift the
writer is always under the influence of Swift the stylist, a happy
derivative of Swift the rhetorician. In certain aspects of composition, the unconscious writer rules, but I have no wish to deny him
his autonomous conscious role in the selection and design of his
work. It is this conscious forceful being who is after all the subject
of any Swift study.

Appropriately enough, this study opens with a review of the
criticism elicited by Swift's style from his time to ours. The many
senses in which the word *style* has been used during that period
lead to an attempt at definition in the second chapter. After a
formal statement of my own assumptions and the procedure which
is based on them, I proceed to the examination of the style itself,
moving from the most clearly observable phenomena to those
which require the most delicate nicety of technique. The sum of
my observations about the style of Swift and his literary peers is
tested by reference to the case of a contested work, *A Letter of
Advice to a Young Poet*, which has been admitted into the canon,
ejected from it, and finally relegated to a limbo of dubious attributions by successive editors of Swift. It is my hope to add a
measure of certainty to the status of this piece.

But whether I succeed in carrying conviction on this point or
not, I shall feel that I have succeeded in my aims if I have collected a body of verifiable information about Swift, as well as about
those who are his companions in this research, and if by my proposed method I have forwarded by even one step the study of
style and the study of Swift.

The stress on method is evident in my title "A Quantitative

Approach to the Style of Jonathan Swift". I have not hoped to give a full or a conventional literary description of Swift's style. My intention has been deliberately partial and quantitative because only within those limits could I hope to accomplish what I had set out to do.

I. THE REPUTATION OF SWIFT'S PROSE STYLE

The style of Jonathan Swift has always attracted attention and the reputation of his prose, purely as language, has had a comforting stability. Not all reputations fare so well. Many authors, during their lives and later, fluctuate in public esteem like commodities on a financial exchange. But Swift and especially his prose have maintained the status of blue chips. This is not to say that their level has always been the same, but it has always been high in the opinion of most readers and critics.[1] Though Addison in one period, Johnson in another, and doubtless others at various times, have achieved the topmost place, Swift has always been among the leaders, and during the twentieth century his prose has surely received more praise than any other in English. The most cursory inspection of anthologies, histories of literature, manuals and guidebooks, not to mention specialized studies of English prose, must surely lead to such a conclusion. An anthology of English prose which did not award Swift a major place would be inconceivable today.[2] It is probable that no great prose writer

---

[1] See Donald M. Berwick, *The Reputation of Jonathan Swift, 1781-1882* (Philadelphia, 1941), passim.
[2] A survey of some twentieth-century collections will support this position. Henry S. Pancoast, ed., *Standard English Prose,* 2d. rev. ed. (New York, 1905), gives Swift 24 pages, compared with 15 for Addison, 13 for Dryden, 25 for Johnson, 26 for Burke and Carlyle, 28 for Arnold, and 53 for Macaulay. Herbert Read and Bonamy Dobrée, ed., *The London Book of English Prose* (London, 1932), in selections of a page or two, give 4 to Swift, Gibbon, Hazlitt, Johnson, Milton, Newman and the Bible, but only one to Addison. In *An Oxford Anthology of English Prose,* ed. Arnold Whitridge and John Wendell Dodds (New York, 1937), Swift receives 38 pages, Addison 10, Johnson 23, Gibbon 5, Hazlitt 40, Carlyle

has been more widely read.[3] In the words of Herbert Read, "the continued vitality of [his] style is a great consolation to the theorist",[4] even though that vitality may be nourished largely in the nursery.

But critics since Swift's day have not been content merely to praise his prose style: they have in a variety of ineffective ways attempted to characterize, describe and analyze it. For the most part, they have gone about it with directness and assurance.

Lord Orrery sounded the dominant themes for most of his successors: clarity, propriety, simplicity. Because he had known Swift personally and because he was first in the field, his comments carried great weight. Nothing, however, could have been more damaging to an accurate understanding of Swift's literary style than his Olympian praise:

His style was masterly, correct, and strong: never diffusive, yet always clear; and, if we consider it in comparison with his predecessors, he has outdone them all, and is one, perhaps the chief, of those few select English writers, who have excelled in elegance and propriety of language.[5]

Orrery did not offer to particularize these points of praise because he felt secure that they would not be challenged. In this aspect of Swift's reputation, as in others, Orrery's word became almost the gospel.[6] Before Johnson, one writer and critic after

75, and Arnold 62. In a recent anthology, *Eighteenth-Century Prose, 1700-1800,* ed. D. W. Jefferson (Harmondsworth, 1956), which consists of short extracts, Swift is represented by six pieces, more than Addison, Fielding, Hume, Goldsmith, Gibbon or Johnson. It is surely significant, too, that these editors all select different passages.

[3] Apart from the Bible (a translation), there is generally only one book which it is possible to suppose that everyone in the English-speaking world has read and that book is *Gulliver's Travels.* It must be admitted that *Robinson Crusoe* is a contender for the honor and at one time *Pilgrim's Progress* would have outstripped both.

[4] *English Prose Style* (Boston, 1955), p. xiii.

[5] John, Earl of Orrery, *Remarks on the Life and Writings of Dr. Jonathan Swift* (London, 1752), p. 234.

[6] Orrery's book was extremely popular and influential. Berwick (p. 7) wonders whether the nineteenth-century view of Swift as inhuman could have developed if Orrery's book had not been published.

another dutifully echoed Orrery's laudatory generalities, with barely noticeable variations and scarcely any difference of opinion.[7] Only two detractors, Goldsmith and Hume, dared to deviate from the tradition, and they raised interesting issues.

Goldsmith, in a passage in which he compares Swift to Charles D'Avenant and a certain Trenchard, both political pamphleteers of the period, takes a position far from the main road:

They were followed by Dean Swift, who, though in other respects far their superior, never could arise to that manliness and clearness of diction in political writing for which they were so justly famous.[8]

Goldsmith adds that all three were exceeded by Bolingbroke, whose style was excellent, though he did not understand the subjects he wrote on. It is questionable whether Goldsmith's implied definition of style has much to contribute to this investigation. But the slurs on both the clarity and the manliness of Swift seem to require explanation. Why did Goldsmith wish to deny to Swift what everyone so readily granted him? Like Johnson, he may have transferred a dislike of Swift the man to his works; or he may, at least with respect to the "manliness", have been alluding to the theory of Swift's physical impotence.[9] At any rate, since Goldsmith does not offer any elucidation of the unmanly diction, the comment may be disregarded in its substance and merely recorded as an instance of the perverseness of impressionistic descriptions of style.

Scarcely any more importance attaches to Hugh Blair's comment, which returns to Swift the manliness that Goldsmith would have denied him, but Blair is at least in the center of the tradition:

He is esteemed one of our most correct writers. His Style is of the

---

[7] "On one point ... most commentators agree. The excellence of Swift's dry, severe, concise style, his superb control of word and tempo, are only once questioned in the pre-Johnsonian era – and then by the Scotchman, David Hume" (Berwick, p. 16). Goldsmith must be added to this minority, but he was an Irishman. Among those who continued in Orrery's wake were Delany, Deane Swift, Beattie, Shenstone and Gray.

[8] Oliver Goldsmith, *The Bee,* No. VIII, in *The Works of Oliver Goldsmith,* ed. P. Cunningham (New York, 1881), III, 138.

[9] This was first suggested in print by Orrery, p. 113.

plain and simple kind; free from all affectation, and all superfluity; perspicuous, manly, and pure. These are its advantages. But we are not to look for much ornament and grace in it.[10]

By the time of Blair, praise of Swift's style included references to his lack of ornament and elegance, qualities which the writings of Johnson and Gibbon were thought to contain.[11]

Although Gibbon in his *Decline* did not try to write like Swift, he formed his style on those of Swift and Addison:

By the judicious advice of Mr. Mallet, I was directed to the writings of Swift and Addison; wit and simplicity are their common attributes: but the style of Swift is supported by manly original vigour; that of Addison is adorned by the female graces of elegance and mildness.[12]

It may be that this tribute to Swift's manliness is only the consequence of Gibbon's love of antithesis, but the praise of simplicity and vigor is by now standard.

A self-consciousness about Scotticisms and a great interest in language doubtless made Hume a severer critic than an English Hume might have been, and it is understandable that he castigated Swift in defiance of the English.[13] Some of his criticisms, however, merely anticipate the Johnsonian formulation:

I know your affection for *wherewith* proceeds from your partiality to Dean Swift, whom I can often laugh with, whose style I can even approve, but surely can never admire. It has no harmony, no eloquence, no ornament and not much correctness, whatever the English may imagine.[14]

[10] *Lectures on Rhetoric and Belles Lettres,* 4th ed. (London, 1790), II, 144. This book was first published in 1783.
[11] According to the findings of William Kenney, the preferred quality of prose during the late eighteenth century was energy. Addison was considered especially deficient in this, his style being variously called "weak", "feeble", "enervated", whereas Johnson's was "vehement", "forcible", "nervous". In this context, Johnson's praise of Addison must be recognized as lukewarm ("Addison, Johnson, and the 'Energetick' Style", *Studia Neophilologica,* XXXIII (1961), 103-114).
[12] *The Memoirs of the Life of Edward Gibbon,* ed. G. B. Hill (London, 1900), p. 122.
[13] A discussion of the interesting question of Scotticism may be found in the apparatus of *Boswell's Life of Johnson,* ed. G. B. Hill, rev. L. F. Powell (Oxford, 1934-1950), I, 439, fn. 2 and Appendix G, p. 549.
[14] *Letters of Hume,* ed. J. Y. T. Greig (Oxford, 1932), II, 194.

The most interesting item in this list of aspersions is that dealing with correctness. For the most part, Swift was accepted as a model of propriety, although a number of grammarians took exception to some of his constructions.[15] Hume's keen awareness here may have originated from his study of English as "a dead language", a procedure that often yields a higher notion of correctness than is common among vernacular speakers.[16]

Despite their literary eminence, neither Hume nor Goldsmith had much personal effect on the course of Swift's literary reputation. But Johnson's measured praise of Swift's style revealed that a change of critical ideals of prose style had taken place, a change which must entail the consequent revaluation of Swift as a stylist:

In his other works [aside from *A Tale of a Tub*, which Johnson considers unique and above Swift's other productions] is found an equable tenour of easy language, which rather trickles than flows. His delight was in simplicity . . . He studied purity; and though perhaps all his structures are not exact, yet it is not often that solecisms can be found: and whoever depends on his authority may generally conclude himself safe. His sentences are never too much dilated or contracted; and it will not be easy to find any embarrassment in the complication of his clauses, any inconsequence in his connections, or abruptness in his transitions.

His style was well suited to his thoughts, which are never subtilised by nice disquisitions, decorated by sparkling conceits, elevated by ambitious sentences, or variegated by far-sought learning. He pays no court to the passions; he excites neither surprise nor admiration; he always understands himself, and his reader always understands him: the peruser of Swift wants little previous knowledge; it will be sufficient that he is acquainted with common words and common things; he is neither required to mount elevations nor to explore profundities; his passage is always on a level, along solid ground, without asperities, without obstruction.

This easy and safe conveyance of meaning it was Swift's desire to attain, and for having attained he deserves praise, though perhaps

---

[15]   Hugh Blair, Horne Tooke and others may be found mentioned in Sterling A. Leonard, *The Doctrine of Correctness in English Usage, 1700-1800* (Madison, 1929), pp. 251 ff.

[16]   This tendency is equally observable in foreign students of English, whose knowledge of formal grammar is usually superior to that of native speakers. The point about English as a dead language is made in the material referred to in footnote 13.

not the highest praise. For purposes merely didactick, when something is to be told that was not known before, it is the best mode, but against that inattention by which known truths are suffered to lie neglected it makes no provision; it instructs, but does not persuade.[17]

From 1781 to the latter end of the nineteenth century, this conception of Swift's style as *merely* pure, simple and clear stands out against a generalized background of praise in the older tradition.[18] To Johnson, Swift's virtues as a writer are virtues of little consequence, virtues it was not worth cultivating. But even Johnson, for all his reservations, felt that these virtues were generally recognized and had achieved the force of a received opinion.

With an irony that Swift might have appreciated, the low point in the reputation of his style coincided with the notable edition of his works produced by Walter Scott in 1814. The Augustans were no longer admired or even much read.[19] The great period of English prose was now seen to be the Jacobean, and the special heroes of the Romantic period were Taylor, Hobbes, and Barrow.

Coleridge, though willing to do justice to Swift, was fully in accord with this trend, against what he considered to be the prevailing opinion: "From the common opinion that the English style attained its greatest perfection in and about Queen Anne's reign I altogether dissent." [20] Though Hooker and Taylor could not be matched, in a lower sphere Swift might be recognized: "Swift's style is, in its line, perfect; the manner is a complete expression of the matter, the terms appropriate, and the artifice concealed. It is simplicity in the true sense of the word." [21] The

[17] Samuel Johnson, "Swift", in *Lives of the Poets,* ed. G. B. Hill (Oxford, 1905), III, 51-52.
[18] "Much the same sentiments [about the excellence of Swift's style] have been repeated time and again since . . . The idea of 'proper words in proper places' becomes a shibboleth in the history of Swift criticism; and the student eventually grows to welcome even the slightest defection from the common opinion" (Berwick, pp. 47-8).
[19] "Addison and Swift are now not at all read; Johnson and Gibbon very rarely; – yet Swift is the best writer that ever was, in his peculiar style." Robert James Mackintosh, ed. *Memoirs of the life of . . . Sir James Mackintosh* (London, 1835), II, 475, entry dated 1830.
[20] Samuel Taylor Coleridge, *Select Poetry and Prose,* ed. Stephen Potter (London, 1933), p. 319.
[21] *Ibid.*

term "perfect" is new but will continue to be seen in this context. Simplicity, true or other, has hardly had a moment's respite.

The reviewer of Scott's edition in 1816 espoused less elevated but similar ideals: "Junius and Johnson [were] the first who again familiarized us with more glowing and sonorous diction – and made us feel the tameness and poorness of the serious style of Addison and Swift." [22] Although Jeffrey admits that Swift was the most vigorous writer of his time, he goes further than Johnson in denigrating his style:

> Of his style, it has been usual to speak with great, and, we think, exaggerated praise. It is less mellow than Dryden's – less elegant than Pope's or Addison's – less free and noble than Lord Boling-broke's – and utterly without the glow and loftiness which belonged to our earlier masters. It is radically a low and homely style – without grace, and without affectation; and chiefly remarkable for a great choice and profusion of *common* words and expressions.[23]

However out of fashion Jeffrey's comment may seem today, it is recognizably in accord with the critical tendency of his epoch and it has an interior consistency. But De Quincey's perverse and capricious argument, though it proceeds from the same aesthetic source, seems to court illogic in order to discredit Swift's merits. Arguing that Swift's style was not a model of excellence, De Quincey proposes three points: Swift's merit is merely "ver-nacularity", or lack of artifice; whatever excellence he had was shared by his contemporaries (Defoe, Dampier); like them, he wrote on subjects specially suited to his simple, dull, unadorned style. But if he had had to emulate Taylor or Browne, his real limitations would have appeared.[24] After this, the trend to detrac-tion more or less ends and the standard view proceeds unhampered till modern times.

In retrospect, all these commentators, praisers and detractors alike, have some things in common. They seem to agree in the terms they apply to Swift's style (*simple, clear, vigorous*), though

[22]   Francis Jeffrey, *Edinburgh Review*, XXVII (September 1816), p. 8.
[23]   *Ibid.*, p. 56.
[24]   Thomas De Quincey, *Tait's Magazine* (September 1847), in *Collected Works* (London, 1890), XI, 17-18.

none go to any trouble to specify the extension of these figurative terms [25] or even to illustrate with examples. It is difficult not to conclude that they agree mainly because of their preconceptions, their willingness to accept the prevailing opinion without trying to verify it by a detailed examination of the style itself. The perpetuation of the tradition that Swift's style was simple, clear, vigorous, by means of a self-hypnotic unconscious plagiarism can be explained by reference to three factors.[26]

The difficulty of discussing style except as synonymous with diction is evident in nearly all these writings. That this is a consequence of the classical division of styles according to the level of the words is equally self-evident. Consequently, the vaguest references to certain abstract qualities (for example, simplicity) satisfied all concerned. When a more individual judgment was required, some metaphors could be invoked (grace, manliness). But the necessity of specifying qualities which were difficult to isolate was circumvented by the simple proceeding of identifying the style that one approved of with the ideals of style then current. Swift's style was called simple, clear and vigorous in part because there was general agreement that Swift's style was good and because simplicity, clarity and vigor were good qualities for a style to have. When these qualities were no longer valued so highly and Swift's style was no longer quite so well thought of, denigratory variants of these qualities were applied: *homely, common, plain, poor*. At no time was an attempt made to discover what simplicity in style consisted of or how it could be illustrated with quotations

[25] Descriptions of style almost by necessity use terms figuratively. A *low* style, for example, is not such by virtue of anything it contains but only by comparison with some imagined scale. If a *simple* style were one which consisted of simple sentences, that would be a literal description. But since a simple style is intended to be compared to other simple ("once-folded") things, as distinguished from complex (or "braided") things, it may be seen that the metaphorical extension is considerable. When the terms used involve such non-literary conceptions as limpidity, masculinity, energy, nervousness, the interpreter's task is beyond aid.
[26] Sometimes the plagiarism could be overt. William Monck Mason, in *The History ... of St. Patrick* (Dublin, 1820), presents as his own a condensed version of Johnson's comment in *The Life of Swift* (ed. cit., p. 51) on the variety of Swift's style (pp. 431-2). Berwick quotes this without comment (p. 82).

from the pages of Swift's works. This was felt to be unnecessary because the whole issue had been settled by Swift himself. In a variety of places in his works, Swift had allowed himself to express his ideals of style: "that Simplicity, which is one of the greatest Perfections in any Language",[27] "Their Stile is clear, masculine, and smooth, but not Florid; for they avoid nothing more than multiplying unnecessary Words, or using various Expressions",[28] "They are expressed in the most plain and simple Terms",[29] "I should be glad to see you the Instrument of introducing into our Style, that Simplicity which is the best and truest Ornament of most Things in human Life . . .",[30] "I rather chose to relate plain Matter of Fact in the simplest Manner and Style . . .",[31] "Two Things I will just warn you against . . . flat, unnecessary Epithets; and . . . old, thread-bare Phrases . . ."[32] The fact that personal ideals of style need not coincide with actual practice regularly escapes all those who consider an author the best critic and final authority on his own work. Ideals of style are goals toward which the writer is striving, not accurate descriptions of his practice. Moreover, as will be shown, the mechanism of style-production is mainly unconscious and beyond the reach of any voluntary modification resulting from the application of abstract ideals. In view of these factors, it is difficult to escape the conclusion that most of the criticism of Swift's style until the twentieth century has been of very little value.

In the late nineteenth century, the impressionistic descriptions take on more color but they make no especial contribution to the understanding of Swift's style. To be sure, the themes of simplicity, clarity and vigor continue to be heard but the combinations give the appearance of novelty. There is the beginning of an awareness that the old tradition of generalities is useless, but the new material

---

[27]   *Proposal*, in *The Prose Writings of Jonathan Swift*, ed. Herbert Davis (Oxford, 1939-in progress), IV, 15. All citations of Swift, unless otherwise indicated, are to this edition (hereafter called *Works*).
[28]   *Gulliver, Works,* XI, 121.
[29]   *Ibid.*, 120.
[30]   *Tatler*, 230, *Works*, II, 177.
[31]   *Gulliver, Works*, XI, 275.
[32]   *Letter to a Young Gentleman, Works*, IX, 68.

comes from the same old bin. Samuel Butler, surely a disciple of
Swift in spirit, with typical perversity dismisses the necessity of
taking pains with style: "I never knew a writer yet who took the
smallest pains with his style and was at the same time readable." [33]
But he admits that the writer should be concerned about the
reader's convenience. Though he points out that a terse style may
be more fatiguing than a diffuse one,[34] a point applicable to an
understanding of Swift, he concludes more or less in the usual
fashion: "Swift is terse, he gets through what he has to say on
any matter as quickly as he can and takes the reader on to the
next." [35]

Twentieth-century criticism begins tamely enough with a few
comments by G. A. Aitken in *The Cambridge History of English
Literature*. Aitken re-introduces the notion of perfection, dormant
since Coleridge but soon to have a great vogue, in addition to the
usual reference to clarity and precision. He also borrows some
terms applicable to the person of Swift to describe the style, which
he calls forceful and grave.[36] This kind of transfer or interchange
between the qualities of the man and his work, though practiced
in a small way by Goldsmith, Gibbon and their contemporaries,
is now to provide a device for seeming to talk about style without
actually doing so. For example, Brownell comments on the lack of
warmth he perceived in Swift's character.[37] His comment departs
from convention when he notices that Swift's "simplicity is more
highly organized than superficially appears".[38] This observation
represents such a break with tradition that it is easy to understand
why it passed unnoticed. It is far from rejecting the attribute of
simplicity, but it is a start toward understanding.

Herbert Read's study of English style, which appeared midway
between the World Wars (not a period of great sanity), supports

[33]   *Samuel Butler's Notebooks,* ed. Geoffrey Keynes and Brian Hill (London, 1951), p. 290. A conjectural date for these comments is 1897.
[34]   *Ibid.,* p. 66. In the context in which it occurs, this point seems unrelated to the Ciceronian-Senecan opposition.
[35]   *Ibid.,* p. 287.
[36]   "Swift" in *The Cambridge History of English Literature,* ed. A. W. Ward and A. R. Waller, IX (Cambridge, 1912), 128.
[37]   William C. Brownell, *The Genius of Style* (New York, 1924), pp. 112-3.
[38]   *Ibid.,* p. 112.

a claim for Swift's rank as a stylist of unrivalled power and interest with a compound of references to simplicity, clarity and purity illustrated with examples. His main statement is remarkably sweeping and the appositive in the second sentence remarkably obscure:

Swift is the only one of [those] prose writers in whom we may confidently expect no organic and inevitable lapses. The prose style of Swift is unique, an irrefrangible instrument of clear, animated, animating and effective thought. English prose has perhaps attained here and there a nobler profundity, and here and there a subtler complexity; but never has it maintained such a constant level of inspired expression.[39]

Behind the "irrefrangible instrument" and "animated, animating" thought are two things: a desire to claim a measure of perfection for Swift and an inability to do so with existing means of description. If the result is obscurity, there is at least a gain over the easy "simple" explanation. The use of telling examples is a step toward objective description. All in all, however, the yield is not substantial in facts about Swift's style. For some of these it will be necessary to examine the results of more professional scholars. The findings of those who take up style on the way to something else are alike in their failure to produce anything concrete.

A herd of impressionistic images elbow each other in the critical biography of Swift by W. D. Taylor, the tenth chapter of which purports to be (but is not) entirely about Swift's style: "it is hard round crystalline", "like an athlete sweated down to sinew and muscle who knows how to reach his goal"; "it is *the* nervous style".[40] This is not very informative, and one concludes after reading that Taylor had a high opinion of Swift's style but no very good idea of how to express it. But to read the comments of the novelist Maugham is to wonder whether he is talking about another writer altogether. Maugham is explaining how he trained himself to become a good writer by practising on *A Tale of a Tub:*

The prose of Swift enchanted me. I made up my mind that this was

---

[39]   *English Prose Style*, p. xiii.
[40]   W. D. Taylor, *Jonathan Swift* (London, 1933), p. 255.

the perfect way to write ... [But] it is a tiresome allegory and the irony is facile. But the style is admirable. I cannot imagine that English can be better written. Here are no flowery periods, fantastic turns of phrase or high-flown images. It is a civilized prose, natural, discreet and pointed. There is no attempt to surprise by an extravagant vocabulary. It looks as though Swift made do with the first word that came to hand, but since he had an acute and logical brain it was always the right one, and he put it into the right place. The strength and balance of his sentences are due to an exquisite taste ... I found that the only possible words were those Swift had used and that the order in which he had placed them was the only possible order. It is an impeccable prose.

But perfection has one grave defect: it is apt to be dull. Swift's prose is like a French canal ... Its tranquil charm fills you with satisfaction, but it neither excites the emotions nor stimulates the imagination. You go on and on and presently you are a trifle bored. So, much as you may admire Swift's wonderful lucidity, his terseness, his naturalness, his lack of affectation, you find your attention wandering after a while ...[41]

And so, allowing Swift to bore him, Maugham takes up Dryden whom he proceeds to describe impressionistically.

But it may be unfair to expect critical responsibility from an admitted amateur critic. On the other hand, when a writer presents himself with the credentials of an expert and writes a book called *Style*, as F. L. Lucas does, it may be just to expect something more than mere imagery. However, only imagery is provided:

Luckily for us, the style of Swift himself was a good deal more than proper – or improper – words in proper places. Into its ruthlessly swept and garnished body there entered the spirits of scorn and hate and pride and indignation, but also of courage and independence, of frustrated affection and even of something like compassion.[42]

It cannot be supposed that these "spirits" can actually be detected as formal elements in the style; one must assume that Lucas put them there. He proceeds to lament Swift's lack of those images that charm rather than wound: "That is partly why, to me, he is

---

[41] W. Somerset Maugham, *The Summing-Up* (New York, 1957 [1938]), pp. 20-1.
[42] (London, 1955), p. 126.

on the whole an unattractive writer – bleak, monotonous, and depressing, though impressive, like a Pennine moorland – not like the Highlands." [43] As is easily seen, Lucas's fondness for imagery is betrayed in each of these comments; he does not so much criticize Swift's prose for what it is as he rebuilds it as he would like it to be, most plainly when he denies that he is doing so, as in this final comment:

It is idle to wish, as Swift trots like a lean gray wolf, with white fangs bared, across his desolate landscape, that he were more like a benevolent St. Bernard; he would cease to be Swift. Being what he was, he made a striking addition to the infinite variety of the world; but one Swift seems to me quite enough. And his style is of interest as showing both what trenchancy the presence of imagery can give, and how much charm and colour its absence takes away. [44]

The vagueness of this kind of criticism is not mitigated by the false concreteness of animal or landscape similes. Nothing is told that is of any value. It is not because it is subjective that it is valueless but because the subjectivity is irresponsible, general and misty.

After a string of disconcerting generalities, [45] it is a welcome surprise to find in Wilson Knight's criticism of Swift's irony several concrete references to the actual details of style: "Swift's narrative may seem colourless [in *A Tale of a Tub*], but the materials within are not. The plainness consists rather in continual emphasis on noun and verb with rejection of the *qualifying* adjective." [46] In fact, Swift's satire operates in a simple description of action: "Having the right nouns ready, he has only to attach the verb." [47] Swift's "fine use of the active verb" [48] is everywhere evident, the best point being made in action statements. In *Battle of the Books,* he relies on "concrete nouns and active verbs with

---

[43] *Ibid.,* pp. 209-210.
[44] *Ibid.,* p. 210.
[45] "Swift's prose is noted for control and reserve. He is a master of lucidity and understatement." G. Wilson Knight, "Swift and the Symbolism of Irony", *The Burning Oracle* (London, 1939), p. 115.
[46] *Ibid.,* p. 117.
[47] *Ibid.,* p. 119.
[48] *Ibid.,* p. 122.

scarcely an adjective to assist".[49] It is good to come finally to nouns and verbs and adjectives, even though Knight has no figures to assist his observations. Does he mean that Swift uses nouns and verbs and fewer adjectives than average? Are active verbs merely transitive verbs? How many is *scarcely* and are qualifying adjectives descriptive or limiting? Obviously there can be no answer to these questions because Knight's reference to these grammatical details is the result of subjective impression and not of exact study. Still the realization that style must be talked about in terms of its actual mechanisms constitutes a significant advance, however unsatisfactory the immediate results. At least there is an awareness that Swift used verbs, nouns, and adjectives rather than simplicity and purity and clarity as the vehicles of his expression.

Interest in the particulars of style, however, does not make much progress in the work of those who might be called theoretical students of style — those who take up the matter of Swift's style incidentally or as subsidiary to some larger purpose, those at any rate who are not considering style as a practical matter. It is necessary to look to those who have an axe to grind if we are to find much regular or systematic reference to grammatical categories and to particular words or expressions. These are the students of Swift's canon. Their purpose is the attribution of some new work to Swift (or the rejection of an accepted or dubious work) by internal evidence.

Despite the appearance of exactness produced by the citation of relevant passages and the sometimes extensive parallels offered as evidence, most scholars are suspicious of the method of internal evidence and resort to it only in desperation. The general distrust of internal evidence usually attaches to the method itself but it actually arises in all probability from the practices of those who have used it. That this distrust has some basis can be shown by considering the demonstrations offered in connection with the few canon problems in Swift bibliography.

About Swift's major productions there is now scarcely any doubt. To be sure, Johnson questioned whether Swift could have

49   *Ibid.*, p. 130.

been the author of *A Tale of a Tub* [50] and the *History of the Four Last Years of the Queen* was considered uncertain for a long time,[51] but neither of these works is now suspected. About certain minor items some doubt has arisen. Herbert Davis, the most recent editor of the Prose Works, in line with his conception of the canon-problem in Swift editing as the exclusion from the canon of the things he did not write,[52] recently relegated to an appendix of dubious attributions *A Letter to a Young Poet*, partly on the basis of certain criteria of style.[53] And H. Teerink in 1925 tried to credit to Swift on a similar ground the John Bull pamphlets he was then editing.

Apart from some external matters and the kinship of ideas in *A Tale of a Tub* and the pamphlets, Teerink leans heavily on a set of parallels of expression and of style. He cites fifty-nine expressions which may be commonly found in Swift's works and in *John Bull*, for example, "I need not tell you", "The Parson (of the Parish)", "Let that be as it will", "Pen, ink and paper". These are distinguished from the parallels of style, such as the wide use of "happen'd", the beginning of sentences with "It has been wisely observ'd", and the use of pairs and triplets of verbs and the like. Phrases like "so much for . . ." and references to the "following account" are also characteristic.[54] Finally, the transgression of the sequence of tenses "is a peculiarity which is sometimes found in Swift's works".[55]

The case, it can be seen, revolves mainly around matters of diction. Two answers to Teerink's claim speedily demolished it.

---

[50]   Johnson was reluctant to credit Swift with the *Tale* because it was above his usual power ("Swift", *Lives of the Poets, ed. cit.*, III, 10, 51). He was also doubtful of the *History* (*Ibid.*, pp. 27-8). Gray, however, found "the manner . . . careless [with] little to distinguish it from common writers" (*Correspondence of Thomas Gray*, ed. Paget Toynbee and Leonard Whibley (Oxford, 1935), II, 566-7).

[51]   The matter is summarized in Davis's Introduction to Volume VII, *Works,* p. ix f.

[52]   Herbert Davis, "The Canon of Swift", *English Institute Essays 1942* (New York, 1943), p. 135.

[53]   Introduction, *Works,* IX, xxiv f.

[54]   H. Teerink, ed., *The History of John Bull* (Amsterdam, 1925), pp. 119-129.

[55]   *Ibid.,* p. 129.

Mayo dismissed the parallels by pointing to the diffusion of the terms at the time and the possible effect of the intimacy between two friends.[56] Arbuthnot's biographer, Lester M. Beattie, refutes the argument in detail. Of the 59 parallels of expression, he shows that 36 occur only once in *John Bull* and 12 only twice, and 20 only once and 10 only twice in the relevant works of Swift. Few occur often enough to be typical and few of those are common in Swift. Only four expressions are frequent in both authors and they include such common phrases as "his wife and children", "I need not tell you", "a cuff on the ear", and "who the devil". Thus the seeming weight of the accumulated parallels is dispelled by reference to common speech or other normal circumstances.[57]

As he had earlier disapproved of the use of internal evidence for the purpose of positively identifying a dubious work,[58] so Davis now found it convenient to use it for reaching a negative decision about *A Letter of Advice to a Young Poet*.[59] After first taking up the biographical evidence militating against the attribution, he proposes the following reasoning in support of his position. He brings in another pamphlet of the time – *The Right of Precedence between Physicians and Civilians Enquir'd Into* (1720) – which had been fathered on Swift but specifically disavowed by him after Curll reprinted it. Then he cites a number of resemblances between the *Letter* and this supposititious work as evidence of his suspicion that both were written by the same hand (not Swift's), especially since these resemblances diverge from Swift's own practice. They include mechanical devices of connection, heavy use of parenthetical phrases and of adjectives and a tendency to worry figures of speech.[60]

[56] T. F. Mayo, "The Authorship of the *History of John Bull*", *PMLA,* XLVI (March 1930), 274-282.
[57] *John Arbuthnot: Mathematician and Satirist* (Cambridge, Mass., 1935), pp. 36-42.
[58] "On the evidence of style alone we ought to be able to say: that is certainly *not* his work. But we should perhaps hesitate to say: this is so like him that there can be no doubt he wrote it" ("The Canon of Swift", p. 135).
[59] See Chapter VII, below, for a full discussion of this work.
[60] *Works,* IX, xxvi-xxvii.

Whether he is right or wrong about the attribution, Davis is at least proceeding in a manner distinct from the usual subjectivity and vagueness.[61] He not only attempts to specify the grounds for believing the work uncanonical and the style un-Swiftian, but he also does not rely entirely, as many have done, on purely lexical factors, such as favorite words and phrases or the presence or absence of a particular part of the vocabulary. Connectives, parenthetical expressions, the frequency of adjectives – these are all aspects of style which it is appropriate to cite in this context. Of course, Davis gives no formulation for his concept of a Swiftian style. What he has is an auditory sense for Swift's style developed from years of close study of Swift's text. Such a sense can produce a highly sensitive instrument for measuring genuineness, but it is intuitive and personal. As it is not based on extensive and systematic observation, it does not operate from verifiable fact but from an impression – in the case of a highly skilled and trained reader, a very accurate impression. Davis's ear may be an excellent, even a foolproof, ear, but that confers no special validity on his comments about Swift's frequency of adjectives or parenthetical phrases. These impressions might easily be in error without impugning his intuitive accuracy. Unfortunately no data of the sort that he needed were available and he was therefore compelled to extrapolate from his impressions.[62] Essentially, Davis is on the right track, both in his conception of style and in his reliance on specific data. That a detailed and systematic body of these is lacking is a condition of the study of style at the present time.[63]

It is significant that Davis's rejection of the attribution was contested by a scholar who presented not evidence but a competing theory. In fact, in Fussell's view, the writer does not always speak in his own identity but assumes a mask to suit the needs of the ostensible speaker. Fussell borrows this theory of the *persona*,[64]

[61] But see his theory about Swift's "conciseness", p. 38, below.
[62] Limited data about Johnson, Addison and some contemporaries are available, but these figures are about special aspects of style, e.g., parallel structures, doublets.
[63] Whether Davis's conjectures were accurate will appear below.
[64] The theory of the *persona* in Swift is also discussed by John M. Bullitt, *Swift and the Anatomy of Satire* (Cambridge, Mass., 1953); Martin Price,

which he modifies by adding the provision that the writer with each *persona* assumes a new style as well. Thus, he concludes, it is dangerous to speak of Swift's style, since he has "except in the letters, some of the poems, the sermons, and 'straight' works like *A Proposal for Correcting ... the English Tongue ...* no style at all, ... [but] a whole stable of dramatic styles".[65]

It cannot be gainsaid that Swift assumes a variety of poses in his many works and that the theory that these are so many personalities has a certain plausibility. The next step is obvious. The enactment of these personalities is so deeply felt, says Ewald, "that it modifies even Swift's style: for evidence one need only notice the sweeping allusions and daring images of *A Tale of a Tub*, the impersonal calculations of *A Modest Proposal,* the blunt counselling of the author of the *Letter to a Young Clergyman*, and the plain narrative of Gulliver." [66] Here as in Fussell's argument it becomes clear that the definition of style is so far broadened that it takes in the substantive aspects of the work to the exclusion of the formal ones. If "blunt counselling" is a characteristic of style, then Gulliver's narrative is indeed plain.

These excesses of the *persona* theorists proceed from a loose use of terms and the understandable desire to prove a case to the hilt. But the term *personality* cannot responsibly be bandied about to cover a few strokes of character found in a ten-page pamphlet. It is to be expected that these writers, in their devotion to a revived new rhetoric, would construe style to mean rhetorical figures, and it is plain that such a procedure will yield only controversial generalities and mere speculation.

Not much greater precision has resulted from the effort to consider the eighteenth-century prose writers as members of a literary family, a sort of stylistic movement. The general feeling has been

---

Swift's Rhetorical Art (New Haven, 1953); W. B. Ewald, Jr., *The Masks of Jonathan Swift* (Oxford, 1954); and Ronald Paulson, *Theme and Structure in Swift's Tale of a Tub* (New Haven, 1960).

[65]   Paul Fussell, "Speaker and Style in *A Letter of Advice to a Young Poet* (1721) and the Problem of Attribution", *Review of English Studies,* X (1959), p. 64.

[66]   Ewald, p. 184.

that the excellence of the prose of the early eighteenth century
was of a rather uniform character and its best exemplars, like
Addison and Steele, hard to tell apart.[67] This view, perhaps derived
from R. F. Jones's studies of the program of the Royal Society,
reigned for some time, but it has been found powerless to explain
much of the excellence of the Augustan style. James Sutherland
rejects the importance of the Royal Society in shaping the new
style of the Restoration. He prefers to find the explanation in the
dominance of the aristocratic tone in the intellectual and literary
life of the period. The well-bred conversation of gentlemen was
poised, unemphatic, easy, witty, clear and impersonal.[68] These
characteristics, he claims, can be found in Dryden, Addison, Swift,
and Fielding, who with some others comprise the early stream of
eighteenth-century prose. The later style, exemplified by Johnson,
Gibbon and Burke, was concerned with attracting and holding
attention with elaboration and challenging it with difficulty.
Sutherland finds it easier to characterize the later, less attractive
stream, than the earlier. He can only say that Addison had "a
sort of neutral quality".[69] The disadvantages of studying styles in
families are evident to Sutherland himself, who emphasizes the
necessity of remembering and listening for the individual voice of
the writer, though he despairs of being able to characterize it.[70]

Herbert Davis believed that he could name the essential quality
of all Swift's writing, a conciseness which marks all his work in
unmistakable ways:

---

[67]   "A delicate ear and subtle observation are needed to discern a recur-
rent trait, especially in writers who, like many Elizabethan dramatists or
eighteenth-century essayists, use a uniform style." René Wellek and Austin
Warren, *Theory of Literature* (New York, 1949), p. 184. The implication
is that they cannot be distinguished.
[68]   James R. Sutherland, *On English Prose* (Toronto, 1957), pp. 66-8.
[69]   "Some Aspects of Eighteenth-Century Prose", in *Essays . . . Presented
to D. Nichol Smith,* ed. J. R. Sutherland and F. P. Wilson (Oxford, 1945),
pp. 94-5.
[70]   D. W. Jefferson warns against the trend of making an Augustan stylist
out of Swift. His roots lie in the seventeenth century and constantly harp-
ing on his simplicity conceals this kinship with the flamboyant great stylists
of the earlier period ("An Approach to Swift", in *From Dryden to Johnson*
(Harmondsworth, 1957), pp. 230-1.

But in all these different forms of writing, and even in his most hurried as well as his most deliberate work ... Swift is a master of conciseness, unequalled and unmistakable by reason of that quality alone, which gives a flavour as of salt to all his work, and preserves it from certain levels of dullness, banality, or mere impoverishment of style liable to appear in the writings of all his contemporaries.[71]

This conciseness is equally terseness, economy, functionality and urging to action. Davis can find the quality in the structure of the whole work and of the sentence. The conception of such a quality (uniform in his works, absent in his contemporaries') can only be applauded. But whether "conciseness" is objective enough to serve is problematic. Despite Davis's enthusiasm, as an editor he does not have much confidence in such a characteristic or such a procedure. Conciseness, in any case, is relative and dependent on the training of the observer. Donald Davie, however, says that Swift's primary quality is irony, which he uses to suspend his reader in a series of demoralizing choices. He concludes that Swift's writing was not satiric or concise.[72]

This sort of disagreement is characteristic, as we have seen, of the entire history of the criticism of Swift's style, and it symbolizes the futility of approaching such a problem with such imprecise methods. In part, the difficulty lies in not realizing the dangers of subjectivity (or proceeding in their despite). But even more significant is probably the lack of agreement about what is being discussed. Style, in most of the opinions we have examined, seems to be an extremely vague matter, the target of various preconceptions and unconscious assumptions. To be sure, a firm definition of style is not easily come by: the whole question is complicated by the intrusion of a variety of non-literary factors. Before proceeding to formulate a definition which will serve as the basis of the study which follows, it may be well to review some definitions of style and some methods which have been used to study it.

[71]   Herbert Davis, "The Conciseness of Swift" in *Essays ... Presented to D. Nichol Smith,* p. 16.
[72]   "Irony and Conciseness in Berkeley and Swift", *Dublin University Magazine,* Oct.-Dec. 1952, pp. 20-29.

II. THE PROBLEM OF STYLE

When the author of the recent book, *The Style of Don Juan*,[1] explains his purpose and choice of title, he first makes reference to the classical theory of styles, which he considers important for an understanding of *Don Juan*. But he quickly passes on to the candid admission that he needed a title which did not promise a new or complete interpretation of the poem. He therefore settled on *style*, a term which, aside from its rhetorical connotations, implies an interest in an author's ways of shaping experience, in his vision.[2] In other words, he wanted a title which would not bind him to a precise task but which had the proper semantic aura. The choice he made illustrates one of the problems of style today.

There is much evidence to indicate that the word has become fashionable. A preoccupation with "the origins of the acutely pragmatic national style"[3] is the basis of another book, *The American Style*. In expatiating on this theme, one of the contributors to this work tries to define the matter he is supposed to be investigating: "How men cope with ... problems as they go about their business reflects what is here called a national style."[4] There is no doubt that the contributors to this volume are indeed studying something. It is possible to guess that they chose to call it *style* because of the vagueness and expressiveness of the word rather than its exact meaning.

If we may judge by the twenty-nine subdivisions of meaning

---

[1]   George M. Ridenour, *The Style of Don Juan* (New Haven, 1960).
[2]   *Ibid.*, pp. x-xii.
[3]   Ed. Elting Morison (New York, 1958), p. viii.
[4]   W. W. Rostow, "The National Style", *ibid.*, p. 247.

given in the latest edition of Webster's unabridged dictionary,[5] compared with the twenty of the previous edition,[6] it is obvious that the word is not losing its popularity. This apparent increase of nearly fifty per cent does not signify that many new meanings have arisen. Rather, a variety of new applications for existent meanings have developed,[7] as for example to describe the carriage of an animal, the combination of shape and ornament in certain artifacts, or a manner of dancing.[8] The meaning previously cited under "style of life" and labelled "*Psychol.*" is now simply listed as one of the senses of style.[9] Some innovation is noticeable under the verb entry ("to style a manuscript") and under the gerund *styling*, in the sense of adding a stylish quality to something.

All this suggests that the modern user of English at least dimly senses the complex and sophisticated notion summarized by the term *style* and its derivatives. Perhaps it appeals to his sense that the mysterious totality which constitutes any real or synthetic organism can only be invoked as a whole, as if it were a tutelary deity. There is in fact more than a hint of reverence for word-magic in the popular use of this term and the notion it represents. But there is scarcely any sense of the relation between matter and manner which is a prerequisite to any mature treatment of the subject.

Surely style needs to be discussed from a more analytical point of view and for this a critical vocabulary is required. Although a number of disciplines are cooperating to this end, a proper vocabulary does not yet exist, at least in English. A good beginning for such an undertaking would be a definition of the term itself.

The material object which gave rise to the complex modern term was the pointed stake, employed in military operations and

---

[5] *Webster's Third New International Dictionary* (Springfield, 1961), s.v. style.
[6] *Webster's New International Dictionary of the English Language,* Second Edition (Springfield, 1954); this edition was originally published in 1934.
[7] It may also show a greater precision on the part of the new editors in discriminating among closely-related meanings.
[8] Senses 6a(3), 6b(2), and 4d in *Webster's Third,* s.v. "style", n.
[9] Sense 4c(2).

agriculture, that the Romans called *stilus*.[10] The name also was applied to the pointed tool used to scratch on wax tablets. The use of the same term for two different, though similarly-shaped objects, required no great play of the imagination, but when it was applied to the scratches themselves – to the writing – a metonymic leap of considerable implication had been made. After that, it was an easy step to the whole composition, the assembly of scratches on the wax tablets. But Classical Latin did not progress to the modern sense of the term.[11] That was a development which began in Late Latin and emerged fully only in the modern European languages.[12]

In English, the history of the derivative *style* has followed a similar but more extensive path. The twenty-six items given by the *Oxford English Dictionary* may be divided into three major classes of meaning which arose in order: writing tool, writing or manner of writing, manner or fashion in general. The second of these classes contains the conflicting senses of the word.

The literary meanings of *style* are basically three, with subdivisions. The earliest meaning, which dates from the fourteenth century is "characteristic manner of expression . . . considered in regard to clearness, effectiveness, beauty and the like",[13] as in "Therefore Petrak writeth / This storie which with heigh stile he enditeth." [14] Manner of composition, in this sense, is equally applicable to a group or literary school, a genre, a nation, a period or an individual, as "Euphuistic style", "Italian style", "ancient style", "Miltonic style". The remaining two senses developed during the Renaissance. First, the word was refined to specify the formal rather than the substantive aspects of literary com-

---

[10] *Stilus* was later misspelled *stylus* by confusion with the Greek for column.

[11] Charlton T. Lewis and Charles Short, *A New Latin Dictionary* (New York, 1907), s.v. "stilus". This work gives the Classical Latin equivalents as *sermo, oratio, dictio, dicendi modus, ars, forma.*

[12] Alexander Souter, ed., *A Glossary of Later Latin* (Oxford, 1949), s.v. "stilus", gives the sense "language" and indicates it must not be sought before the third century. Incidentally, *style* is closely related to *stigma, stick, stimulus,* all of which look back to the primary meaning.

[13] OED, s.v., "style", n., sense 13.

[14] Chaucer's "Clerk's Tale", ll. 1147-8.

position.[15] Then, by a regular process of melioration, it came to mean *good style*, as *poetry* is frequently used to mean *good poetry*.

These three meanings (expression, form of expression, good form) tend in practice to merge and overlap. How much they do may be realized by considering the range of terms used as synonyms for *style: manner, mode, expression, way, language, fashion, diction,* among others. The interaction between these terms and the notion of style is vaguely reciprocal. The trajectory of meaning from pointed stick to modern style, in all its variety, though it may be traced, cannot be accounted for, except in the sketchiest way (metonymy, specialization, melioration). The influences acting upon the users of a language which lead them to adopt this or that variation of meaning at a given time are extremely mysterious. There can be no positive method for reaching the minds of those who have left us no record of their thought. But, by examining the root-metaphors of these synonyms, we may be able to gain some insight into the minds of the modern users of the term. It may be possible, that is, to find the limits of the extension of a term by making a collection of the primitive notions which surround it.

Language and *manner* are very closely related to the physical body of the user of language, one through his tongue (*lingua*) and the other through his hand (*manus*). Both of these buried figures of speech have a continuing life in the consciousness of the modern reader and writer in such expressions as "slip of the tongue", "the hand of the writer", or even, at a slight remove, "the voice of the writer". The writer may also be visualized as taking part in a process. As a maker, he is prefigured in the origin of *poet*. In the process of making (*fashioning*), he is presented as a producer of words, an artisan. *Expression* implies a more laborious process of "squeezing out", recalling a wine-press. *Diction* symbolizes the gap between wordless and verbal statement, its ultimate derivation being from *showing*, presumably by pointing.

More elaborate concepts are concealed in *way* and *mode*. In

---

[15] This is what *Webster's Third* describes as "aspects of literary composition as distinguished from content or message" in sense 2a(2), s.v. "style", n.

way there is the suggestion of a choice of routes to be travelled from the same origin. The quantitative aspect of *mode* (from *modus*, a measure) reflects a willingness to believe that a man's words are a measure of something about him. All together, these words seem to stress the individual nature of the concept of style, in its origins and its current uses. They may be easily distinguished from two words of related meaning: *system* and *method*. That they are related is emphasized by the presence of the idea of *way* in the word *method*.[16] A method is an investigation after the event. *System*, however, derives from a collection of objects placed together, thus an arrangement of principles. Both of these terms imply a procedure leading to a goal, a notion absent from *style* which is concerned with the way itself. The distinction in exactness is quite evident in the difference between *systematic* and *methodical*, on the one hand, and *stylish,* on the other.

In comparison with such precise terms as *system* and *method, style* has no clear-cut nucleus but rather an outline of amorphous dimensions which tends to collect meanings within itself. In mentalistic phrase, it is a word trying to express the inexpressible. How this situation came about has been documented with etymological data stemming from the ancients. But, as has been seen, they did not use the protean modern term,[17] though they were much concerned with the thing itself. Most of the theories which still govern the thinking of those who worry about style had their origin in Greece and Rome.

The ancient theory of style (Style as ornate form) is probably older than Plato.[18] Of the two modern theories (Style as a reflection of the individual and Style as meaning), the first has its roots in the ancient past and the second is modern. "The theory

---

[16] The components of *method* are Greek: *meta*, after; and *hodos*, way.

[17] Its ubiquity is illustrated by the fact that some form of the same word is used in most European languages, e.g.: French *style,* Italian *stile,* Dutch *stijl,* Spanish and Portuguese *estilo,* German and Danish *Stil,* Czech and Polish *styl,* and Norwegian, Swedish, Romanian, Irish, Serbo-Croatian, Bulgarian and Russian *stil* (with suitable transliteration).

[18] It may have originated with Plato's teacher, Gorgias, who was born half a century earlier (in 483 B.C.) and who doubtless inherited some ideas from his own predecessors.

of ornate form" as Croce has named it,[19] requires a fundamental separation between content and form. Aristotle held this view and, in urging the student of rhetoric to learn not only what to say but also how to say it, clearly implies the independence of thought from its linguistic clothing.[20]

The analogy between applied rhetorical ornament and clothing appropriate to the occasion becomes most evident in the classification of styles practised by the Roman theorists.[21] The author of *Rhetorica ad Herennium*, for example, was supposedly the first to classify styles into the Grand, the Middle, and the Simple, which are distinguished mainly by diction.[22] Quintilian's extensive and detailed treatise represents the culmination of the rhetorical view of style, with lists of figures of speech and figures of thought.[23] The system espoused by these rhetoricians was based on a belief in ideas unrelated to their form, on a hierarchy of occasions (linked to the hierarchy of styles), on teachability of style from models to the virtual exclusion of individuality, and on the dominance of diction as an expressive feature of style. This system, refined and subtilized, was carried over into the Middle Ages without much change.[24] In fact, this tradition concerning style

[19]   Benedetto Croce, *Aesthetic,* tr. D. Ainslie (New York, 1958 [1909]), p. 422.
[20]   *Art of Rhetoric,* tr. J. H. Freese, Loeb Classical Library (London, 1926), Bk. III, Ch. 1, p. 345. Aristotle elsewhere shows a belief in the organic unity of the work of art, but his commitment to the ancient view is surely reflected in such a statement as "written speeches owe their effect not so much to the sense as to the style" (p. 349). In this passage, the translator renders *lexis* as *style.*
[21]   This view was popular in the eighteenth century: Chesterfield says "Style is the dress of thoughts", *Letters to his Son, Philip Stanhope, Esq.,* 11th ed. (London, 1800), II, 303, in the letter dated November 24, 1749 O.S. William Melmoth cites an unidentified passage from Addison: " 'there is as much difference between comprehending a thought cloathed in Cicero's language and that of an ordinary writer, as between seeing an object by the light of a taper or the light of the sun' ", *Letters on Several Subjects by the Late Sir Thomas Fitzosborne, Bart.* (London, 1748), p. 162.
[22]   *Rhetorica ad Herennium,* tr. Harry Caplan, Loeb Classical Library (London, 1954), Bk. IV, Ch. 8, p. 253.
[23]   *Institutio Oratoria,* Bk. IX, passim.
[24]   See Charles Sears Baldwin, *Medieval Rhetoric and Poetic* (New York, 1928), pp. 304-5, where a list of figures drawn from the *Rhetorica ad Herennium* is reproduced.

has had adherents until the nineteenth century, reflected especially in handbooks of rhetoric used in schools.[25]

However influential this theory may have been, exceptions to it existed in the ancient world, and they may have furnished if not the basis at least the sanction for one of the modern theories, style as a reflection of character. Even with uniform education and similar outlook individuals think differently, and this difference is reflected in their mode of expression. Naturally enough, the modern development of this view may be found in the writings of Montaigne, to whose assertion on behalf of the individual we continue to be indebted: "Comme à faire, à dire aussi je suy tout simplement ma forme naturelle . . ." [26] "Est-ce pas ainsi que je parle par tout? me représente-je pas vivement? suffit! J'ay faict ce que j'ay voulu: tout le monde me reconnoit en mon livre, et mon livre en moy." [27] When this is compared with Plato's notion, the distant original of Montaigne's opinion, that virtue will express itself in eloquence (as in graceful dancing),[28] the basic difference between the ancient and modern viewpoints can be detected. The belief has persisted, however, that a thoroughly bad man could not write a good book.[29] Plato's argument seems built out of a belief in the equality of ideals. Thus goodness in the abstract leads to excellence in specialized performance. There is clearly no room for the individual in this system.

What seems at first glance to be a more modern collection of views can be found in Cicero and Seneca. Cicero rejects the theory of set styles in favor of a range arising out of varied subject matter and personal preference.[30] Seneca connects the degeneracy

[25]   E.g., Richard Whately, *The Elements of Rhetoric* (London, 1828); Alexander Bain, *English Composition and Rhetoric* (London, 1866).
[26]   *Essais,* ed. A. Thibaudet (Paris, 1946), Bk. II, Essai 17, p. 625.
[27]   *Ibid.,* Bk. III, Essai 5, p. 848.
[28]   *Republic,* tr. Paul Shorey, Loeb Classical Library (London, 1953), Bk. III, Ch. 11, p. 255.
[29]   George Orwell addresses himself to an aspect of this question relating to Swift in "Politics *vs.* Literature", in *Selected Essays* (Harmondsworth, 1957), pp. 138 ff. The history of this belief is touched on by M. H. Abrams, *The Mirror and the Lamp* (New York, 1958), p. 229.
[30]   *Brutus,* tr. G. L. Hendrickson, Ch. XXI, p. 77; *Orator,* tr. H. M. Hubbell, Ch. XVI, p. 345; Loeb Classical Library (London, 1952).

of morals with the corruptions of style (an idea borrowed later by Swift) and even finds the defective character of Maecenas reflected in his faulty style, full of inversions and "surprising thoughts".[31] He seems modern in not only rejecting fixed styles but insisting that style is dominated by usage and changes constantly. After coming as close to a respect for individuality as to admit that errors may not be the result of a debased mind but rather the reflection of a peculiar temperament, Seneca concludes that the soul must be guarded from contamination because it emits expression. A sound soul will produce a vigorous and manly style. This is obviously not very divergent from Plato's conception of the *vir bonus*.[32]

The individualist view has grown steadily since Montaigne, as an increasing number of maxims demonstrates. Pascal's "Quand on voit le style naturel, on est tout étonné et ravi, car on s'attendait de voir un auteur, et on trouve un homme",[33] is less well known, though more pungent, than Buffon's famous dictum. Not "le style est l'homme même", but "le style n'est que l'ordre et le mouvement qu'on met dans ses pensées" [34] represents Buffon's contribution to the growth of the individualist theory. The number of statements of this view after Buffon is large.[35] But the view has become so well established in this century that it has achieved the status of an unconscious (or unspoken) assumption and as a result is no longer stated in axiomatic form. As diluted into the misapplied "Style is the man", it is the predominant popular

---

[31] *Epistulae Morales,* tr. Richard M. Gummere, Loeb Classical Library (London, 1953), Epistle CXIV, III, 303-5. The translator renders "hoc sensus miri" as "surprising thoughts" (304).

[32] In this context the earlier statement of *Demetrius on Style:* "everybody reveals his soul in his letters. In every form of composition, it is possible to discern the writer's character, but in none so clearly as in the epistolary", may, in spite of its seeming modernity, be disregarded as atypical or ambiguous. The citation is the translation of W. Rhys Roberts, Loeb Classical Library (London, 1960), p. 441.

[33] *L'Œuvre de Pascal,* ed. Jacques Chevalier (Paris, 1941), p. 831. Cf. "L'éloquence est une peinture de la pensée" (p. 834).

[34] "Discours sur le style", in *Œuvres Philosophiques de Buffon,* ed. Jean Piveteau (Paris, 1954), pp. 500, 503.

[35] For English examples, see Abrams, pp. 226-235.

view, though it coexists at times with the theory of ornate form.[36]
No inconsistency seems to be felt by those who hold those essentially inimical opinions, perhaps by reason of the minor importance usually attached to theories of style, since any compromise
offering pragmatic satisfaction makes theoretical consistency unnecessary.

The latest modern theory of style, however, involves no compromise whatever. It postulates that there can be no segmentation
between the thought (or "intuition") and its form or expression. Croce, the most important advocate of this theory, states it
thus:

> Every true intuition or representation is also *expression*. That which
> does not objectify itself in expression is not intuition or representa-
> tion, but sensation and mere natural fact. The spirit only intuites
> in making, forming, expressing. He who separates intuition from ex-
> pression never succeeds in reuniting them.[37]

The implications of this aesthetic theory are far-reaching for the
theory of style. Obviously it follows that no intuition has any
reality until it has achieved expression. In turn this denies the
possibility of a choice among means of expression for a given intuition. The intuition is unique with the individual and is so to
speak identical with the expression, which is thus also a delinea-
tion of the will of the particular individual. Here then is the
coalescence of the two modern views of style, as meaning and as

---

[36] A compromise of all three theories can be found in Sumner Ives, *A
New Handbook for Writers* (New York, 1960), pp. 274-319.
[37] *Aesthetic*, p. 8. I. A. Richards, *Principles of Literary Criticism* (New
York, n.d.), in a chapter entitled "Truth and Revelation Theories", mentions what he considers to be Croce's "confusion between value and com-
municative efficacy" (p. 255). He also cites with approval the comment of
Giovanni Papini, in *Four and Twenty Minds*: "If you disregard critical
trivialities and didactic accessories, the entire aesthetic system of Croce
amounts merely to a hunt for pseudonyms of the word 'art', and may
indeed be stated briefly and accurately in this formula: art=intuition=
expression=feeling=imagination=fancy=lyricism=beauty. And you must
be careful not to take these words with the shadings and distinctions which
they have in ordinary or scientific language. Not a bit of it. Every word is
merely a different series of syllables signifying absolutely and completely
the same thing" (*ibid.*, fn. 4).

a reflection of the individual.[38] In the progress from the early rhetorical to the modern organic view, it seems as if style itself has disappeared. If style is acknowledged as distinct from content, each may be examined separately. But if style and content are so interfused that every change in the one affects the other, there is no style or there is no meaning, at least as analyzable entities. Thus, according to the modern theory, every possible arrangement of the same set of words represents a different meaning. To take an illustration, does each of the following statements have a different sense?

Only the miserable confess the power of fortune.
Only by the miserable is the power of fortune confessed.
The power of fortune: only the miserable will confess it.
The power of fortune is confessed only by the miserable.[39]

The changes involve word-order and the adjustment of function words and inflections to syntactic necessity. In the Crocean view, these are not alternative phrasings but substantive changes: because they are different expressions, they convey different meanings.[40]

There is no question that this is an attractive view logically. It seems to accord with present-day psychological emphases on minute and unconscious significances. Moreover, it is to some extent congruent with the experience of writers and speakers, who have found that there are no real synonyms, no two ways of saying exactly the same thing. But this Crocean theory entails some

[38] An interesting corroboration of this theory is furnished by a non-theoretician, Ernest Hemingway: "In stating as fully as I could how things really were, it was often very difficult and I wrote awkwardly and the awkwardness is what they called my style." A. E. Hotchner, "Hemingway Talks to American Youth", *This Week*, Oct. 18, 1959, p. 11.

[39] Only one of the four was written by Swift. The others are restatements of the original. The implication is that, if the version composed by a great literary artist is difficult to distinguish from casual variations of it, then the unitary theory is to some extent weakened. See "Thoughts on Various Subjects", *Works,* I, 245.

[40] A brilliant demonstration tending to support the Crocean theory may be found in Raymond Queneau, *Exercices de Style* (Paris, Gallimard, 1947), in which the same trivial incident is told in one hundred different ways, only some of them stylistic.

difficulties, partly because it dispenses with the necessity of style, term and notion, and because, logic apart, *some* alternatives seem to be equivalent.[41] If style and meaning are in fact identical, a student of style must study meaning or be merely working with phlogiston. If he studies meaning, he is no longer mainly or even at all concerted with those details of the literary text which are usually called "stylistic", but is planted helplessly before the entire work without a method of approach.

Further, there are unexpected implications in the organic view. If any external aspect of the text is alive with meaning, then any change, not only of the words themselves, affects the meaning. The text is embedded in a context which includes the size and shape of the letters, the margins on the page, the paper and binding of the book, the reader and attendant circumstances of reading, his state of mind, the time of day and a host of other variables over which the author can have no control. Ultimately, no literary statement can have the same meaning twice and any comment about it is likely to be true only for the commentator and perhaps not even for him on a subsequent occasion. Thus, the implications of this organic view reduce all criticism, including that of meaning, to futility. In order to salvage something usable for the study of style, it becomes necessary to return to the modern theory and see whether it may not permit an accommodation.

The perplexity engendered by the logic of the Crocean position has produced not a little ingenuity in the finding of solutions. The problem clearly is how to go on studying style (words, metaphor, arrangement) without seeming to overturn the essential identity of form and content.[42] The solution to the problem seems to lie in an appropriate re-definition of meaning, according to some modern students of the problem.

John Middleton Murry, who seems to be a thorough-going

[41]   What, for example, is the substantive difference between "the prose of Swift" and "Swift's prose"? Such alternative phrasings are regularly considered equivalent in composition in order to avoid repetition or alliteration or too long a sequence of prepositional phrases.
[42]   The problem is reminiscent of the dilemma faced by seventeenth-century Englishmen, who were at once admirers of Shakespeare and adherents to French Aristotelianism.

Crocean dismisses the whole question with "style is not an isolable quality of writing; it is writing itself".[43] But he is not actually ready to dismiss it; he wants to examine it from the viewpoint not of the reader (who is style-oriented) but that of the writer, who is most conscious of effects. He therefore presents Stendhal's maxim as the best thing on the subject, provided some qualification may be made of a key term: "Le style est ceci: Ajouter à une pensée donnée toutes les circonstances propres à produire tout l'effet que doit produire cette pensée." [44] But *pensée* is not be taken literally: "it is a general term to cover intuitions, convictions, perceptions, and their accompanying emotions before they have undergone the process of artistic expression or ejection." [45] That this is only a version of the Crocean view is evident. That it is not a satisfactory resolution of the problem is suggested by the content of Murry's book, which seems devoted more to literary criticism than to what is usually associated with discussions of style.[46]

No such objection can be lodged against the work of W. K. Wimsatt, whose book about Johnson's style[47] is exclusively devoted to what the term usually suggests. His awareness of the Crocean dilemma is sharpened by Croce's explicit rejection of rhetorical categories, something that Wimsatt cannot spare, for his examination of Johnson's style proceeds along rhetorical lines (Parallelism, Antithesis, Inversion, even Chiasmus). He finds a solution in the tendency of works to mean something, at all times, whether the writer has expressed what he intended or not. Thus bad style is a deviation, not of words from meaning but of the meaning conveyed from the meaning intended. Even when the fault of style is "awkwardness", the meaning is conveyed completely. The awkwardness is a missing part of the meaning or a contrary or irrelevant meaning which is unnecessarily present, but which is

---

[43] *The Problem of Style* (Oxford, 1922), p. 77.
[44] From *Racine et Shakespeare,* as quoted by Murry, p. 79.
[45] *Ibid.*
[46] His dependence on the notion of perfection suggests a contamination by Platonic ideas. See, for example, pp. 34, 36, 45, 67, 84, 88, 99, etc. . . .
[47] *The Prose Style of Samuel Johnson* (New Haven, Conn., 1941).

disregarded because the writer's intention can be inferred.[48] The real difficulty is in deciding what the author ought to have said: "It is the only difficulty, for it is the only question, and it is one we implicitly answer every time we judge style." [49] It is done, he contends, by a constant reference of the detail to the "central and presiding purpose".[50] Faults of style can be classed and presumably so can merits, though Wimsatt concedes that useful classification can also be done by those who continue to keep style and meaning separate. He concludes: "That which has for centuries been called style differs from the rest of writing only in that it is one plane or level of the organization of meaning . . . it is the furthest elaboration of the one concept that is the center." [51] It is difficult to conclude that this definition is anything but a pretext designed to permit the critic to get on with his job of analyzing Johnson's style. The furthest elaboration of meaning still requires the critic to have an impossibly accurate knowledge of the author's intention.

Much less subjectivity marks the work of a recent scholar who has attacked this problem. Richard M. Ohmann[52] tries to provide a justification for the study of style as a main concern of literary critics, by means of a philosophical argument, in a volume devoted to the "concept of style as a writer's conscious or subconscious choice among alternatives offered by a language for the ex-

[48]   *Ibid.*, p. 10. Cf. the remarkably similar comment of Hemingway, p. 49, fn. 38, above.
[49]   *Ibid.*
[50]   Cf. Leo Spitzer's circular procedure, p. 66, below.
[51]   Wimsatt, p. 11. An interesting variant of Wimsatt's formulation is expressed by George Steiner, in a review of John Updike's *The Centaur*: "It is both fashionable and logically cogent to deny the hoary distinction between form and content, to proclaim that they are indivisible. But . . . they are indivisible only where we are dealing with literature in the most serious, fully realized sense; only where the writer's medium strikes us as inevitable because it is controlled, from within, by pressure of adequate vision. Where such a vision is in default, form and content can and will drift apart. Style, the manipulation of image or verbal sound, will make its independent claims", "Half Man, Half Beast", *Reporter*, XXVIII (March 14, 1963), 52.
[52]   "Prolegomena to the Analysis of Prose Style", in *Style in Prose Fiction*, ed. Harold C. Martin, English Institute Essays, 1958 (New York, 1959), pp. 1-24.

pression of thought or feeling".[53] Ohmann criticizes the compromise which considers style as a part of meaning because in his opinion it is difficult to establish the limits of meaning as style, as opposed to meaning as "not-style".[54] He begins with the notion of experience as an infinite set of possible relations between events and the person experiencing them, relations which differ between any two people. Because of the infiniteness of experience, then, no available categories of thought can be made to fit any given person's response to events. "What nature does offer to experience, however, and experience to language, is a constant *formlessness.*" [55] In the search for order, each person selects the "perceptual forms" most useful to him, "though most often the choice is unconscious and inevitable".[56] These primitive choices which underlie a writer's prose represent the basis of his epistemology, his particular sorting of perceptions, although of course this task has already been performed in part by the writer's native language.[57] The "epistemic" bias of his language limits a writer's linguistic choices while it encourages his originality, which can help him to overcome the deficiency of his language by the creation of words, and metaphors, by changing syntax. Even short of this possible extreme, his choices remain considerable and meaningful. That a writer may be given to abstraction, a peculiar use of the present tense, or an avoidance of causal words, signifies a habit of meaning, that is, a particular way of classifying experience.[58] Thus, the problem is resolved: by preserving for the writer a kind of choice (an inevitable prerequisite for the study of style), the choice among the components of the world-stuff by means of his particular mental predisposition to classify this way or that. Unfortunately, this kind of choice seems to be no more a choice than the alternatives it was designed to supplant. As Ohmann admits, the decision may be unconscious and pre-verbal.

---

[53]   In the words of the editor, p. xi.
[54]   *Ibid.,* p. 3. He pretends (p. 14) to exonerate Wimsatt and Murry from having resorted to this compromise, but it is clear that he cannot be sure.
[55]   *Ibid.,* p. 8.
[56]   *Ibid.,* p. 9.
[57]   *Ibid.,* pp. 10-11.
[58]   *Ibid.,* pp. 13-14.

By the time the writer comes to this "choice", the intellectual machinery governing his outlook upon the world has already been determined and it is no more a true choice than the selection of reading matter by a person who can read only English.

The difficulty with any organic theory is that it precludes the dissection into parts which is both a convenience and a necessity for the successful study of detailed organization. The same problem exists in medicine, wherein the student of human ailments is required to reject the convenient division of disease into psychic and somatic or in the study of psychology, in which the customary division into thought and feeling must be exorcised for a genuine understanding of the mind. But any organic theory is a corrective, rather than a method. By overstating the unity of aspects often ruthlessly dichotomized, such a theory brings into closer contact what ought to be considered parts of the same thing. It does not, however, furnish a procedure for dealing with the reconstituted unity. The only possible result, if analysis is to proceed at all, is to acquire a respect for the whole and a consciousness of the totality, even while separating what seems to be inseparable. If "theoretical paralysis" is to be avoided, Austin Warren and René Wellek observe, "process and work, form and content, expression and style, must be kept apart, provisionally and in precarious suspense, till the final unity".[59]

If, then, the process of writing is considered as a continuum leading from thought to expression, it may be possible to formulate a practical solution to the dilemma posed by the organic view. If the influence of thought or conceptualization is strongest at the origin and diminishes as expression is approached and the influence of expression or form grows as the former diminishes, the two being co-extensive, it can be seen that the two processes are kept together and yet separate for the process of analysis. They are, it may be said, like two wedges which, fitted together, make a perfect quadrilateral. A vertical section of the figure, at whatever point, intersects both areas. But if the section is made near the end belonging to expression, only a small part of thought is involved. In non-metaphoric terms, the consideration of style can

[59]   *Theory of Literature* (New York, 1949), p. 188.

never exclude the simultaneous consideration of meaning, but if the style is examined at the level of literal expression the influence of the component of meaning can be reduced to negligible size for the purpose of the examination.[60] The totality remains intact in spirit, as the study remains in constant tension between the poles of thought and expression, but the tendency is constant toward the verbal and literal side, which is to say the study of style rather than of thought (meaning).

That style can be studied, regardless of the theoretical justification for it,[61] can be verified by a glance at the more than two thousand items listed in a recent bibliography of work in Romance stylistics alone.[62] That the problems of style have been attracting increasing interest in recent years is evidenced by a number of books containing the proceedings of groups met for the purpose of discussing problems of style and form. The English Institute in 1958,[63] the International Federation for Modern Languages and Literatures in its Seventh Congress at Heidelberg in 1957,[64] the Conference on Style at Bloomington, Indiana, in 1958,[65] all brought together large numbers of people interested in the study of style. Significantly, the difficulty of the problem was recognized by the variety of approaches represented at two of the meetings.

The International Congress contributed to this task by confronting students of style working with traditional approaches in a

[60] Cf. "Here the word style will be used as a convenient designation of the linguistic structure which underlies and indeed constitutes a work of literature." R. A. Sayce, *Style in French Prose* (Oxford, 1953), p. 1.

[61] Students of style have something in common with the bumblebee that did not know it lacked adequate wing surface to fly, according to the findings of aerodynamics engineers. It therefore continued to fly. In a sense they are also like psychologists who know that their intelligence tests measure something which they cannot define and are reduced to defining intelligence as that which intelligence tests measure. A similar problem of definition is discussed in Raymond B. Cattell, "The Nature and Measurement of Anxiety", *Scientific American*, CCVIII (March 1963), 96-104.

[62] Helmut Hatzfeld, *A Critical Bibliography of the New Stylistics* (Chapel Hill, 1953).

[63] Martin, see p. 52, above.

[64] Paul Böckmann, ed., *Stil- und Formprobleme in der Literatur* (Heidelberg, 1959).

[65] *Style in Language*, ed. Thomas A. Sebeok (New York, 1960).

dozen or more languages[66] and compelling them to consider the possible virtues of alternative methods. The Conference was frankly interdisciplinary and at the risk of speaking to uncomprehending audiences, linguists, poets, critics, philosophers, psychologists, folklorists, anthropologists and statisticians presented papers attacking the subject from many sides. There was in all this activity nothing new except the simultaneity, for style like anything elusive and fascinating, has been long studied in various ways.

However variegated the particular methods, they all have much in common, for studies of style can have but few aims. They can hope to teach how to write or how to understand writing; they can try to understand or identify an author or group of authors; they can contribute illumination to another subject, such as linguistics, psychology, statistics, anthropology, or the history of ideas.

The use of illustrious models as incentives and examplars in the study of composition was one of the foundations of rhetoric. Though no longer basic, this procedure is still considered valuable.[67] The categories devised by the rhetoricians are still useful in literary study, but they serve more as convenient labels than as fundamental constituents of the style process. Although not much is known about the relation of thought to language, it is considered unlikely that the simplified psychology underlying the rhetorical figures can be anywhere near the mark.[68] But the study of styles as an aid to developing skill in writing is clearly incidental to the study of an author's style as a prelude, or as part of the attempt, to understand him or his methods of composition. Most of the work to be considered has resulted from a concern with the

[66] The book itself contains articles written in German, English, French and Italian.

[67] Nearly all college composition courses are based on sets of "readings", some of which are undoubtedly proposed as models for emulation, if not imitation.

[68] "The study of language is an integral part of the study of thinking. Unfortunately psychologists have little to offer ... so far their studies have been exploratory." Robert Thomson, *The Psychology of Thinking* (Harmondsworth, 1959), p. 181. This suggests, as Thomson says passim, that thought involving reasoning of a complex kind cannot be carried on without language.

author, his psychology, his creativity, his mind and his personality.[69]

The most common approach to styles of authors by literary critics and historians has been the subjective or intuitive, sometimes called "impressionistic". It is an eclectic procedure in which the critic refers to passages which have struck him in terms of categories drawn from grammar, rhetoric, aesthetics and whatever other fields he may be acquainted with. Or he may simply describe adjectivally the impression which the writer has made upon him. Such criticism is readily found in older critical studies, in which it occupies some pages toward the end of the book, sometimes (if the subject is a notable "stylist") a whole chapter, but it is not lacking in more recent work.[70] It seems almost to be an afterthought, added after everything of importance has been settled, or an unpleasant necessity, fulfilled because of tradition. The vocabulary of these studies is unstable, and the terms used seldom bear any precise application. Burke's style, for example, is "noble, earnest, deep-flowing".[71] Sterne, however, has no style, but "it is a perfectly clear vehicle for the conveyance of thought".[72] On the other hand, Sir Thomas Browne has only style (no substance), but he clothes this non-existent substance in splendors, "turning the rough yarn of statement into heavy cloth of gold".[73] The two styles of Joseph Conrad have, respectively, "murky splendour" and "elastic suavity".[74] Fanny Burney's sentence-structure is occasionally "natural".[75] These figures of speech

[69] Here belong, presumably, such sophisticated rhetorical treatments as those of Wimsatt on Johnson, and that of Martin Price, *Swift's Rhetorical Art* (New Haven, 1953). Although these studies make use of rhetorical categories, they are in some part historical studies, dealing with the meaning and function of these categories during the periods considered.

[70] John Morley, *Burke* (New York, 1879), Ch. X, "Burke's Literary Character"; H. D. Traill, *Sterne* (London, 1882), Ch. X, "Style and General Characteristics"; Edmund Gosse, *Sir Thomas Browne* (New York, 1905), Ch. VII, "Language and Influence"; Richard Curle, *Joseph Conrad: A Study* (London, 1914), Ch. IX, "Conrad's Prose"; Eugene White, *Fanny Burney, Novelist* (Hamden, Conn., 1960), Ch. V, "Style".

[71] Morley, p. 210.

[72] Traill, pp. 142, 143.

[73] Gosse, pp. 190, 192.

[74] Curle, p. 181.

[75] White, p. 55.

reveal most of all the helplessness of the writers to deal with the question, a weakness of which they seem vaguely aware. But the usefulness of such treatment cannot be easily estimated. It is doubtful whether it provides more than merely a generalized approval.[76] A number of modern studies operate more responsibly within the same impressionistic tradition, making their subjective points by means of a substantial number of examples or the juxtaposition of an author's views on composition to appropriate instances of his practice.[77]

The limitations of such a procedure must have become apparent earlier than is commonly supposed. The nineteenth-century faith in the power of science to solve every problem yielded a number of results in the realm of stylistic study. The turn of the century was the great age of laboriously-compiled concordances.[78] A concordance, even though painfully compiled by human hands, implies scientific objectivity, doubtless the result of its dependence on quantitative evidence. In any case, the labor that goes into such an index always has a potential usefulness. Not all quantitative work can claim so much.

Enumerative methods applied to literary work have, at least, the advantage of a very ancient tradition. The standardization of the Homeric text was accomplished by Alexandrian scholars, who compiled lists of words appearing in the text (and nowhere else) and of *hapax legomena* (words appearing only once).[79] Similarly, the Masoretic text of the Bible was safeguarded by devoted scholars, who counted the verses and words of each book and

[76]   As was inferred by the student who wrote at the top of the page containing Traill's speculations about Sterne's style: "Style good".
[77]   For the first type, see H. L. Bond, *The Literary Art of Edward Gibbon* (Oxford, 1960), Ch. VII, "Language"; for the second, Mary Lascelles, *Jane Austen and Her Art* (Oxford, 1939), Ch. III, "Style".
[78]   Biblical, 1894, 1897, 1900, etc.; Shakespeare, 1895; Milton, 1894.
[79]   G. U. Yule, *The Statistical Study of Literary Vocabulary* (Cambridge, 1944), pp. 7-8. Cf. J. E. Sandys, *A History of Classical Scholarship* (New York, 1958): "The scholars of Alexandria were ... concerned with the verbal criticism of the Greek poets, primarily with that of Homer... They were the earliest examples of the professional scholar and they deserve the gratitude of the modern world ..." (I, 144). The study of *hapax legomena* has a place in modern "stylo-statistics". See Gustav Herdan, *Type-Token Mathematics* ('s-Gravenhage, 1960), pp. 66-8.

determined its middle word and middle letter.[80] Their modern
descendants derived their stimulus from observing the success of
scientific methods in all fields of human endeavor. Professor
Lucius A. Sherman of the University of Nebraska, having noted
the improvement in chemistry classes after the students were
permitted to perform experiments themselves (instead of merely
watching the instructor's demonstration), found that similar successes attended his introduction of objective laboratory methods
into the study of English Literature. The usual lecture method
was profitable, he had discovered, to only a few of the best
students, and, in any case, it failed to exploit the literary or
linguistic elements common to both Chaucer and Shakespeare.[81]
The actual research upon which his objective method was based
arose from an interest in the genealogy of the English sentence.
In a series of articles by Sherman and two of his students, a
number of conclusions were reached about English sentence-
structure.[82] Sherman found that, despite a gradual decrease in
sentence-length (measured in number of words) between Thomas
More and Macaulay, a remarkable consistency existed in any
single writer's average sentence-length. For example, Thomas
More's *Richard III* averages 53 words per sentence; by De
Quincey's time, the average is down to 32. But Macaulay's average
of 23-plus is entirely his own peculiarity. Sherman counted the
words of all the sentences in Macaulay's *Essays* and his *History
of England* and found a constant average of a little over 23 words
per sentence in any sample larger than 500 periods. This he
ascribed to the author's sentence-sense, the ability to cast a

[80]   The Numerical Masorah is treated in *The Jewish Encyclopaedia* (New
York, 1901-6), s.v. "Masorah".
[81]   The chemical analogy may be found in the preface to his *Analytics of
Literature* (Boston, 1893).
[82]   Lucius A. Sherman, "Some Observations upon the Sentence-Lengths in
English Prose", and "On Certain Facts and Principles in the Development
of Form in Literature", *University of Nebraska Studies,* I (Oct. 1888),
119-130 and I (July 1892), 337-366; George W. Gerwig, "On the Decrease
of Predication and of Sentence-Weight in English Prose", *University of
Nebraska Studies,* II (July 1894), 17-44; Carson Hildreth, "The Bacon-
Shakespeare Controversy", *University of Nebraska Studies,* II (Jan. 1897),
147-162.

"mind-full" into an independent syntactic unit. The writer seems subject to "some conception or ideal of form which, if it could have its will, would reduce all sentences to procrustean regularity . . .".[83] The study of a variety of other authors, at various stages of their writing lives, convinced Sherman that he had discovered a constant characteristic in sentence-length and that, therefore, other constants must exist:

if it were true that each author writes always in a consistent numerical sentence average, it would follow that he must be constant in other peculiarities, as proportions of verbs, substitutes for verbs, conjunctions etc. . . . if a sufficiently large sample were taken as the basis.[84]

Some of the peculiarities were sought for by a student of Sherman's (Gerwig), who observed that modern writers used fewer than the half-dozen verbs in each sentence affected by their literary ancestors. The modern tendency was to suppress the superfluity of finite verbs by such means as apposition and verbals and to write more simple sentences.[85] Gerwig devised a percentage-of-clauses-saved index as a measure of modernity of style and tirelessly examined a great range of authors in considerable detail. Unfortunately industry is not proof against error, and a least some of Gerwig's and Sherman's work was invalidated by their ignorance of statistics and experimental design.

The consistency of the sentence-length averages for Macaulay was shown by Moritz to be the result of the uniformity of the material tested: history and essays.[86] A similar bias, he showed, had infected all of Sherman's selections. He was easily able to demonstrate very wide ranges of sentence-length in individual authors both German and English by examining works in different genres. Further, he pointed out, the decreases of predication-average and increases of simple-sentence average were not merely parallel, as Gerwig had thought, but were functionally

[83]   "On Certain Facts . . ." p. 353.
[84]   *Ibid.,* p. 350.
[85]   Gerwig, p. 18.
[86]   Robert E. Moritz, "On the Variation and Functional Relation of Certain Sentence-Constants in Standard Literature", *University of Nebraska Studies,* III (July 1903), 229-253.

related.[87] Although this discussion did not invalidate all of what Sherman and his students had done, it apparently showed the danger of venturing into the territory of science unarmed, for little work of this type appeared during the two decades following Moritz's article.[88]

In the same tradition of numerical tabulation but more carefully qualified in both procedure and conclusions are some articles by Robert R. Aurner.[89] It is the apparatus of clause diagrams, bar-graphs and the like, which is interesting, as it seems to represent a continuing expression of the yearning of a segment of the literary community to reach a level of precision with the sciences.

The next full-scale manifesto of the scientific approach to lit-erature came from the hand of Edith Rickert,[90] who had been im-pressed by the power of code and cipher analysts to bring sense out of meaningless symbols during the First World War. The book was an attempt "to substitute for the impressionistic, hit-or-miss, every-man-for-himself, method of approaching literature" [91] some "graphical and statistical methods" through which the several strands of style "may be understood with a definiteness and certainty impossible through reading alone".[92] She was aware that her methods were neither rigorously scientific nor really original. As far as it is possible to tell, her suggestions has very little in-fluence. [93] The defect of these methods (from Sherman to Edith

[87]   As one went down, the other was bound to go up: as the use of finite verbs per sentence decreased and sentences became shorter, the percentage of simple sentences naturally rose. Moritz even presented a formula by means of which either could be computed if the other was known: $P\sqrt{S}$ $= C$, where P is the predication-average, S the simple-sentence percentage, and C a constant (13.57). *Ibid.,* p. 250.
[88]   Interest continued, however, in the study of the Saxon-Romance com-ponents of the vocabulary.
[89]   "Caxton and the English Sentence", *Wisconsin Studies in Language and Literature,* XVIII (1923), 23-59, and "The History of Certain Aspects of the Structure of the English Sentence", *Philological Quarterly,* II (1923), 187-208.
[90]   *New Methods for the Study of Literature* (Chicago, 1927).
[91]   *Ibid.,* p. 6.
[92]   *Ibid.,* p. 7.
[93]   One derivative result is Howard L. Runion's "An Objective Study of the Speech Style of Woodrow Wilson", *Speech Monographs,* III (Oct. 1936). It is interesting to compare this dispassionate and colorless study

Rickert) is that they seem to represent a mere emulation of the outward aspect of the sciences. The mathematical and statistical aspects were only half-understood and the results were negligible and always seemed suspect to more traditional scholars. For that reason, the historical study of style has been far more influential.

The historical approach is well-established in literary studies and, though it has its detractors, it so permeates the thinking of literary scholars that they do not even think of it as a method. Historicism is the invisible outward limit which guides overt methods. Sherman, for example, and Aurner later, cast their researches into the form of studies of the prose sentence beginning with Caxton and ending with some near-contemporary. Their *method,* however, was not historical but enumerative. But there are also students of prose form who have openly adopted the historical approach and have made comments about the progress of English prose style and the forces that have directed it by examining writers as representatives of their time rather than as individuals speaking in their own unique voices.

Within the historical approach itself, the dominant problem in dealing with style is identifying the styles of particular periods and accounting for the changes which seem to have taken place. A standard history such as Krapp's [94] presents an examination of samples and a discussion of characteristics in terms of some generally-useful categories (form of the sentence, diction) without being primarily concerned with the motive power behind the changes.[95] The Classical influence, for instance, can be detected in every genre and form up to about 1850 by anyone intent on pursu-

---

with the highly subjective, hostile and vigorous book of William Bayard Hale, *The Story of a Style* (New York, 1920), which seems to have been inspired by political motives.

[94]   George Philip Krapp, *The Rise of English Literary Prose* (New York, 1915).

[95]   "the main point . . . has been to trace the growth of a temper and attitude of mind towards the use of speech, to show the development of taste and feeling for prose expression . . .", *op. cit.,* p. xiii. The emphasis is on the panorama not on factors influencing the changes in the landscape. A more limited conspectus is George Saintsbury's *A History of English Prose Rhythm* (London, 1912).

ing that pervasive element.[96] A more pointed attribution of causes and results, however, concerns itself with such matters as the Ciceronian and Senecan styles.[97] Another side of the matter, the influence of the Royal Society, was suggested long ago by Joel E. Spingarn[98] and extensively developed and elaborated by R. F. Jones, with whose name it is now usually connected.[99] Jones acknowledges the difficulty of analyzing style and limits himself to "pointing out those more obvious influences that are combined and reflected in speech and writing . . . ignoring other factors that may escape detection".[100] No quarrel can be picked with the conclusions of R. F. Jones or George Williamson [101] except that they do not seem to account for the very important individual element, and in fact, deliberately exclude it. It is obvious that in any period a variety of writing patterns can be found. Of necessity, the historian pressing a point is constrained to select representative illustrations. Even when he is aware of contradictory tendencies, he is bound to underrate the likelihood that within a highly mannered style, such as the Ciceronian, there were important individual variations, differences so great that they obscured the significance of the common pattern. The brilliant demonstration offered by Jones,[102] contrasting two versions of Glanvill's *Vanity of Dogmatizing*, one earlier and one later than his exposure to the Royal Society's program of prose reform, is not wholly convincing because it does not consider the possible tendency of a "late"

[96]   E.g., J. A. K. Thomson, *Classical Influences on English Prose* (London, 1956).
[97]   See the well-known work of Morris Croll and also George Williamson, *The Senecan Amble* (London, 1951).
[98]   Introduction, *Critical Essays of the Seventeenth Century* (Oxford, 1908), I, xlvii.
[99]   "Science and English Prose Style in the Third Quarter of the Seventeenth Century" [1930] and "The Attack on Pulpit Eloquence in the Restoration" [1931], both reprinted in *The Seventeenth Century* (Stanford, 1951).
[100]   "Science and English Prose Style . . .", p. 75.
[101]   As explanations for the undoubted change which took place in the last quarter of the seventeenth century, they are rejected by James R. Sutherland, *On English Prose* (Toronto, 1957), pp. 56, 66-7. He favors the influence of aristocratic conversation.
[102]   *Ibid.*, pp. 91 ff.

style to diverge from an early one, often in the direction of "simplicity". Whatever the undeniable truths uncovered by the historical study of style,[103] it affords no more than a negative value to the student of an individual author's style. Historical influences are abstractions of a high order and their effect, even their existence and applicability, are impossible to measure. A more concrete method, whatever its theoretical justification, implies a more successful resolution of the style-problem. Everyone interested has heard of and superficially pays homage to the Ciceronian-Senecan squabble and the influence of the Royal Society, but he does not feel reliably armed with the information because the terms involved (Ciceronian . . .) disguise the inconstancy of the phenomena they refer to. An approach which begins with the stylistic phenomena and carries them back to some historical sequence at least suggests a firmly-grounded empiricism and to that extent it is persuasive. Such a procedure is the study of modern "Stylistics", mainly concerned with the Romance languages, especially French.[104]

Stylistics is related to linguistics and consequently is much concerned with structures definable in grammatical or philological terms.[105] The stylistic device is considered a conscious deviation from the linguistic norm of a writer's period.[106] In fact, to the stylistician only that which is beyond the neutral common denominator qualifies as style. Where there is an alternative available, the possibility of a stylistic choice exists. For example, the French adjective may be placed before or after the noun it modifies, subject to a complicated list of exclusions. The consistent or even the occasional use of the unexpected word-order represents a stylistic device. Obviously such a method depends on a

[103]   It is useful in isolating the ideals of prose style which govern certain periods and exert an influence on criticism, if not on practice.
[104]   Hatzfeld, p. 15.
[105]   Synoptic accounts of stylistics may be found in Stephen Ullmann, *Style in the French Novel* (Cambridge, 1957), pp. 1-39; and Pierre Guiraud, "Stylistiques", *Neophilologus*, XXXVIII (1954), 1-12.
[106]   A fresh emphasis is given to the idea of the stylistic device, in a procedure based on context and predictability, by M. Riffaterre, "Criteria for Style Analysis", *Word*, XV (1959), 154-174 and "Stylistic Context", *Word*, XVI (1960), 207-218.

close familiarity with the grammar and the linguistic norms of the period studied.

Though its origins are in linguistics, stylistics proceeds independently and has amassed a diverse body of doctrine also including elements of psychology, statistics, rhetoric, and even information theory. Most followers of stylistics, however, would agree with Ullmann's summary:

At the risk of oversimplification, one might say that everything which, in language, transcends pure communication belongs to the province of style. Whether the choice, and the effects it produces, are conscious or not is fundamentally irrelevant to a purely stylistic inquiry, and it is also most difficult to determine.[107]

The concern, it is clear, is with effects on the reader, not the sources in the writer, and with the particularity of the device itself, its variant forms, its diffusion. Such studies have been highly productive (at least in numbers), although they have tended to the mechanical application to an author of a predetermined schedule of devices.[108] Following the grammars of style provided for the French language by Marcel Cressot [109] and others, some critics have produced treatises examining French prose,[110] individual authors, the use of particular devices in various authors.[111] In such careful scholars as Sayce and Ullmann, this procedure turns up a good many significant insights. It is to be noticed, however, that in a language like French, which has far stricter standards of grammatical propriety than English, the norm is clearer and deviations more readily perceptible. But the insistence on the consciousness of the whole artistic process minimizes,

---

[107] Op. cit., p. 6. But cf. Guiraud, p. 2, who is concerned to distinguish conscious from unconscious choice.

[108] Ullmann (p. 35), mentions a number of Sorbonne theses on the 'language and style' of a given author as offenders in this direction. A better-than-average example in this vein is Joseph-Barthélemy Fort, Samuel Butler l'Ecrivain: Etude d'un Style (Bordeaux, 1935). The inherent defects are visible in the contents of some chapters: Butler's ideas about style, his diction, his imagery, his "styles".

[109] Le Style et ses Techniques (Paris, 1947).

[110] R. A. Sayce, Style in French Prose (Oxford, 1953).

[111] See bibliographies in Ullmann and Sayce; also P. Guiraud, La Stylistique (Paris, 1954), pp. 81-86 and Hatzfeld, Critical Bibliography.

when it does not totally ignore, the considerable component of literary composition which is not subject to consciousness, but represents the unconscious expression of personal tendencies. Besides, despite their disciplined and traditional procedure, some followers of Romance stylistics continue to be bound to something of the impressionism which has been a constant handicap to the criticism of style.[112]

Implicitly connected with this approach is a scholar whose work requires particular mention because of its influence. Leo Spitzer's own "philological circle", with which he tries to bridge linguistics and literary history, parallels Romance stylistics in its notion of the deviation from the linguistic norm and its emphasis on linguistic features of style, but it is also dependent on the idealist position of Croce.[113] Spitzer's technique, however, does not conveniently fit into any classification, partly because it draws on so extensive a set of disciplines and partly because its success is in large part dependent on the method's being applied by Spitzer himself, according to his detractors, who point to its highly subjective aspects, those derived from psychoanalysis.

Not all application of psychology to the study of style need be wholly subjective, however. Psychologists have studied language for some three decades, most recently with the objective means provided by statistics. The aim of the psychologists is not to study style as a literary phenomenon but rather to use the information supplied by literary style in the study of personality.[114] Experimental psychology has produced results in the form of numerical

[112]   Here might be mentioned also the hybrid works (part *modus dicendi,* part style-history, part study of stylistic ideals and devices) represented by such works as Read, *English Prose Style,* and Lucas, *Style,* the first of which is full of judicious criticism and keen historical observations and the second a hotbed of such concepts as 'urbanity', 'sincerity', 'gaiety'.
[113]   For Spitzer's own explanation, see *Linguistics and Literary History* (Princeton, 1948), Ch. I and passim; for the accounts of favorably-disposed scholars, Ullmann, pp. 25-8 and Guiraud, *Stylistique,* pp. 71-77; for a negative view, J. Hytier, "La Méthode de M. L. Spitzer", *Romanic Review,* XLI (1950), pp. 42-59.
[114]   Summaries of work done in this field may be found in Fillmore H. Sanford, "Speech and Personality", *Psychological Bulletin,* XXXIX (Dec. 1942), 811-45 and George A. Miller, *Language and Communication* (New York, 1951) especially Ch. VI, "Individual Differences", pp. 119-139.

data, which could be treated statistically. Unfortunately most experiments depend on unstable definitions or classifications, with the consequence that one experimenter's results cannot be compared with another's and some doubt is cast on the validity of the conclusion, though workers in this field have not been forward to claim too much for their discoveries. One experiment, for instance, required the matching of sets of nine anonymous themes written by a class of students in composition. The three experimenters had very good success in grouping the themes written by individual students, but they were powerless to explain how they did it. They were unable to point to the clues they had used and concluded that they had done so intuitively (that is, they had recognized clues they were not aware of).[115] The verb-adjective ratio devised by Busemann connects emotional stability in children with the use of a low number of verbs for each adjective.[116] The extension of this method to adult literary work (Emerson) revealed wild fluctuations in the writings of the same author, depending on the type of literary work examined. The most obvious variable in such an experiment is the concept of emotional stability, the estimate of which is bound to be vague.[117] A sufficient number of experiments have been made to indicate that results from this approach will eventually be useful to literary students, but to date the yield has been low.

The statistical approach to the study of language and literature, unlike the merely enumerative, is perhaps the furthest removed from the usual activities and the kind of thinking practiced by literary students. In fact, for some time the two have not too happily mixed. The literary workers seem resentful of having their domains invaded by the uncouth practitioners of an obscure ritual, whom they often rightly accuse of fundamental ignorance. The statisticians are either apologetic, attempting to disarm criticism by admitting that they are not entirely qualified for their venture, or aggressively assertive of the possible advantages of a

---

[115] Allport, Walker and Lathers, recounted in Miller, pp. 119-120.
[116] Miller, pp. 127-128.
[117] The divergence between works in different literary genres, here as in Sherman's earlier work, seems to constitute a significant stumbling-block. Any theory of consistent style must give an account of this divergence.

scientific approach to the problems of literary study.[118] It may be asked what the appropriateness might be of an approach to literature which seems equally suited to the charting of beer-drinkers' preferences or the distribution of shirt sizes. Literature is a matter of the spirit to be understood and appreciated by nothing less than the subtlest intellectual effort of trained and sensitive minds. Statisticians concede this point but argue that an opportunity for their science still remains because language is a mass phenomenon (involves a great many small units in various distributions) and statistics is a method for treating masses of any units with a verifiable amount of accuracy. Although an individual work is a unique creation, it is part of the greater enveloping mass of the language, among whose users the author is only one: "What before were regarded as quite unique events, the products of wilful creation, appear now when studied quantitatively as mere variants of typical expenditure of linguistic material . . ." [119] This is not to be taken as rejecting the scope of the individual contribution in composition but as merely narrowing it in some phases. For example, whatever might be the divergence – artistic, ideological – between Dickens and James Joyce, it seems likely that the frequency with which they use the letters, phonemes, and word-sizes in letters and syllables of the English language will be very similar and quite predictable within certain limits.[120] Of course, to say this is only to say that the English language has some features which bind all its users to a certain kind of uniformity. But it also means that on some levels, a writer may be powerless to escape the effect of chance. It is almost as if he were picking words blindly from a bag. Obviously the deterministic threat posed by this view is mitigated by the realization that such uniformity operates at the fundamental level of language and that there is a considerable sphere in which the individual talent may exert itself.

It was to this fundamental level that the founder of statistical

[118]   See, for example, G. Herdan, *Language as Choice and Chance* (Groningen, 1956), p. 1; Yule, *Statistical Study*, pp. 1-2.
[119]   Herdan, *Language*, p. 2.
[120]   *Ibid.*, p. 66.

linguistics addressed himself. George Kingsley Zipf discovered in language the vast number of units in which statistics is most at home and the high repetitiveness which makes categorizing convenient. In investigating "the relationship which exists between the form of the various speech elements and their behavior, in so far as this relationship is revealed statistically", he sought to prepare the way to "the formulation into tentative laws of the underlying forces which impel and direct linguistic expression".[121]

Examining words according to their size in syllables,[122] Zipf found that in German, one-syllable words were used half the time, two-syllable under a third and so on to one lone fifteen-syllable word.[123] To verify the tentative conclusion that short words are more common than long ones, Zipf demonstrated that Chinese [sic], English and Latin accord very closely to the same proposition, whether the measurement be based on morphemes, syllables or phonemes.[124] From this evidence, he formulated a "Principle of Least Effort", which supposedly governs word-length and tends to preserve equilibrium among the various components of language.[125] Statistical linguistics has developed since Zipf's time.[126]

[121] G. K. Zipf, *The Psycho-Biology of Language* (Boston, 1935), p. 3.
[122] He used the count of ten million words of German prose made in 1897-8 by F. W. Kaeding.
[123] Zipf, p. 23. Another investigator's results, based on samples of book length (c. 100,000 words), were very close to Kaeding's, one-syllable words ranging between 48.6 and 52.91 per cent for five prose works of four German authors, with excellent uniformity for two- to six-syllable words, except that one philosophical writer (Jaspers) used fewer two- and more three-, four-, and five-syllable words. The aggregate average for the five, if it could be computed, would probably come very close to Kaeding, the variations being accounted for by individual difference. See William Fucks, "On Mathematical Analysis of Style", *Biometrika,* XXXIX (1952), 125, Table 1.
[124] Zipf, pp. 24-8.
[125] *Human Behavior and the Principle of Least Effort* (Cambridge, Mass., 1949).
[126] He lived long enough to be a member of the "Committee on Quantitative Linguistics" established by the Sixth International Congress of Linguists, Paris, 1948. For a review of work in this field, see John B. Carroll, *The Study of Language* (Cambridge, 1959), pp. 61-5 and Miller, *Language and Communication,* pp. 80-98 and consult Herdan, *Language,* passim.

The application of statistics, rather than mere enumeration, to literary problems, specifically problems of style, or "individual differences" (in the phrase of the psychologists), has moved more slowly. The reason may be sought in the characteristics of statistics itself, which is a means of dealing with masses of units, grouped in discrete quantitative categories. A natural language supplies inexhaustible materials for a count of letters, syllables and phonemes. But the application of this method to the study of an author introduces two difficulties. First, the size of the material (the sample) is vastly reduced. Secondly, the categories applied to the material tend to be less simple and larger in size, shrinking the size of the sample still further. Whereas the number of words available for study in a language has no practical limit and the number of units, therefore, of whatever size, is similarly unlimited,[127] the size of any author's word-hoard is rather modest by comparison, and it becomes smaller as the units into which it is divided become larger.[128] The tendency of analysts of style to design cumbrous and ambiguous categories and to study no more than a fraction of the available units goes far to explain the skepticism with which such attempts are greeted.[129] However, there does not seem to be much doubt that substantial findings in the matter of individual differences between authors can be made by careful workers who are not tempted to claim more than the evidence will allow.[130] The attribution problems involved in

[127] It is not infinite, obviously, but unlimited within the ability of any person to deal with it, especially since it can be generated faster than it can be examined.
[128] A canon of 100,000 words contains fewer than 20,000 units if searched for prepositional phrases, and perhaps no more than 4,000 if sentences are the units.
[129] By Wimsatt, for example, p. 24.
[130] Problems of attribution by internal evidence are well illustrated in a series of articles ("The Case for Internal Evidence") which ran in the *Bulletin of the New York Public Library* in 1957, 1958 and 1959. Part of this material, which rehearsed arguments presented before a Symposium of the English Institute in 1958, combines claims for the value of internal evidence with the most unreliable demonstration of its use for attribution (verbal parallels, areas of interest, peculiarities of spelling). See Arthur Sherbo, "Can *Mother Midnight's Comical Pocket Book* be attributed to Christopher Smart?", *ibid.*, LXI (Aug. 1957), 373-382 and George F. Lord,

the *Imitatio Christi*, which Yule [131] attempted to settle by a study of the nouns it contained as compared with those in the works of two possible authors, may not be considered solved, but they have been taken a certain distance toward that goal. Yule suggests, near the end of his study [132] that a safe minimum in statistical stylistics might be a sample of 10,000 words. But since this may not always be available, as in disputed short tracts, the shortage could be made up for by considering other sections of the vocabulary, excluding only the function words, which might have uniform distribution in any author and thus tend to blur differences.

Just this dearth of sample handicapped the students of the *Equatorie of the Planetis*,[133] tentatively attributed to Chaucer on the basis of a minute study of the percentage of native vs. Romance words (as well as other items). The superiority of the modern treatment of the linguistic evidence lies in its ability to deal with the problem raised by the fluctuation of the native-Romance word ratio with the size of the work.[134] Not many studies of the same type have been conducted, perhaps because attribution-problems of importance are not common. However, various studies have dealt statistically with one stylistic feature or another. Both Elderton [135] and Fucks [136] rely on syllable-counts as tests of authorship with stable properties, Elderton specifying

---

"Two New Poems by Marvell?" *ibid.*, LXII (Nov. 1958), 551-570. The latter explicitly states that though no single piece of evidence is conclusive, the lot amounts "to a strong probability". (p. 564). Some useful cautions may be found in Ephim G. Fogel, "Salmons in Both, or some Caveats for Canonical Scholars", *ibid.*, LXIII (May 1959), 223-236 and LXIII (June 1959), 292-308.
[131] *Statistical Study,* passim.
[132] P. 281.
[133] Ed. Derek J. Price (Cambridge, 1955).
[134] G. Herdan, "Chaucer's Authorship of the *Equatorie of the Planetis*", *Language,* XXXII (1956), 254-9. But see the adverse review of his procedure by C. Douglas Chretien, "A New Statistical Approach to the Study of Language", *Romance Philology,* XVI (Feb. 1963), 299-301.
[135] W. P. Elderton, "A Few Statistics on the Length of English Words", *Journal of the Royal Statistical Society* (Series A), CXII (1949), 436-443.
[136] See fn. 123, above.

samples of 10,000 to 20,000 words for likely stability.[137] The authors each has examined do not coincide, except for Shakespeare. Elderton counted the prose and the verse of *Henry IV, Part I*, whereas Fucks counted the words in *Othello*. The percentages for each word-length correspond very closely and the average number of syllables per word agrees to two decimal places.[138] Such agreement depends on large enough samples, adequately selected, on the careful definition of categories (even in the case of syllables), and of course on accurate counting. That this approach will likely have a place in certain types of literary work seems inescapable, especially in view of the ease with which very large counts may now be made with the aid of electronic data-processing equipment.[139] Manuals of technique and bibliographies of past work have been published[140] and concordances been produced with the aid of this newest of all research tools.[141] Projects of even greater scope have been announced: Samuel Johnson's works, the *Iliad* and the *Odyssey*, St. Paul, Junius, the authors of the *Federalist* have all been subjected to quantitative analysis.[142] It is understandable that the introduction of such a technological advance as the electronic computer into literary study should stir some opposition.[143] Even the printed book and the typewriter were

---

[137] P. 443.

[138] Elderton (Verse): 1-syllable, 78.4; 2, 16.5; 3, 4.1; 4-5, 1.0. Average word-length in syllables: 1.28 (p. 441). Fucks: 1, 78.81; 2, 15.11; 3, 4.95; 4, 1.16. Average: 1.287 (p. 125).

[139] See Andrew D. Booth, L. Brandwood and J. P. Cleave, *Mechanical Resolution of Linguistic Problems* (London, 1958).

[140] Pierre Guiraud, *Les Caractères Statistiques du Vocabulaire* (Paris, 1953), *Problèmes et Méthodes de la Statistique Linguistique* (Dordrecht, 1959), and *Bibliographie Critique de la Statistique Linguistique* (Utrecht, 1954), 2500 titles; also G. Herdan, *Language as Choice and Chance,* and *Type-Token Mathematics.*

[141] E.g., Dryden and Matthew Arnold.

[142] A Johnson project has been under way at Michigan State University for some time. The Homer study of James T. McDonough, Jr., is described in "Classics and Computers", *Graduate Faculties News-Letter* (March, 1962), pp. 4-5. For Junius and the *Federalist,* see Appendices G and D. News of a project designed to distinguish the genuine Epistles of St. Paul from the spurious (by means of a test based on the frequency and patterning of *kai*) is contained in *Time,* LXXXI (March 15, 1963), p. 56.

[143] And yet the London *Times Literary Supplement* published a series of

not unopposed at their introduction, and Swift himself may be numbered among those taking a short view of the quantification of literature.[144] Nonetheless, the advantages of such equipment seem too great to discard. If it is remembered that electronic machines are merely clerks who can count and sort at very high speed and only under human instruction, it may be realized that objections to their use are not entirely rational. It is obviously not the tool but the wielder of it who is the responsible party. Statistics is a means of processing data and of evaluating their predictive accuracy, and electronic-data processing equipment is a means of doing this more rapidly than the unaided mind and pencil can do it. The quarrel must be with the assumptions, and the definitions according to which the study is undertaken. It is when these are not plainly stated that untrustworthy results are produced. Therefore, as the first step toward introducing rigor into this study of style, let the major assumptions be stated along with the basis on which they rest and the consequences which are expected to follow.

articles and a correspondence about the advantages for humane studies of technological aids (March-June 1962). These have all been collected into a pamphlet entitled "Freeing the Mind".
[144] *Works,* XI, 168.

III. PRINCIPLES, ASSUMPTIONS AND METHODS

It is dark on a side street of a large city. A man tries to open a closed window and when it resists he takes a glass-cutting tool out of his pocket and makes a small triangular hole in the window glass just below the point where he judges the lock to be. He slides his hand through the opening, releases the catch and, raising the window, quietly enters the building he is about to burglarize. The whole operation has taken less than a minute because the burglar is a professional, who works efficiently and without distraction. He is so cool that his hand hardly trembles as he shapes the hole in the glass into an inverted isosceles triangle with a broad base; that is his unconscious trademark and it will be ultimately responsible for his capture because the police have a file of criminals, arranged according to their modes of operation or criminal styles.

The burglar, who might have been at a loss without a regular method, has developed one as a way of dealing with the challenges he faces. Because he is a member of a sub-culture (the professional criminal), his basic choices are culturally limited. If he decides to be a burglar, he follows the criminal procedures he has become familiar with from his teachers and associates (the bearers of the tradition). Because he is a professional with an opportunity to develop competence through practice, he acquires technique, but because he is an individual he leaves traces of his individuality in the preferences he expresses. These no doubt reflect some underlying tendency in himself, which mysteriously comes to the surface, as in the triangular hole. Although he may be captured as a result of his consistency (because his style is known), he might have been captured earlier if he had faced the challenge of the closed window by simply throwing a brick through it. In other words, his style is an ordered rather than a patternless response to the challenges offered by the hazard of experience (the locked window). The style of a writer may be considered in a similar context. Considerably over-simplified, the task of a writer is to respond effectively to certain challenges of his profession. The writer's challenges are not concrete, like the burglar's, but they have a similar reality. Broadly, the writer must respond to the necessity of presenting material in a persuasive or a moving way; or he must find a logical sequence to impose on the disorderly array of facts he has collected. His response to these challenges is always conditioned by his culture, the choices available in his language in his time and place. But it is also limited by the choices he makes deliberately for the effect on the reader. And finally it is given form by those he is impelled to make by some unconscious predisposition.[1]

Sometimes these three components – cultural, rhetorical, expressive – cannot be readily distinguished. For instance, a piece of ancient pottery found by an archaeologist may be traced to its proper time and culture with hardly any hesitation by the expert cognizant of styles in pottery, that is, by one who knows the limits of available choice for the potter in that particular place and moment. The artist's individual contribution, his further refinement of choices, is not so easy to elicit, however. And to distinguish between what the potter-artist chose to convey and the decoration he felt impelled to add to the vessel may well be impossible.

In literature, the position is clearer. The writer's culture (his period, usually), may be easily specified, sometimes within a very few decades. But this cultural aspect of style represents merely a secondary phase of the study of any individual writer's style.[2] The

[1] R. Barthes, *Le Degré Zéro de l'Ecriture* (Paris, 1953), distinguishes these three components as *langue, écriture* and *style proprement dit,* as cited by P. Guiraud, *La Stylistique* (Paris, 1954), p. 94.
[2] It is taken into account in the choice of writers to be compared with Swift. See p. 279, below. Style as a cultural phenomenon is interestingly treated by A. L. Kroeber, *Style and Civilizations* (Ithaca, N. Y., 1957).

major concern is the personal aspect, in its two phases: (1) the deliberate choice of effective means of communication (the usual sense of *style* for most critics); and especially (2) the unconscious expression of the writer's personality in his writing. That this unconscious reflection of the writer's personality in his work is consistently diffused through all his writings is the major assumption of this study.

The study of personality being a branch of psychology, it may be appropriate to accept the results of psychologists who have specialized in this field.[3] In their opinion, literary style is an expressive movement of the personality (like handwriting), guided and directed by its deepest recesses functioning effortlessly and unconsciously.[4] As the personality matures, style changes with it. But, in a sense, it is the product of the mature personality which alone can be reflected as a consistent pattern. Though literary style is studied in vocabulary and sentence-structure, it is not merely to be found in mechanical carriers; it must be studied as an aspect of the total personality.[5] Gordon Allport summarizes well this entire assumption:

Style is an expressive form of slow growth; it is not something ready-made, picked at random to be donned mechanically. It develops gradually from within; it cannot for long be simulated or feigned. Behind the manifestations of an individual's style stretches a whole life history, back to the cradle and his first departures from the schedule prepared for him and all other infants. Style is the gradual externalization of the inner peculiarities and unique characteristics of the individual. Convention and fashion may set limits upon style, prescribing the frame of the moment within which one's style (of clothing, writing, painting, script, conversation, music, recreation and what-not) must be constrained. For the time being, these limits are rigid; only a genius is able to tear loose from the current frame of mode or convention and create a new idiom (that will determine the frame of the future). But even within these limits no personality, whatever the culture, repeats exactly the style of another.[6]

[3] The views cited are given on the authority of Gordon W. Allport, *Personality* (New York, 1937), a standard text. Similar views may be found in Sanford, *op. cit.*, p. 814, who cites Dewey, Sapir, Kantor as progenitors.
[4] Allport, p. 466.
[5] *Ibid.*, pp. 490-1.
[6] *Ibid.*, p. 493.

Consequently, the uniqueness of an author shows consistently in his style, regardless of the subject-matter or the conventions of the medium or the period.[7] It may progress with maturity, but it is not subject to the sort of influence that conscious activity suffers. Though one cannot deny that a writer is at liberty, in revising, to modify his material as he wishes, he can only modify it in certain ways. Revision is usually no more than a slight change of sentence-structure or the replacement of individual words. The underlying layer is seldom touched because the writer is, in some sense, not aware of it. He sees past or through it. In the same way, his remarks on literary composition and his overt criteria of style are generally unreliable guides to his own writing. They represent standards of general currency and, being consciously applied, can have only a superficial effect on his own writing. One may modify one's conduct but one is unable to change one's personality.

Thus, three points are united in this assumption: (1) that style reflects personality; (2) that this is an unconscious process; and (3) that in mature writers the process is consistent. Two of these components lead in turn to further assumptions which are my remaining theoretical foundations.[8] That the process of composi-

---

[7] This assumption seems to have become common in the most recent studies of the style of individual authors. It is implicit in the *Federalist* project (see Appendix D). Ellegård, *Statistical Method*, is clearly dependent on a version of it (pp. 8-9). Even the Rev. Mr. Andrew Morton, studying St. Paul's Epistles, refers to "the theory that every writer has certain subconscious, invariable writing habits", *Time*, *loc. cit.* Richard M. Ohmann, *Shaw: The Style and the Man* (Middletown, Conn., 1962), seems to be accepting the idea when he announces his work to be "an effort to specify the modes of expression he [Shaw] finds most congenial ... [and] ... a discussion of his habitual patterns of thought and feeling..." (pp. xi-xii), but he does not finally commit himself.

[8] This insistence on sound theoretical foundations may be a pointless concession to traditional ways of conducting research. I might have allowed my assumptions to remain unstated, on the intuitive level, and have set out immediately to measure all and anything that struck me. That this might be a sound procedure is suggested by the *Federalist* Projectors: "If obvious methods fail, the systematic explorations of a very large pool of variables may strike oil. Routine drilling paid off for us more than clever thoughts about words and other variables that ought to discriminate", "Inference in an Authorship Problem", Press Release dated September 9, 1962 (p. 20).

tion is in some part unconscious leads to the implication that it may be most easily observed in an involuntary or automatic aspect of writing. That the process is consistent leads to the possibility that it may be measured.

What happens in a writer's mind while he is writing is not known. The ancient view held that he found ideas first, arranged them in an appropriate order, found words in which to clothe them, combined these words in appropriate grammatical forms and then submitted the result to the public. It now seems improbable that ideas can be manipulated without words but quite possible that the writer's mind projects a syntactical mold for a sentence at the same time as it handles the complex interaction between word and idea.[9] That is, while the sentence is mentally in suspension, a certain outline is planned for it, in which the individual places for words are designed in grammatical rather than semantic terms. One word may be later replaced by another of the same or different meaning, but the pattern remains roughly similar. Far more extensive activity would be necessary to change the general structure of the thought.

A natural inference from this process is that the individual choice of word is far more readily tampered with than the grammatical mold. The writer can change words at will, in revising, with a minimum of effort. He does not have to recast the sentence in order to substitute one word for another and he goes through this process of synonym substitution as a regular part of the discipline of writing and revision. The selection of a grammatical framework for his thought is a far more complex procedure, one which proceeds in great part below the level of conscious thought, at least while the process of literary composition is going on at the usual rate.[10] It takes more effort to modify the syntactical structure of thought than the lexical component. There is less

[9] I cannot cite specific sources for these two constructs, but most readers will recognize the former as one that permeates older works of rhetoric and psychology. The second one is a compound of the ideas of modern schools of psychology, communication engineering, and such anthropological-linguistic ideas as the Sapir-Whorf hypothesis.
[10] The comment of a grammarian on this process is cited in Chapter VI, fn. 13, below.

economy in structural revision because it is far-reaching, each affected unit having influence on related ones, until considerable care must be taken to avoid logical or grammatical impropriety. Further, there is a loss of economy in the move from the unconscious handling of structure to conscious revision. Thus it seems probable that vocabulary is intimately connected with Style (1), the rhetorical level, but that emphasis on syntax will reach Style (2), the expressive level.

The search for the truth of personality and of culture in the unconscious realm is a commonplace in an age whose scholarship is in so many ways Freudian. In the depths of his imagery, says Kenneth Burke, the artist cannot lie.[11] It is not carrying this thought too far to extend it to grammar. In his syntax, the writer is expressing himself more fully than in his vocabulary. Can it be because he does not realize that he is doing so, blinded as he is by the overwhelming semantic luster of the words? It is no mere accident that *style* has always had *diction* as a synonym. However interesting the study of vocabulary may be for other uses, in eliciting the personal, unconscious style, it must be set aside in favor of grammar. Thus the analyst of Shaw's style comes forward with the opinion: "It would clearly be preferable if the only categories used in the actual description of a style were formally defined, grammatical – not semantic." [12] But he doubts whether modern grammars of English are rigorous enough, whereas the old grammars are contaminated by semantic influence.[13] Obviously the discovery of suitable grammatical categories is essential for the success of the sort of description of style that I am making. But it is comforting to find that one's intuitive and theoretical views are confirmed by a recent Swift biographer: "The

[11]   Cited by Herbert J. Muller, *Science and Criticism* (New Haven, Conn., 1943), p. 155.
[12]   Ohmann, p. xiv.
[13]   His doubts may be considered excessive. In the old grammar a noun is described in terms of its meaning – it is the name of a place, person . . . – but in the new it is described by means of the formal signals it embodies (terminal *s* in plurals, use with *the*, possible function with *is*, etc. . . .).

heart of Swift's literary effectiveness is not his vocabulary but his syntax." [14]

The search for Swift's syntactical consistency is based on the belief – indeed the necessity – that such consistency is characteristic of all his work, regardless of subject matter. Most studies of style specify, as we have seen, that this or that peculiarity is limited to prose of a certain type or on a certain subject. It has seemed to me necessary to go beyond this, to find a description which was insensitive to such changes. If the style truly derives by unconscious agency from the personality of the writer, no discounts or compromises should be necessary. In other words, if a peculiarity has been discovered which is directly the result of some aspect of the personality of the writer, it should logically be present in all his writings. This principle I follow with Swift, expecting that if the same man wrote both *Gulliver's Travels* and *A Tale of a Tub*, they should have fundamental stylistic characteristics in common, subject only to two reservations. Men change with time and so do their personalities and therefore their styles. The only works I have excluded from this examination of Swift's prose are those few which appeared over his signature, such as the *Proposal* (1712), the *History*,[15] the *Journal to Stella*, his correspondence and personalia, as well as the Dialogues in *Polite Conversation*. These are considered atypical works, because of their mode of publication and in view of the fact that Swift's reputation depends almost wholly on the works he published anonymously.

Before the establishing of grammatical categories can be effective, something must be said about measurement. Unless quantities can be measured, they are only qualities and may only be handled impressionistically, if at all. Even if the assumptions previously made are granted, nothing will be accomplished if the presence

---

[14]   Irvin Ehrenpreis, *Swift: The Man, His Works and the Age* (London, 1962), p. 177. Ehrenpreis's comments on the styles of Swift and Temple are an unfortunate mixture of observed peculiarities and adjectives like *graceful, direct, charming* and phrases like *nervous syntax* and *simplicity of phrase and language* (pp. 180-1).

[15]   But note that the *History* is used in Ch. VII, below, as a control. There is no guarantee that the atypical works would not accord with the anonymous, but for the sake of excluding all unnecessary variables atypical works were mainly left out.

of certain peculiarities of style cannot be observed in quantitative terms. If the artist is, in Flaubert's impressive phrase, like God in the creation, present everywhere and visible nowhere,[16] the measurement of peculiarities of style must stop before it has begun, because some sort of visibility is necessary to any objective measurement. To be sure, some things are not readily visible to the naked eye. In the same way, there are characteristics of style that might escape observation and still be there, ready to be resolved with the proper optical instrument.[17]

Granted the possibility of measurement, what of the desirability of dealing with quantities that can be measured? It has often been the boast of students of humane letters that they were dealing with the unmeasurable matters of the spirit. This claim has not always been accurate. Any work of literary scholarship, opened at random, will probably yield a statement suggesting that a certain influence is greater than another, that some event has a greater probability of occurrence than another, or that a given source is the most likely antecedent of some literary masterpiece. What are all these but imprecise quantitative statements? And if imprecise statements are acceptable, why should formulations striving for greater precision be viewed with suspicion?[18]

Even if the objection about the propriety of mensuration is met, the more weighty objection which is behind it must be considered, that is, whether the things which can be precisely measured are really the significant ones. In any rigorously-conducted research, the investigator begins by being faced with the whole problem, baffling in its organic unity. In order to deal with it, he must analyze, break up and divide the unity into components which can be treated objectively without violating the spirit of literary inquiry. The ultimate aims of literary study must be kept

[16] Gustave Flaubert, *Correspondance*, Deuxième Série, 1850-4 (Paris, 1889), p. 155. The original reads: "L'auteur dans son œuvre doit être comme Dieu dans l'univers, présent partout, et visible nulle part . . ." It is used as an epigraph by Caroline Spurgeon, *Shakespeare's Imagery* (Cambridge, 1935).

[17] This question is taken up in Ch. VI, p. 204 f., below.

[18] On the question of measurement, see H. J. Eysenck, *Sense and Nonsense in Psychology* (Harmondsworth, 1958), pp. 182-3.

always in mind while the student is devising suitable categories for quantitative treatment of his text. It is too obvious to dwell on, yet it always needs mention, that there must always be, in any quantitative inquiry involving a literary figure, an aim beyond the mere obtention and manipulation of quantities. Statisticians, to whom the materials of literature and economics are indifferently suitable, may find themselves exempted from this necessity. But the student of literature must frame his categories in such a way that he has the conviction that he is measuring something that he feels is significant, not something which is merely measurable.

The use of significant categories unfortunately raises a problem which the present state of knowledge about the relation of thought to writing and of language to style makes insoluble. The most effective categories would necessarily be such as might serve to distinguish one personality from another. These could perform this task most effectively if they had a given correspondence to grammatical, syntactical, inflectional or other categories. Of course, we do not know that they do so correspond and so we are at liberty to concoct new categories to which we may attach sub-jective personality equivalents[19] or we must use existing categories in the hope that they coincide in some way with personality traits. The latter proceeding seems the more sensible, if only be-cause it moves from the known to the speculative.

The use of such grammatical categories as form-classes and function-classes (suitably modified) in the later chapters of this study is in accord with this view. But, to begin with, a more personal response to Swift's text seemed to be in order, one which would emphasize the literary nature of the bond between the writer and the analyst of style. On this basis, I began by reading the works of Swift with careful attention to such peculiarities as I might observe to be present in Swift and absent from the work of his contemporaries (at least in the same degree).[20] I collected

[19] This is the frequent sin of neo-rhetorical critics of style, who observe a peculiarity which they erect into a category (for example, negativism – use of words meaning *no*) and on the basis of meager evidence, without controls, ascribe an equivalent personality trait to an author. Neither the category, the evidence, nor the interpretation is justified.

[20] This procedure owes something to Spitzer's "philological circle", for

examples of these features of his style and then rendered the procedure objective by an actual count in the work of Swift and
various other authors. This mode of proceeding, though it begins
with an intuition, ends with the concrete data in a form which
may be verified.

The closest to the writer's consciousness of these peculiarities is
the making of lists, or catalogues, or series, or accumulations, as
they are variously called. Under the heading of "Seriation", this
organizing principle of Swift's thought is considered from a variety
of analytical and interpretive aspects. It is the first to be studied
because it is the most obvious feature – other have noticed it –
and the most rhetorical. It is followed by a discussion of Swift's
way with connectives. This peculiarity, which has not previously
been noticed, seems to operate mainly on the expressive level. It
opens the way to the most recondite aspects of Swift's style, those
which may only be elicited by detailed grammatical analysis.

---

which see *Linguistics and Literary History,* pp. 10-15. Ellegård's study of
Junius begins with a similar "subjective impression" corrected by objective
methods (*A Statistical Method,* pp. 22-3).

IV. SERIATION

It is a commonplace of rhetoric that the use of more words than necessary constitutes redundancy and that redundancy is a defect to be avoided in good writing. In the eighteenth century, not only rhetoricians but literary men might be found laying down the law about this violation. George Campbell says in his authoritative text: "It may be established as a maxim that admits no exception ... that the fewer the words are, provided neither propriety nor perspicuity be violated, the expression is always more vivid." [1] Addison, in the *Tatler*, urges pleaders to banish all "synonymous terms and unnecessary Multiplications of Verbs and Nouns".[2] Swift in a variety of places inveighs against "multiplying unnecessary Words, or using various Expressions",[3] and warns against "the Frequency of flat, unnecessary Epithets".[4] And in fact most handbooks of rhetoric are still very strict about wordiness. Though this rule doubtless has its useful side, there is much more to the matter than amateur rhetoricians have realized.[5] Modern communications theorists have taught us that redundancy is a useful

[1] *Philosophy of Rhetoric*, 7th ed. (London, 1823), p. 362.
[2] No. 253, November 21, 1710. *The Works of ... Joseph Addison* (Birmingham, 1761), II, 343.
[3] *Gulliver's Travels, Works*, XI, 121.
[4] *Letter to a Young Gentleman, Works*, IX, 68.
[5] It is surprising how unreliable professional writers are on the subject of writing success: Swift is consistently confusing his ideals with his performance, Butler is affectedly unconcerned about style: *Samuel Butler's Notebooks*, ed. G. Keynes and B. Hill (London, 1951), pp. 290-1; Maugham is elaborately irresponsible: *The Summing-Up*, passim. *The Writer on His Art*, ed. Walter Allen (New York, 1948), is a collection of such useless advice. Perhaps this is a kind of confirmation of the hypothesis that style is an unconscious mold of the mind and that neither conscious theories of

safeguard of meaning, protecting the message against garbling, inattention and other obstacles.[6]

The ancients also had respect for the uses of excess or fullness.[7] Numerous figures of speech used by the ancient rhetoricians represent ways of saying more than the minimum, from which it may surely be inferred that they had at least a suspicion that brevity (minimal statement) was not the last word. Modern studies of meaning have equally suggested that nothing can be retrenched from a statement without the loss of some particle of what must be the author's meaning or effect. These differences of opinion surely suggest a human willingness to cling to opinions for which there is no warrant. For brevity, simplicity and clarity, men seem to hold an unreasoning fondness, something like the love of unity that Arthur Lovejoy called "metaphysical pathos".[8] And they are inclined to credit those whom they approve of (as they approve of Swift's style) with these master-qualities, more as accolade than as accurate description.

In reading Swift's works with any attention, one cannot fail to be struck by the frequency with which one comes across catalogues or sequences of syntactical units of various size.[9] One observes

---

style nor advice as to the adoption of particular idiosyncrasy can have much influence on the writer anxious to improve. In Platonic terms, all he can do to improve is to come closer to being a *vir bonus*.

[6] See Miller, *Language and Communication,* pp. 102 ff., for a general discussion.

[7] Redundancy, or whatever else it may be called – prolixity, pleonasm, tautology, copiousness and the others given – all agree in referring to what is more than the minimum.

[8] *The Great Chain of Being* (Cambridge, Mass., 1948), pp. 12-13.

[9] They have been previously noticed by Teerink (p. 126), Gertraut Zickgraf, *Jonathan Swifts Stilforderungen und Stil* (Marburg, 1940), pp. 42 ff., who treats them as types of sentence-structure, as well as by Martin Price, *Swift's Rhetorical Art* (New Haven, 1953), p. 21 ("frequent lists of parallel terms"), D. W. Jefferson, *From Dryden to Johnson* (Harmondsworth, 1957), p. 241 ("destructive juxtapositions of words"), Bonamy Dobrée, *English Literature in the Early Eighteenth Century: 1700-1740* (Oxford, 1959), p. 459 ("lumping together ... activities"), Ronald Paulson, *Theme and Structure in Swift's Tale of a Tub* (New Haven, 1960), p. 69 ("Juxtapositions", "lists", "series"), and J. Holloway, "The Well-filled Dish: an Analysis of Swift's Satire", *Hudson Review,* IX (Spring 1956), p. 27 ("important device ... for insinuation is the catalogue").

The surprising observation of Jan Lannering, *Studies in the Prose Style* time after time that illustrations are seldom given in pairs or triplets but in disorderly accumulations, variously connected and sometimes of great length. An examination of several texts of Swift suggested to me that this might well be a stylistic peculiarity of his. This possibility seemed unusual because some recent studies of eighteenth-century style revealed that formal parallelism was characteristic not only of Johnson, but of Addison and by implication of the whole group of Augustan writers,[10] who have more than once been credited with a uniform style.[11] They were especially attracted to the careful and planned grouping of items (nouns, adjectives, verbs) in twos and threes (doublets and triplets). That this rhetorical device is akin to amplification is clear to the commentators on Addison's and Johnson's styles.[12] Though Swift is not a frequent user of this sort of parallelism, his practice is fully in the spirit of amplification. It deserves the name Lannering borrows from the ancients to characterize Addison's use of doublets: *copia* or *copia verborum*.[13]

To the classical rhetoricians, *copia verborum* was not a formal device of style (like inversion or irony) but rather a vague ideal, not unlike the feeling about having a large vocabulary which prevails today. Cicero, for example, explaining the advantage to the orator of using his mind to the fullest, says that "a plenty of things will beget a plenty of words".[14] Quintilian advises the reading of the older Latin dramatists, who may help the student to acquire a rich vocabulary, despite their mediocre literary value.[15]

---

of Addison (Uppsala, 1951), must be set down alongside these: "Swift's peculiar sense of economy of style makes him communicate his thoughts with the force of terseness rather than of amplification and multiplication" (p. 30). This blindness must be traced to the fossilized tradition of Swift-style criticism discussed above (Chapter I). Lannering had the evidence before him but preferred to trust to the commonplaces of the tradition.

[10]   Wimsatt, *op. cit.,* Ch. I, passim; Lannering, p. 54.
[11]   Wellek and Warren, p. 184.
[12]   Lannering, pp. 54-5; Wimsatt, p. 15.
[13]   P. 54.
[14]   "Rerum enim copia verborum copiam gignit", *De Oratore,* tr. H. Rackham, Loeb Classical Library (London, 1960), Bk. III, Ch. xxxi, II, 99.
[15]   "Multum autem veteres etiam Latini conferunt ... in primis copiam verborum", *Institutio Oratoria,* tr. H. E. Butler, Loeb Classical Library (London, 1958), Bk. I, Ch. viii, I, 151.

The main idea in both these writers is the praise of richness in a vocabulary. It is hardly necessary to do more than glance at the Urquhart translation of Rabelais to realize that copiousness, as represented by long lists of words, was practiced in English earlier than Swift's time. In the coincidence of this stylistic tendency, Swift's and Rabelais's names are again brought together. Pope, in some well-known lines,[16] established the connection, which was elaborated by Voltaire a few years later.[17] Swift was a ready reader of French and in fact owned the Lyons 1558 edition of Rabelais's works, which he had annotated in his own hand.[18] Source-seekers for the origins of *Gulliver's Travels* have made some efforts to establish Swift's debt to Rabelais,[19] and students of *A Tale of a Tub* have noted some parallels,[20] while some have sought to refer the resemblance to Swift's connection with the seventeenth-century tradition of English prose rather than the Augustan.[21] Whatever the value of these speculations, it remains that Swift and Rabelais have in common the tendency to construct catalogues of words, which likely emerges from a common intellectual and emotional attitude, rather than indicates a debt of one man to the other.

Swift, Addison and Johnson agree in their general adherence to the principle of multiplication, but there is a crucial distinction between Swift's undisciplined or informal method and Addison's and Johnson's careful and formal adherence to customary models. These doublets and triplets from Johnson illustrate the usual formal pattern: "consonance and propriety", "incessant and unwearied diligence", "reproach, hatred and opposition", "her physick of the mind, her catharticks of vice, or lenitives of pas-

[16] "Whether thou chuse Cervantes' serious air/Or laugh and shake in Rab'lais' easy chair . . .", *Dunciad* (1728), Bk. I, ll. 19-20.
[17] *Letters Concerning the English Nation* (London, 1733), pp. 213-215.
[18] Harold Williams, *Dean Swift's Library* (Cambridge, 1932), Item 42, p. 50.
[19] W. A. Eddy, *Gulliver's Travels: A Critical Study* (Princeton, 1923), pp. 57 ff.
[20] William B. Ewald, Jr., *The Masks of Jonathan Swift* (Oxford, 1954), pp. 24, 37; Paulson, pp. 7-8, 72-6.
[21] Jefferson, *From Dryden to Johnson,* p. 231.

sion".[22] Swift builds his multiplied structures not merely of words two or three at a time, but accumulates words, phrases and clauses in seemingly unending series. It is almost as if he could not begin to express enough within the confines of a doublet or triplet. The following series of gerunds from *Gulliver's Travels* typically exemplifies his method:

... vast Numbers of our People are compelled to seek their Livelihood by Begging, Robbing, Stealing, Cheating, Pimping, Forswearing, Flattering, Suborning, Forging, Gaming, Lying, Fawning, Hectoring, Voting, Scribling, Stargazing, Poysoning, Whoring, Canting, Libelling, Free-thinking, and the like Occupations.[23]

This sequence from the *Journal to Stella* well shows Swift's unwillingness or inability to follow regularity of form: "You visit, you dine abroad, you see friends; you pilgarlick; you walk from Finglass, you a cat's foot."[24] On the basis of evidence now to be examined, he seemed dedicated to numbers higher than three.

The test of the observation that Swift was fonder of such lists than other authors was based on the definition that a list is any easily perceptible sequence of items approximately similar in some structural feature and numbering four or more.[25] The controls are Dryden, Defoe, Steele, Addison, Goldsmith and Johnson: five random samples of 2000 words from each.[26] Lists are classified according to the size of the units: words, phrases and clauses. The results justify expectation, as shown in Table 4.1.

---

[22] All four examples are taken from Wimsatt, pp. 35, 20.

[23] *Works,* XI, 236.

[24] Ed. Harold Williams (Oxford, 1948), II, 388, under date October 20, 1711. This example is given despite the fact that the *Journal,* as a "signed" work, is not considered typical of Swift's style.

[25] This definition more or less coincides with that of Ohmann, *Shaw,* who finds the "long series" peculiarly characteristic of Shaw's prose. After some apologetic disclaimers about the necessity of statistical evidence, Ohmann reveals that Shaw has a frequency of 2.7 lists per thousand words, compared with values of 1.6 for his contemporaries, the whole based on samples of 2600 words (Appendix I).

[26] A list of the passages used in all the tabulations in this and the next chapter may be found in Appendix I. An explanation of the basis on which the samples were chosen may be found in Appendix II.

TABLE 4.1

*Frequency of Lists in 10,000-word selections from
seven eighteenth-century writers*

	Dryden	Defoe	Steele	Addison	Goldsmith	Johnson	Swift
Words	5	1	9	7	2	3	14
Phrases	1			1	5	1	6
Clauses	2		1	1	2		9
Total	8	1	10	9	9	4	29

Owing to the small size of the unit samples, the distribution is not uniform, but certain predictions may be made on the basis of the figures. For the reader of Swift, this means that he may expect to find an average of one list of some kind on every page (assuming a page of 300-400 words), though random variation may require him at times to go several pages without finding any. By comparison, in the prose of Dryden, Defoe, Steele and Addison, a list is only to be found once in three pages (about 1000 words), in Johnson's, once in ten or so, and in Defoe, the reader will find one in twenty-five pages.

Moreover such lists are not for Swift what they seem to be for Addison and the others, merely expanded triplets. Whereas theirs are for the most part sequences of four words, Swift's lists range widely in length and in size of unit as well as in variety of structure. Of his 29, only eight are sequences of 4 words; the remainder include six groups of 5 items, three of 6, two of 7, and four of 8 or more, among which may be counted one of 11 and one of 19 items. It is not going beyond the evidence to say that the tendency to multiply words, phrases and clauses is a deep-seated element of Swift's style.

This tendency has been noticed before, but suitable inferences have not always been drawn. Teerink, in his attempt to show that Swift wrote the John Bull pamphlets, makes this observation: "The peculiarity of joining together verbal forms into strings of two or three and even more . . . is a phenomenon which occurs so frequently in Swift's works . . . that the bare mention of the fact

without submitting special evidence, will suffice." [27] Teerink seems
to be saying that Swift is a frequent user of doublets and triplets,
though he presents no evidence. On the other hand, Lannering,
who had made a number of counts and presents figures, contends
that Swift does not use word-pairs or triplets with any frequency
comparable to Addison's, and is thereby misled into thinking that
Swift has no use for copiousness. Lannering's figures show that
Addison used nearly two doublets per hundred words and Swift
fewer than one.[28] It is clear that Lannering was in error about
Swift's affinity for multiplication; was he also mistaken about
Swift's use of doublets and triplets? The matter can be settled by
means of a tabulation recording the frequency of these formal
devices.

Table 4.2 shows the percentage of doublets and triplets in five
2000-word samples of Defoe, Addison, Goldsmith, Johnson, Gibbon and Swift.

TABLE 4.2

*Percentage of doublets and triplets in 10,000-word
samples from six eighteenth-century writers*

	Defoe	Addison	Goldsmith	Johnson	Gibbon	Swift
Doublets	1.11	1.55	1.30	1.72	2.98	1.51
Triplets	.19	.10	.23	.14	.23	.16
Total	1.30	1.65	1.53	1.86	3.21	1.67

[27] It is not clear what *verbal forms* means, whether *verbs* or *verbals,* or
merely *words.* If the more limited meaning is taken, the statement is in-
accurate; therefore, it may be wiser to lay the ambiguity to Teerink's non-
native English and to interpret *verbal forms* to mean *words. The History
of John Bull,* ed. H. Teerink (Amsterdam, 1925), p. 126.
[28] See fn. 9, above, for his statement, and *op. cit.,* pp. 25 ff., for his
figures, of which the following is a summary. The number of word-pairs
per 100 words in a group of Addison's *Tatlers* and *Spectators* varies thus:
2.00, 2.52, 1.50, 1.47, 1.85, 1.56, 1.70, 1.55, 2.45, 2.87, 1.65, 2.67, 1.56.
The relative values he found in Swift's works were 0.77, 0.00, 0.13, 0.59,
1.22, 1.35 for *Tatlers* 66, 67, 68, and "298", and *Examiners* 31 and 32. The
significant point about the Swift values is that the first three are drawn
from works which are *not* by Swift, at least in part, and certainly not

It is easy to observe that Gibbon, as might be expected by anyone who has ever read a page of the *Decline*, is predominant in the use of these forms. Although Defoe is the lowest of the lot, there is hardly any important difference among these writers, except for Gibbon. In particular, the identity of frequency for Swift and Addison is of interest, because it goes counter to Lannering's findings.[29] The consciously selected artifice (doublet and triplet) is undifferentiated in the practice of these two writers. But in the higher arithmetic of seriation, which may reflect the intensity of mental energy – an unconscious factor –, there is a large and important difference. This finding argues against the value of formal rhetorical categories in the description of style.

The rhetorical categories are of little use in the classification of series. Such figures as balance, antithesis, parallelism, repetition, and other types of multiplication, all touch the stylistic feature of seriation but are not congruent with it. They are the consciously-adopted element of composition, as opposed to the heedless output of internal pressures. The abundance of energy and fertility that may be expressed in seriation is too organic to be easily disposed into classes. In fact, though a series can be recognized without difficulty, it cannot be defined more exactly than *an array of analogous syntactical units, numbering more than three, in close proximity.*

Most simply, series can be subdivided into two types: sequences of words and sequences of groups of words, mixed groupings being considered as belonging to the predominant type.

---

authenticated works. Davis (*Works*, II), cites "298" as 20 of Harrison's continuation but does not mention 66 and places parts of 67 and 68 in an Appendix entitled "Contributions to the Tatler and Spectator attributed to Swift or containing hints furnished by him". Moreover, Lannering's figures diverge from Wimsatt's, who found that Johnson used more doublets than Addison. Lannering contests this finding by casting doubt on the randomness of Wimsatt's samples.

[29] The tabulation also supports Wimsatt against Lannering in the matter of whether Addison or Johnson uses more doublets. An additional detail of possible interest is the regular predominance of nouns as components. The ratio is about two to one over adjectives and verbs combined. Adjectives and verbs appear about equally, except in Gibbon and Goldsmith, where adjectives appear twice as often as verbs.

Swift's commonest sequence is the string of nouns or names, which can be found in any syntactical position (subject, direct object, predicate nominative, object of a preposition), but perhaps most frequently toward the end of a sentence:

Temperance, Industry, Exercise and Cleanliness, are the Lessons equally enjoyned . . .[30]

To this Passion he has thought fit to sacrifice Order, Propriety, Discretion and Common-Sense, as may be seen in every Page of his Book . . .[31]

. . . without Jealousy, Fondness, Quarrelling or Discontent.[32]

Adjectives are less common, for example:

. . . whom he knew to be ignorant, wilful, assuming and ill-inclined Fellows.[33]

Verbs and verbals also occur; finite verbs:

Whoever hath an Ambition to be heard in a Crowd, must press, and squeeze, and thrust, and climb with indefatigable Pains . . .[34]

past participles:

. . . whether Stewed, Roasted, Baked, or Boiled . . .[35]

Infinitives:

. . . we hope to gather Materials enough to Inform, or Divert, or Correct, or Vex the Town.[36]

and gerunds:

. . . Sentence of Death, with all the Circumstances of Hanging, Beheading, Quartering, Embowelling, and the like . . .[37]

The number of items varies very greatly, from four, the commonest, to forty-six, but in all the series containing more than

[30] *Gulliver, Works,* XI, 253.
[31] *Remarks on Tindal, Works,* II, 70.
[32] *Gulliver, Works,* XI, 253.
[33] *Examiner* 17, *Works,* III, 25.
[34] *Tale of a Tub, Works,* I, 33.
[35] *Modest Proposal, Works,* XII, 111.
[36] *Intelligencer I, Works,* XII, 29.
[37] *Drapier's Letters, Works,* X, 67.

seven items the forms involved are nouns or nominals, except for one series of thirty-one verbs.

Another difficulty in the way of sorting these series lies in their irregularity. Of the selected sample of series taken to illustrate the types,[38] no regular example was found with more than thirteen items. By *regularity* is meant the conformity of the items in the series to a given part of speech or construction. Here are regular, irregular, and chaotic series:

I am not in the least provoked at the Sight of a Lawyer, a Pick-pocket, a Colonel, a Fool, a Lord, a Gamester, a Politician, a Whoremunger, a Physician, an Evidence, a Suborner, an Attorney, a Traytor, or the like . . .[39]

Their next Business is, from Herbs, Minerals, Gums, Oyls, Shells, Salts, Juices, Sea-weed, Excrements, Barks of Trees, Serpents, Toads, Frogs, Spiders, dead Mens Flesh and Bones, Beasts and Fishes, to form a Composition . . .[40]

Are those detestable Extravagancies of Flanders Lace, English Cloth of our own wooll, and other Goods, Italian or Indian Silks, Tea, Coffee, Chocolate, China-ware, and that profusion of Wines, by the knavery of Merchants growing dearer every Season, with a hundred unnecessary Fopperyes . . .[41]

The regular series consists of thirteen nouns of uniform kind, (types of people) all objects of the preposition *of*. The irregular sequence numbers eighteen nouns, objects of the preposition *from*, of which fifteen are unmodified, one is followed by a prepositional phrase, and two are part of a compound nominal modified by an attributive noun with adjective. These are irregularities, but the pattern remains clearly discernible, that is, a series of nouns. This is not true of the chaotic series, in which the basic pattern is difficult to uncover, though the reader feels that there is one, or at least that there is a series. It is not even clear how many items it

---

[38]   The total illustrative sample includes 200 citations, representing every volume of *Works* (which does not include epistolary matter), except Vol. V, which appeared too late to be included. These 200, by rough estimate, probably constitute one-fifth of all Swift's series.

[39]   *Gulliver, Works,* XI, 280.

[40]   *Ibid.,* pp. 237-8.

[41]   *Answer to unknown Persons, Works,* XII, 79.

contains, whether what comes after "other Goods" is in apposition or in series with it. There is an adjective with noun, another
with a prepositional phrase, limiting adjective with noun, two
alternative adjectives with a noun, four nouns, and a noun with a
prepositional phrase. But no dominant type emerges, though for
convenience it has been classed with nouns, since there are four
of them.

A more readily classified feature of series is the means by
which the items are connected. There are three basic types: the
normal, the asyndetic and the polysyndetic. Normal arrangement
in English requires a connective (*and, or*) between the last two
members of a series:

... the Office of what we now call Prime Ministers; Men of Art,
Knowledge, Application and Insinuation...[42]

Asyndetic connection is really no connection at all, the items
merely being separated by commas:

... the Bulk of the People consisted wholly of Discoverers, Witnesses,
Informers, Accusers, Prosecutors, Evidences, Swearers...[43]

Polysyndetic connection involves the use of a conjunction between
all adjacent items, as this sequence of five alternative adjectives
shows:

... so partial, or treacherous, or interested, or ignorant, or mistaken,
are generally all Recommenders...[44]

or this of four additive nouns:

... they are every Day dying, and rotting, by Cold and Famine, and
Filth, and Vermin, as fast as can be reasonably expected.[45]

Hybrids are occasionally found, in which there is an alternation
of connected and unconnected items:

He is a Person fully qualified for any Employment in the Court, or
the Navy, the Law, or the Revenue...[46]

[42] *Intelligencer, Works,* XII, 47.
[43] *Gulliver, Works,* XI, 175.
[44] *Badges to Beggars, Works,* XIII, 139.
[45] *Modest Proposal, Works,* XII, 114.
[46] *Advancement of Religion, Works,* II, 62.

But this type might just as easily be taken for a pair of doublets, except for the commas between items, which suggest a series.[47] However, in this next sequence of six nouns, the three apparent doublets are separated by commas and may therefore not constitute a hybrid:

> If I display the Effects of Avarice and Ambition, of Bribery and Corruption, of gross Immorality and Irreligion . . .[48, 49]

As is perhaps predictable, the hybrid connection is found most often in the chaotic sequence:

> We have many Sorts of small Silver Coins, to which they are Strangers in England; such as the French Three-pences, Four-pence Half-pennies, and Eight pence–Farthings, the Scotch Five-pences and Ten-pences; besides, their Twenty-pences, and Three and Four-pences . . .[50]

The usual method of indicating that a list is not complete (that the possibilities are too vast to be compassed within the limits of the given discourse) is the use of the formula *etc.* . . ., though it is usually frowned on in most formal literary situations.[51] The strategy of this "continuator" has received very little attention,[52] although the International Society for General Semantics calls its

---

[47] Whether these are Swift's commas introduces the difficult question of the printer's responsibility for punctuation. Davis suggests (*Drapier's Letters,* Oxford: Clarendon, 1935, pp. lxviii-lxix) that Swift was often very careful in his revision of proofs and early editions. Comparison of manuscripts with printed copies supports this view, but the matter is speculative at best. Throughout this study, the assumption is made that Swift was responsible for the words but that the printer might be blamed for all but the end punctuation.

[48] *Examiner 25, Works,* III, 68.

[49] The seeming contrast between the members of each pair suggests that they are doublets and the lack of such contrast in the earlier quotation suggests that it probably is a series, but this sort of criterion (semantic) has been generally avoided in the classifying and tabulation of these types because of its uncertainty.

[50] *Drapier, Works,* X, 38.

[51] See, for example, Porter G. Perrin, *Writer's Guide and Index to English,* 3d ed. (Chicago, 1959) where the use of this device is limited "primarily to reference and business usage" (p. 521).

[52] Ohmann, in his study of Shaw's style, has observed a similar device, to which he gives the name "continuant" (p. 9).

journal *Etc.*, to suggest that everything about a given matter cannot be said and that in fact, the larger part is always left unsaid. It is not uncommon, however, for speakers and writers to fall back on *etc.*, when they cannot call to mind the items constituting a purported list. But whether it is used dishonestly to suggest more items than are actually available or, practically, to save space, the continuator is regularly used only after a short series, usually two or three, though in scientific use it may occasionally follow one unit. With Swift the continuator seems never to be used with lists of less than four and frequently with much longer lists. That is, neither of the two usual reasons for it is involved in Swift's practice. Because he always seems to have an unlimited supply of material and because he is obviously not interested in saving space, it is necessary to look elsewhere for the purpose.

But, in fact, the bare *etc.* is not very common in Swift's writing. Out of the group of 200 illustrative examples, twenty-eight (14 per cent) had continuators of some sort. Of these twenty-eight, three were *etc.*'s, five were *and the like*, and one *or the like*. The remaining nineteen took the most varied and elaborate forms. Basically, they fall into two groups, of which the first is closer to the usual form of *etc.* . . ., that is, to suggest a further quantity. Examples range from the simple "and others",[53] "with many more",[54] "and so of the rest",[55] to the more cumbersome "with several others of the same stamp",[56] "besides many others needless to mention",[57] and the really top-heavy "These are only a few among many others, which I have been told of, but cannot remember." [58] The emphasis can be heightened with numbers, as "and Forty more",[59] or "and a Thousand other Things".[60]

The other type of continuator can also operate with numbers, "with ten thousand other Misfortunes",[61] but an additional ele-

[53]   *Works,* I, 105; VIII, 33.
[54]   *Works,* XI, 230.
[55]   *Works,* III, 77.
[56]   *Works,* VI, 130.
[57]   *Works,* XI, 172.
[58]   *Works,* X, 58.
[59]   *Works,* II, 29.
[60]   *Works,* XI, 228.
[61]   *Works,* II, 76.

ment is here introduced. The last words of the continuator compel that the items preceding be recognized as members of the class *misfortunes*. These classifying continuators may be literal: "and other Places of Profit",[62] "or any other superior Gift of human Minds",[63] "and other Geometrical Terms",[62] "and all other Priests".[65] They prevent misconception for those unacquainted with the exotic, technical, or esoteric terms presented: "Rhombs, Circles, Parallelograms, Ellipses",[66] "Bramines, Persees, Bonzes, Talapoins, Dervizes, Rabbi's".[67] Or they simply emphasize the class.

A more important purpose is behind the other classifying use of this device, which may be called satiric. At the end of a list of items whose classification has not been stated, the classifying continuator throws the preceding items into an unexpected light. The effect is startling in the "Letter to Lord Middleton", one of the *Drapier's Letters*:

I had been long conversing with the Writings of your Lordship, Mr. Locke, Mr. Molineaux, Colonel Sidney, and other dangerous Authors . . .[68]

It is much more predictably ironic in this section of *Gulliver's Travels*:

These unhappy People were proposing Schemes for persuading Monarchs to chuse Favourites upon the Score of their Wisdom, Capacity and Virtue; of teaching Ministers to consult the publick Good; of rewarding Merit, great Abilities, and eminent Services; of instructing Princes to know their true Interest, by placing it on the same Foundation with that of their People: Of chusing for Employments Persons qualified to exercise them; with many other wild impossible Chimaeras . . .[69]

Although Swift, whether from fatigue, inattention or haste, oc-

---

[62] *Works,* VII, 97.
[63] *Works,* XII, 38.
[64] *Works,* XI, 147.
[65] *Works,* IV, 33.
[66] *Works,* XI, 147.
[67] *Works,* IV, 33.
[68] *Drapier, Works,* X, 86.
[69] *Gulliver, Works,* XI, 171.

casionally permits a neutral simple continuator like *etc.* to pass his pen, his resort to neutral continuators has the purpose of emphasizing numerousness or of supplying a further aid to clarity to the reader by classifying the list he has been given, and sometimes both.

The satiric continuator in a sense checks the mere copiousness of the series by implying an intended order in the items presented. The likelihood of a conscious satiric intention is considerable. But those series which are not furnished with a continuator do not permit the inference of an intended order. Yet the desire for some sort of order or pattern is insistent in any serious reader. If he is not able to elicit a pattern, his response is likely to be puzzlement or hostility. Either case involves a loss of meaning. When Swift's series are examined closely, it is difficult to discover the organizing principle, the reason why the items are given in the order in which they appear. It may be well to begin by seeking formal elements in the design of the shorter series.

Alliteration of two or three contiguous elements of a series is frequent: "Philosophy, Poetry, Politicks, Law, Mathematicks and Theology . . .",[70] "Customs, Languages, Fashions, Dress, Dyet and Diversions",[71] "the Park, the Play-House, the Opera, the Gaming Ordinaries",[72] "France, Popery, the Pretender, and Peace without Spain . . ." [73] Occasionally, a longer series is alliterative: "Questions, Answers, Replies, Rejoinders, Repartees, and Remarks . . .",[74] "Court, or Church, or Camp, or City, or Country . . ." [75] Assonance is sometimes noticeable: "Anabapt*ist*, Pap*ist,* Muggletonian, Jew or Sweet Singer",[76] "Halters, Gib*bets*, Fag*gots*, Inquisition, Pop*ery,* Slav*ery,* and the Pretender",[77] "As*gill*, Tind*all*, Toland, Coward . . .",[78] "a Bri*dle,* a Sad*dle,* a Spur,

[70] *Ibid.,* p. 166.
[71] *Ibid.,* p. 193.
[72] *Works,* IX, 20.
[73] *Works,* VII, 28.
[74] *Works,* IV, 111.
[75] *Works,* I, 115.
[76] *Works,* IV, 31.
[77] *Works,* IV, 81.
[78] *Works,* II, 29.

and a Whip . . .".[79] These literal and phonetic similarities are not sufficiently artful to be credited to any deliberate artistic purpose. They seem rather the unconscious tendency of the man who enjoyed word-games with Sheridan and who pursed his mouth while writing to Stella.

If, however, a comparison is made of several analogous lists, such as Swift habitually provided in describing anything under his scrutiny, it can be realized that no discernible pattern informs the ordering. For instance, in a number of places, he has occasion to allude to what might be called the institutional aspects of a nation. Here are five such sets:

. . . Laws, Language, Religion, or Government . . .[80]

. . . Religion, Laws, Language, Manners, Nature of the Government . . .[81]

. . . Manners, Religion, Laws, Government, and Learning . . .[82]

. . . Laws, Government, History, Religion, or Manners . . .[83]

. . . Government, Religion, Law, Custom, Extent of Country, or Manners and Dispositions of the People.[84]

It is noteworthy that, although three of the items appear in all five series and one in four, no two sets have the same order or anything approximating visible uniformity. Another group taken from his religious polemical writing lists types of sectarians who would be benefitted if religious toleration were extended to Dissenters:

. . . any Anabaptist, Papist, Muggletonian, Jew or Sweet Singer . . .[85]

. . . Papists, Atheists, Mahometans, Heathens, and Jews.[86]

. . . Atheists, Turks, Jews, Infidels and Hereticks; or which is still more dangerous, even Papists themselves . . .[87]

[79] *Works,* XI, 225 – all italics supplied.
[80] *Polite Conversation, Works,* IV, 117.
[81] *Free Thoughts, Works,* VIII, 95.
[82] *Gulliver, Works,* XI, 90.
[83] *Ibid.,* p. 150.
[84] *History, Works,* VII, 69.
[85] *Mr. Collins's Discourse, Works,* IV, 31.
[86] *Sentiments, Works,* II, 7.
[87] *Sacramental Test, Works,* II, 115.

Here only two items are common to all three sets (Papists and Jews) and they are differenlty placed in each series. Though we can infer the satiric intention from the outlandish character of some of the items, there is no detectable reason for the particular order of each series.

That there must be a human order in these lists is axiomatic: the order could not be entirely random. The ordering, however, is the product of some deeply-felt rhythm which the external eye cannot read. But here again it is necessary to distinguish between the expository and the satiric purpose. In the expository list, the information provided by the units is presented casually, in response to some unclear internal injunction. The purely expository narrative of Gulliver yields this list of languages, which might have been ordered in a number of ways:

I spoke to them in as many Languages as I had the least Smattering of, which were High and Low Dutch, Latin, French, Spanish, Italian, and Lingua Franca . . .[88]

Alternative orders can be easily devised: according to chronology, familiarity, geographical dissemination, alphabetical sequence. But none of these, nor any discernible one, is used; the list seems utterly without pattern, except for the propriety of *Lingua Franca* in last place.[89] Again, the mockery of Bickerstaff alludes to events in four European countries:

As for the most signal Events abroad in France, Flanders, Italy and Spain, I shall make no Scruple to predict them in plain Terms . . .[90]

Though the purpose is satiric, no effort is made to present the names in a particular or effective order. A comparison of two parallel lists may show the contrasting operation of the two motives. The first, written later and in a calmer retrospect, refers to the political slogans hurled by the Whigs at the Tory Administration:

[88]   *Gulliver, Works,* XI, 15.
[89]   It might be claimed that Swift deliberately chose the disorderly presentation in order to simulate realism, as the list might occur to Gulliver in any order. But such an explanation explains nothing.
[90]   *Bickerstaff, Works,* II, 144.

France, Popery, the Pretender, and Peace without Spain, were the
Words to be given about at this mock Parade . . .[91]

The second represents a contemporary contribution to the controversy itself, in the form of a sarcastic commentary on a book
proposing the slogans:

. . . as if the Pope, the Devil, the Pretender, and France were just
at our Doors. . .[92]

The four items in the first (expository) list are all genuine political
slogans, arranged with some attention to alliteration. Swift's comment on them is external to their arrangement: he does not use
the arrangement as a part of his comment. He refers to them as
"words" and treats them as relative abstractions. But in the
polemical list, the three items referring to people have been per-
sonified and a spurious fourth ("the Devil") has been added.
The presence of this addition serves to throw doubt on the others,
as does the action – "[they] were just at our Doors" – imputed
to the group. This principle of construction is frequent in Swift's
satiric catalogues; that is, mingling some items of dubious or low
social or moral standing with a number of items he wishes to de-
precate, as if there were no difference between them. Thus:

. . . a very particular Description of the Persons, Dresses, and Dispositions of the several Lords, Ladies, Squires, Madams, Lawyers, Gamesters, Toupees, Sots, Wits, Rakes and Informers . . .[93]

This may be usefully contrasted with the expository list which begins in much the same way and in which the arrangement is determined by precedence:

. . . a huge Train of Dukes, Earls, Viscounts, Barons, Knights, Es-
quires, Gentlemen, and others . . .[94]

This mingling effect is heightened by the use of a neutral continuator, which stresses the equality of all the items:

I am not in the least provoked at the Sight of a Lawyer, a Pick-
pocket, a Colonel, a Fool, a Lord, a Gamester, a Politician, a

[91]   *History, Works*, VII, 28.
[92]   *Bishop of Sarum, Works*, IV, 61.
[93]   *Intelligencer I, Works*, XII, 31.
[94]   *Publick Spirit, Works*, VIII, 33.

Whoremunger, a Physician, an Evidence, a Suborner, an Attorney, a Traytor, or the like.[95]

The full complexity of the reductive procedure can be noticed in this most impressive catalogue of the human types and vices Houyhnhnmland is free of and which, by implication, Swift would like to see his society free of: [96]

Here were no Gibers, Censurers, Backbiters, Pick-pockets, Highway-men, House-breakers, Attorneys, Bawds, Buffoons, Gamesters, Poli-ticians, Wits, Spleneticks, tedious Talkers, Controvertists, Ravishers, Murderers, Robbers, Virtuoso's; no Leaders or Followers of Party and Faction; no Encouragers to Vice, by Seducement or Examples: no Dungeon, Axes, Gibbets, Whipping-posts, or Pillories; No cheating Shopkeepers or Mechanicks: No Pride, Vanity or Affectation: No Fops, Bullies, Drunkards, strolling Whores, or Poxes: No ranting, lewd, expensive Wives: No stupid, proud Pedants: No importunate, over-bearing, quarrelsome, noisy, roaring, empty, conceited, swearing Companions: No Scoundrels raised from the Dust upon the Merit of their Vices; or Nobility thrown into it on account of their Virtues: No Lords, Fidlers, Judges or Dancing-masters.[97]

Of the nineteen items before the first semi-colon, six are criminal types, two are professional occupations, and the remainder range from exemplars of personality traits to types of men about town. The arrangement is scarcely deliberate except that those especially aimed at (Politicians, Attorneys) are used to season the others. If the list consisted, for instance, of blocks of criminals, per-sonality types, and professions, the effect would be to suggest distinct classes, rather than a uniform criminality diffused through all orders and types of society. Swift willingly charges all of society with the same kind of sin, in a juxtaposition which adds a meaning to "guilt by association". The seemingly indiscriminate ordering has the appearance of a device, though its details may not have conscious sanction.

A formal detail of this catalogue of dispensable persons is the "nesting" of one list within another. In the central section may be perceived a "nested" series of eight adjectives, inserted in the

[95] *Gulliver, Works,* XI, 280.
[96] Cf. W. S. Gilbert's "I've got a little list".
[97] *Gulliver, Works,* XI, 260-1.

mass of forty-six nouns, not counting doublets and triplets of adjectives. This mechanism occurs more frequently in wordgroup sequences.

Lists of word-groups are less easily classifiable than single-word lists because they are seldom as regular as, for example, lists of nouns. This is not to say that they are hard to recognize or that they are ambiguous, except in the sense that one or another type of element may predominate. They may be syntactically divided into phrasal, clausal and full-sentence series.

Under phrasal sequences are included all those in which items consisting of groups of words without a finite verb make up the greater part of the items. This does not exclude the presence in the sequence of isolated single words or of clauses:

... how can she acquire, those hundreds of Graces and Motions, and Airs, the whole military Management of the Fan, the Contorsions of every muscular Motion in the Face; the risings and fallings; the quickness, and slackness of the Voice, with the several Tones and Cadences; the proper Junctures of smiling and frowning; how often, and how loud to laugh; when to jibe and when to flout; with all the other Branches of Doctrine and Discipline above recited.[98]

The sequence begins with three nouns, five phrases of one type and two of another. An even more heteroclite example combines words, phrases and clauses:

Some were undone by Law-suits; others spent all they had in Drinking, Whoring and Gaming; others fled for Treason; many for Murder, Theft, Poysoning, Robbery, Perjury, Forgery, Coining false Money; for committing Rapes or Sodomy; for flying from their Colours, or deserting to the Enemy; and most of them had broken Prison.[99]

Although a measure of regularity exists, the types tend to converge and overlap. Therefore, I have limited the subdivisions of the phrasal type to prepositional and verbal. The prepositional sub-type includes all those in which prepositional phrases are most prominent, whatever other grammatical feature may be present. The most regular form tends to resemble a sequence of nouns, except for the repeated preposition:

[98]   *Polite Conversation, Works,* **IV,** 112.
[99]   *Gulliver, Works,* **XI,** 228.

... by the Laws of God, of Nature, of Nations, and of your own Country . . .[100]

A more common type involves minute variations in each element but an over-all similarity among all the items:

I differed very much from the rest of my Species, in the Whiteness, and Smoothness of my Skin, my want of Hair in several Parts of my Body, the Shape and Shortness of my Claws behind and before, and my Affectation of walking continually on my two hinder Feet.[101]

But there is a curious pattern here, of a type seldom found in the word series: parallelism of the first and third items and the second and fourth, emphasized by the two doublets of nouns and the one of adjectives. Such strict parallel structure is unusual for Swift, though common in the period,[102] but the variations which prevent the balance from being regular enough to call attention to itself are indeed typical of Swift. It would probably be accurate to say that Swift does not seek balance or parallelism but that these rhythmical features obtrude themselves into his unconsciousness. It might even be possible to claim that there is not a perfect parallel structure of any length greater than a few words to be found anywhere in Swift's prose. Even examples that appear to be formally parallel reveal on closer inspection only approximate and mock parallelism:

But their Manner of Writing is very peculiar; being neither from the Left to the Right, like the Europeans; nor from the Right to the Left, like the Arabians; nor from up to down, like the Chinese; nor from down to up, like the Cascagians; but aslant from one Corner of the Paper to the other, like Ladies in England.[103]

Here the parallelism seems rather extensive, consisting of a conjunction, and three prepositional phrases. But one set of coordinates (*the Left, the Right*) does not match the other (*up, down*) and the last element of the sequence throws disorder into the structure in two ways. An alternative form was available, which

[100]   *Drapier, Works,* X, 63.
[101]   *Gulliver, Works,* XI, 221.
[102]   See Wimsatt, Lannering, and others.
[103]   *Gulliver, Works,* XI, 41.

would have helped to preserve the parallel: "but obliquely (or from *Corner to Corner*), like Englishwomen". That he did not adopt the procedure that would have resulted in perfect parallelism is quite consistent with his avoidance of regularity, both in rhetoric and in grammar.

Verbal phrases, including mostly infinitives and gerunds, exemplify the same leaning to irregularity. Infinitives converging to-ward single words:

... a mighty King, who for the space of above thirty Years, amused himself to take and lose Towns; beat Armies, and be beaten; drive Princes out of their Dominions; fright Children from their Bread and Butter; burn, lay waste, plunder, dragoon, massacre Subject and Stranger, Friend and Foe, Male and Female.[104]

Gerund phrases:

... to reduce human Excrement to its original Food, by separating the several Parts, removing the Tincture which it receives from the Gall, making the Odour exhale, and scumming off the Saliva.[105]

Gerund phrases in an extensive list, with marked initial regularity:

Therefore, let no man talk to me of other Expedients: Of taxing our Absentees... Of using neither Cloaths, nor Household Furniture ... Of utterly rejecting ... Of curing the Expensiveness of Pride, Vanity, Idleness, and Gaming ... Of introducing a Vein of Parsimony ... Of learning to love our Country ... Of quitting our Animosities ... Of being a little cautious ... Of teaching Landlords ... Lastly, Of putting a Spirit of Honesty, Industry, and Skill into our Shop-keepers ...[106]

A chaotic example including a mixture of verbal and prepositional items:

Add to all this, the Pleasure of seeing the various Revolutions of States and Empires; the Changes in the lower and upper World, antient Cities in Ruins, and obscure Villages become the Seats of Kings. Famous Rivers lessening into shallow Brooks; the Ocean leaving one Coast dry, and overwhelming another: the Discovery of many Countries yet unknown. Barbarity overrunning the politest

[104]   *Tale of a Tub, Works,* I, 104.
[105]   *Gulliver, Works,* XI, 164.
[106]   *Modest Proposal, Works,* XII, 116, much abbreviated.

Nations, and the most barbarous becoming civilized. I should then see the Discovery of the *Longitude*, the *perpetual Motion*, the *universal Medicine*, and many other great Inventions brought to the utmost Perfection.[107]

The larger the basic structure, the greater the irregularity of the list. Clause-length sequences tend to vary considerably, internally and from one to the other: there are scarcely two identical or regular examples to be found. The favorite type is probably the *that*-clause:

To this it was answered; That ill Princes seldome trouble themselves to look for Precedents; That, Men of great Estates will not be less fond of preserving their Liberties, when they are created Peers: That, in such a Government as this . . .: And lastly, That the other Party . . .[108]

But clauses beginning with *who* may also be found:

. . . another Sett of Men, who by Confession of their Enemies had equal Abilities at least with their Predecessors; Whose Interest made it necessary for them (although their Inclinations had been otherwise) to act upon those Maxims which were most agreeable to the Constitution in Church and State; Whose Birth and Patrimonies gave them Weight in the Nation; And who (I speak of the chief Managers) had long lived under the strictest Bonds of Friendship.[109]

It may escape notice, however, that in the foregoing example the parallelism is only apparent, as only the first and last clauses begin with the relative *who*, the medial two beginning with the pronoun *whose*. The sequence which consists of an initial *who* with a succession of predicates may be considered similar in type, except for the omission of the relative:

. . . the sober deliberate Talker, who proceedeth with much Thought and Caution, maketh his Preface, brancheth out into several Digressions, findeth a Hint that putteth him in Mind of another Story, which he promiseth to tell you when this is done; cometh back regularly to his Subject, cannot readily call to Mind some Person's Name, holdeth his Head, complaineth of his Memory; the whole

107   *Gulliver, Works,* XI, 194.
108   *History, Works,* VII, 20-1, abbreviated.
109   *Free Thoughts, Works,* VIII, 82.

Company all this while in Suspence; at length says, it is no Matter, and so goes on.[110]

Ellipsis of the auxiliary of a compound verb also produces a series of predicates:

How the Pox under all its Consequences and Denominations had altered every Lineament of an English Countenance; shortened the Size of Bodies, unbraced the Nerves, relaxed the Sinews and Muscles, introduced a sallow Complexion, and rendered the Flesh loose and rancid.[111]

True sentences in sequence are rather rare but they can be found.[112] Part of the difficulty they present is the question of how much similarity between elements constitutes a series. The example which follows consists of five sentences beginning with *I* and a first person verb in the past tense, though the first element separates them with an adverb, the fourth is negative with a pro-verb auxiliary, and the last is preceded by a conjunction:

I then descended to the Courts of Justice . . . I mentioned the prudent Management of our Treasury . . . I computed the Number of our People . . . I did not omit even our Sports and Pastimes . . . And, I finished all with a brief historical Account . . .[113]

The pattern is discernible and the characteristic disruption of regularity is visible. The same may be noticed of this sequence in which the five sentences open with the connective *thus* followed (in three of them) by a subject-verb-object sequence, which is inverted in the last two:

For, the Arts are all in a flying March, and therefore more easily subdued by attacking them in the Rear. Thus Physicians discover the State of the whole Body, by consulting only what comes from Behind. Thus Men catch Knowledge by throwing their Wit on the Posteriors of a Book, as Boys do Sparrows with flinging Salt upon their Tails. Thus Human Life is best understood by the wise man's Rule of Regarding the End. Thus are the Sciences found like Her-

[110] *Hints on Conversation, Works,* IV, 88.
[111] *Gulliver, Works,* XI, 185.
[112] In the illustrative sample of 200, seven per cent were counted as sentences, but this figure includes non-freestanding clauses and elliptical clauses.
[113] *Gulliver, Works,* XI, 112-3, abbreviated.

cules's Oxen, by tracing them Backwards. Thus are old Sciences un-
ravelled like old Stockings, by beginning at the Foot.[114]

This series of apparently *independent* clauses really consists of a
sequence of apodoses for the initial *if*-clause:

That, if it had been my good Fortune to come into the World a
Struldbrugg... I would first resolve... In the second Place, I
would from my earliest Youth apply myself... Lastly, I would carefully record every Action... I would exactly set down the several
Changes... I would never marry after Threescore... I would enter-
tain myself...[115]

Significantly, Swift here seems to end his list after the second
item but continues for three more after *Lastly*.

Questions are the simplest large-scale units to identify. But one
might ask whether a series of questions such as this had any common element except the question-mark:

Are not the Taverns and Coffee-Houses open? Can there be a more
convenient Season for taking a Dose of Physick? Are fewer Claps
got upon Sundays than other Days? Is not that the chief Day for
Traders to sum up the Accounts of the Week; and for Lawyers to
prepare their Briefs? [116]

An elliptic series is much more obviously part of a single intention:

Where are more Appointments and Rendezvouzes of Gallantry?
Where more Care to appear in the foremost Box with greater Advantage of Dress? Where more Meetings for Business? Where more
Bargains driven of all Sorts? And where so many Conveniences,
or Incitements to sleep? [117]

But the thought is not be entertained that a series of questions represents a chance collocation of individual intentions. The fact
that five questions occur in a row is formally an important matter,
even apart from the meaning, which tells us how they are related.
The meaning, however, need not be involved in the usual types of
questions:

[114] *Tale of a Tub, Works,* I, 91.
[115] *Gulliver, Works,* XI, 193, abbreviated.
[116] *Argument, Works,* II, 31.
[117] *Ibid.*

Or, hath he been tried for his Life, and very narrowly escaped? Hath he been accused of high Crimes and Misdemeanours? Has the Prince seized on his Estate, and left him to starve? Hath he been hooted at as he passed the Streets, by an ungrateful Rabble? Have neither Honours, Offices nor Grants, been conferred on him or his Family? Have not he and they been barbarously stript of them all? Have not he and his Forces been ill payed abroad? And doth not the Prince by a scanty, limited Commission, hinder him from pursuing his own Methods in the Conduct of the War? Hath he no Power at all of disposing Commissions as he pleaseth? Is he not severely used by the Ministry or Parliament, who yearly call him to a strict Account? Has the Senate ever thanked him for good Success; and have they not always publickly censured him for the least Miscarriage? [118]

Here the length and the similarity of sentence openings compel that the reader notice their seriation. On the other hand, indirect questions, resembling in form the relative clause or predicate type (though they actually are noun clauses), are punctuated and capitalized as if they were individual independent units. An example which illustrates the variety of the question *form* is this thirty-one unit report of the Brobdingnagian King's interview with Gulliver, of which only the first nine are given:

He asked, what Methods were used . . . and in what kind of Business . . . What Course was taken to supply that Assembly . . . What Qualifications were necessary . . . Whether the Humour of the Prince . . . What Share of Knowledge these Lords had in the Laws of their Country, and how they came by it . . . Whether they were always so free from Avarice . . . Whether those holy Lords I spoke of . . .[119]

Word-group sequences, being larger structures than single-word sequences, oftener produce the "nested" group, or series of contrasting type found within a phrasal or clausal sequence, for example, this set of four regular nouns:

. . . with Indignation to hear our noble Country, the Mistress of Arts and Arms, the Scourge of France, the Arbitress of Europe, the Seat of Virtue, Piety, Honour and Truth, the Pride and Envy of the World, so contemptuously treated.[120]

[118] *Examiner* 16, *Works*, III, 19-20.
[119] *Gulliver, Works*, XI, 113, abbreviated.
[120] *Ibid.*, p. 91.

The regular four-noun sequence is the most common type of "nested" insertion, sequences of two and three items (doublets and triplets) not included. The regularity of the insertions, however, does not go counter to the tendency toward irregularity which has been noticed, because it is obvious that the insertion itself constitutes an irregular element in the "host" sequence. In fact, the latter usually being irregular, the "nested" sequence's regularity would constitute an additional departure from balance. Adjectives may be found "nested":

Difference in Opinions hath cost many Millions of Lives: For Instance, whether Flesh be Bread, or Bread be Flesh: Whether the Juice of a certain Berry be Blood or Wine: Whether Whistling be a Vice or a Virtue: Whether it be better to kiss a Post, or throw it it into the Fire: What is the best Colour for a Coat, whether Black, White, Red or Grey; and whether it should be long or short, narrow or wide, dirty or clean; with many more.[121]

Four prepositional phrases appear within the confines of a rowdy lot of *that*-clauses based on the repeated and italicized verb *expect:*

... so the Nation would (to speak in the Language of Mr. Steele) *Expect* that Her Majesty should be made perfectly easy from that side for the future; No more be alarmed with Apprehensions ... The Nation would likewise *expect* that there should be an End of all private Commerce between that Court and the Leaders of a Party here; And that his Electorall Highness should declare Himself entirely satisfied with all Her Majesties Proceedings, Her Treatyes of Peace and Commerce, Her Allyances abroad, Her Choice of Ministers at Home, and particularly in her most gracious Condescensions to his Requests. That he would upon all proper Occasions ... And lastly that he would acknowledge the Goodness of the Queen ...[122]

Though not truly "nested", some contiguous groups are so related (by apposition) as to deserve inclusion in this group:

... protesting it was only an Heap of Conspiracies, Rebellions, Murders, Massacres, Revolutions, Banishments; the very worst Ef-

[121] *Ibid.,* p. 230.
[122] *Free Thoughts, Works,* VIII, 93-4, abbreviated.

fects that Avarice, Faction, Hypocrisy, Perfidiousness, Cruelty, Rage, Madness, Hatred, Envy, Lust, Malice, and Ambition could produce.[123]

The importance of the nesting contrivance must not be exaggerated because the number of such examples is rather small.[124] But it is useful as a demonstration of Swift's tendency to irregularity and as further evidence of his leaning to redundancy, even inserting lists within lists.

The length of the word-group sequences would make them cumbersome and would entail the repetition (especially in the longer ones) of a number of merely structural words, if Swift did not avoid this necessity by a consistent use of ellipsis.[125] This device was congenial to him in more than merely this particular situation, but his practice may be illustrated by his performance here. Commonly some form of the verb *to be* is left out of all units except the initial one:

To instance no more; Is not Religion a Cloak, Honesty a Pair of Shoes, worn out in the Dirt, Self-love a Surtout, Vanity a Shirt, and Conscience a pair of Breeches . . .? [126]

There is nothing unusual in this except the number of items, which compels the reader to remember the omitted element longer than merely until the customary second item. Swift makes a great demand on his readers but he supplies them with helps. The five-unit question is short enough to permit the slight irregularity of the modifying phrase ("worn out in the Dirt"), but in a longer elliptical sequence, the cost of using ellipsis is regularity of form. Any irregularity which affected the reader's ability to recognize the basic design would result in nonsense, something Swift always guarded against. A long sequence, in which the omitted term is the infinitive *to signify*, protects the reader from ambiguity by

---

[123] *Gulliver, Works,* XI, 116.
[124] Eleven in the 200-unit sample, or 5½ per cent.
[125] Ellipsis is defined as the leaving out of any syntactical structure of those words (usually function words) whose existence can be inferred from the context, from their habitual omission (e.g. *that*), or from the initial member of a repetitive sequence.
[126] *Tale of a Tub, Works,* I, 47.

unusual regularity and by careful punctuation[127] (commas between terms, semicolons between units):

> For Instance, they can decypher a Close-stool to signify a Privy-Council; a Flock of Geese, a Senate; a lame Dog, an Invader; the Plague, a standing Army; a Buzard, a Minister; the Gout, a High Priest; a Gibbet, a Secretary of State; a Chamber pot, a Committee of Grandees; a Sieve a Court Lady; a Broom, a Revolution; a Mouse-trap, an Employment; a bottomless Pit, the Treasury; a Sink, a C---t; a Cap and Bells, a Favourite; a broken Reed, a Court of Justice; an empty Tun, a General; a running Sore, the Administration.[128]

Only the extreme familiarity of the type of structure involved, with elliptical *is* or *are*, makes the irregularity of this sequence unambiguous:

> His Features are strong and masculine, with an Austrian Lip, and arched Nose, his Complexion olive, his Countenance erect, his Body and Limbs well proportioned, all his Motions graceful, and his Deportment majestick.[129]

And the departure from parallelism is not very marked, being limited to an adventitious prepositional phrase, a doublet in the fourth item, and a limiting adjective in the fifth. The desire to make the structure clear to the reader leads Swift in the use of this device to come very close to complete parallelism:

> There Crassus drew Liberality and Gratitude; Fulvia, Humility and Gentleness; Clodius, Piety and Justice; Gracchus, Loyalty to his Prince; Cinna, Love of his Country and Constitution; and so of the rest. [130]

The elliptical manner tends to be cumulative, and more elements are left out or the structures are made artificially shorter as the series proceeds:

> I found how the World had been misled by prostitute Writers, to

[127] It is probable that in the Faulkner edition of this work, which Davis used, the punctuation is close to Swift's intentions. Swift's share in this edition and the extent of his cooperation with Faulkner are discussed in Davis's Introduction, *Works*, XI, xxvi-xxviii and fn. 1 on p. xxvii.
[128] *Gulliver, Works*, XI, 175.
[129] *Ibid.*, p. 14.
[130] *Examiner* 26, *Works*, III, 77.

SERIATION 113

ascribe the greatest Exploits in War to Cowards, the wisest Counsel
to Fools, Sincerity to Flatterers, Roman Virtue to Betrayers of their
Country, Piety to Atheists, Chastity to Sodomites, Truth to Informers.[131]

From "to ascribe the greatest Exploits in War to Cowards" to
"Truth to informers", there is a convergence toward the most
economical statement. The same may be noticed in the next example, where the introductory dependent clause is repeated in
variant form as each unit becomes simpler:

... much less that Men are ennobled on Account of their Virtue,
that Priests are advanced for their Piety or Learning, Soldiers for
their Conduct or Valour, Judges for their Integrity, Senators for the
Love of their Country, or Counsellors for their Wisdom.[132]

The sort of pattern represented by the gradual simplification of
the syntactical units of a series is only an occasional event and not
relevant to the examination of sequences of words. The problem
of detecting the informing pattern in Swift's series is, as I have
earlier suggested, of considerable difficulty. And yet it is a problem whose solution is of some importance. We cannot assume that
there is no order, for to do so would be to turn Swift over wholly
to the psychiatrists.[133] For the average reader is only too ready to
assume that a pattern he cannot puzzle out must be the product
of a diseased mind. Such has been the fate of advanced poets,
painters and musicians from the time of Beethoven and Blake to
that of Cage, Pollock and Ezra Pound. Though the individual is
not capable of producing a true random order,[134] he may be able
to simulate its appearance. But careful examination will always
reveal some lack of randomness. When the individual proceeds,
however, without conscious attention to pattern, his work, though

[131] *Gulliver, Works,* XI, 183.
[132] *Ibid.,* p. 116.
[133] Psychoanalysts have already made a number of efforts to appropriate
him, e.g., Ben Karpman, "Neurotic Traits of Jonathan Swift . . .", *Psychoanalytic Review,* XXIX (1942), 26-45, and Phyllis Greenacre, *Swift and
Carroll* (New York, 1955). But see also Norman O. Brown, "The Excre-
mental Vision", *Life Against Death* (New York, 1959), pp. 179-201.
[134] Only a machine, with no interest in its choice, can do so. The individual always selects or rejects on the basis of some predisposition.

patternless in appearance, invariably contains some elements of unconscious rhetoric. Certain preferences exert themselves and are impressed on the material, ready to be discerned by the observer with the key. To determine whether a key can be produced under the stress of the necessity, let us examine a series which seems utterly pell-mell:

... before the Members sat, administer to each of them Lenitives, Aperitives, Abstersives, Corrosives, Restringents, Palliatives, Laxatives, Cephalalgicks, Ictericks, Apophlegmaticks, Acousticks, as their several Cases required ...[135]

At first glance, it seems to be a list without conscious order. The most obvious formal aspect, alliteration, does not seem to have been invoked: the series of initial letters – L, A, A, C, R, P, L, C, I, A, A – fails to bring together the obvious pairs (L, C) or the four A's. But a possibility remains: to examine the meaning. Considering Swift's notorious fixation on the digestive tract, it is not surprising that at least three of the terms refer to it.[136] Of the others, two are concerned with illnesses that plagued Swift himself, and another with the relief of pain in general.[137] An analysis of the series from this point of view suggests a possible interpretation.

These observations, then, permit the speculation that Swift began his list with the digestive items which he so regularly employed to remind mankind of its animality and that the ills to which he was himself subject broke into his consciousness as a kind of counterpoint, the remaining items consisting of such abstruse medical terms as he happened to know.[138] In that sense, the progression from *Lenitives* to *Acousticks* is a move from the satiric to the personal. The formal features, in this case, can only be interpreted by means of the semantic ones, which themselves must be referred to the tendency of the unconscious to arrange its product in accordance with its own logic. It is possible that this

---

[135] *Gulliver, Works,* XI, 172.
[136] *Aperitives, Restringents* and *Laxatives. Lenitive* may mean a soothing medicine or a laxative, according to the *OED*.
[137] *Cephalalgicks* and *Acousticks,* treating headache and hearing, respectively, and *Palliatives.*
[138] Three in four of the remaining terms are the most obscure in the list.

logic may be revealed only when information about unconscious factors is at hand.[139] Something is known about Swift's feeling about the bowels and about his medical history. But knowledge of this sort is not always available. When it is not, exclusive reliance must be placed on such formal features as can be found.

In the following sequence of six activities, for instance, lacking any indication other than Swift's assumed contempt for the lot, examination begins with the grammatical features:

[good-breeding] takes in a great compass of knowledge; no less than that of dancing, fighting, gameing making the circle of Italy, riding the great horse, and speaking French . . .[140]

Three gerunds are followed by three gerund phrases, a perfectly sensible order,[141] which proceeds from the simple to the complex. But the three gerund phrases are all different: the first has a noun as object modified by a prepositional phrase, the second a noun as object modified by an adjective and the third merely a noun as object. The trend of short to long is there reversed, whether the matter be judged by the number of words in each element (five, four, two) or the complexity of each element of structure. The internal arrangement of this illustration, in the absence of more positive data,[141] may be credited to Swift's feeling for irregularity and to his sense of climax.

Climax means obvious motion toward a goal or in a given direction. It can converge or diverge; that is, the units can go from short to long or few to many, or the reverse. A dramatic climax develops in a remark of the King of Brobdingnag:

And yet, said he, I dare engage, those Creatures have their Titles and Distinctions of Honour; they contrive little Nests and Burrows,

[139] This supplies justification for the most seemingly trivial investigation of Swift's mind and personality; but in the personal as distinguished from the artistic realm, who is to say what is trivial?
[140] *On Good Manners, Works,* IV, 217.
[141] The gerunds, it may be noted, are in strict alphabetical order, a fact which may exclude further interpretation, though a case can be made for the parallelism of the phrases with the unit gerunds. If "riding the great horse" – the phrase means being able to ride a charger in battle or tournament – is taken as the equivalent of "fighting", then a parallelism between dancing and Italy, gaming and France, may be glimpsed.

that they call Houses and Cities; they make a Figure in Dress and Equipage; they love, they fight, they dispute, they cheat, they betray.[142]

The three initial clauses are discursive in tone and grammar and become gradually simpler. Then there is a pause (semi-colon) and five identical structures are hurled at the reader. The content of the last five clauses may be noticed to proceed from the customary or praiseworthy (*love, fight*) to the hierarchy of evils (*dispute, cheat, betray*).[143] This kind of climactic series predominates in Swift's work.[144]

On the other hand, the emphatic sequence which proceeds simply or regularly from short to long is rare. A simple example from an early work does not quite fulfill the requirements:

Embroidery, was Sheer wit; Gold Fringe was agreeable Conversation, Gold Lace was Repartee, a huge long Periwig was Humor, and a Coat full of Powder was very good Raillery . . .[145]

The first two items do progress, but the third regresses and the fourth is no longer than the second. However, the last brings the sequence to a climax. This type of progression apparently did not appeal to Swift. His favorite rhythmic vehicle, as suggested by the frequency of its occurrence, is the rising-falling sequence which comes to a point in the center, like a one-humped camel or a normal curve.

This figure can be best illustrated from among Swift's longer lists, which naturally give the greatest scope for variation, but it can be found in the shorter and simpler series as well. For example, this series of twelve nouns describing types of people, a rather common kind of list in Swift's works, shows the characteristic inflation:

---

[142] *Gulliver, Works,* XI, 91.
[143] Swift considered fraud, betrayal of trust, disloyalty, as peculiarly human and particularly vicious crimes, probably deserving the innermost circle. See *Works,* passim, but especially *Gulliver's Travels,* XI, 42.
[144] Some series do not show evident climax and some produce climax by other means than increasing or diminishing size of units. See the example of the drugs, above, for climax of another type.
[145] *Tale of a Tub, Works,* I, 48.

... as likewise of all Eves-droppers, Physicians, Midwives, small
Politicians, Friends fallen out, Repeating Poets, Lovers Happy or
in Despair, Bawds, Privy-Counsellours, Pages, Parasites, and Buffoons ...[146]

There are three nouns, four nouns modified in four different
ways; finally, five nouns. Characteristically, the potential regularity of the arrangement is disrupted by the alliteration of the
Privy-Counsellors, Pages and *Parasites.* In this early example,
there is no coincidence of the formal climax (the central section)
and the supposed semantic climax.

Of course most of the shorter word-group lists, which are more
complex than those made up of single words, illustrate only part
of Swift's rhythmic tendency: irregularity of elements, with a
tendency to make the last element of a series markedly different
from the others. These two examples from opposite ends of Swift's
literary span show the mechanism plainly:

Is any Student tearing his Straw in piece-meal, Swearing and Blas-
pheming, biting his Grate, foaming at the Mouth, and emptying his
Pispot in the Spectator's Faces? [147]

... will find them to have been Servants in good Families, broken
Tradesmen, Labourers, Cottagers, and what they call decayed House-
keepers ...[148]

In the second more than in the first, the outline of the pattern
(longer initial and ending phrases, single words in the middle)
more closely approximates the reciprocal of the peaked figure
characteristic of the long series.

One such long list – an improved model of one just cited –
has already been presented:[149]

Here were no Gibers, Censurers, Backbiters, Pick-pockets, Highway-
men, House-breakers, Attorneys, Bawds, Buffoons, Gamesters, Politicians, Wits, Spleneticks, tedious Talkers, Controvertists, Ravish-

---

[146] *Ibid.,* pp. 66-7. It is also possible to see a climactic progression from
Eves-droppers to *Buffoons.* But are *Parasites* worse than *Bawds*?
[147] *Ibid.,* p. 111.
[148] *Badges to Beggars, Works,* XIII, 135.
[149] It is incidentally the longest series found in all Swift's prose, in the
number of separate units.

ers, Murderers, Robbers, Virtuoso's; no Leaders or Followers of
Party and Faction; no Encouragers to Vice, by Seducement or Examples: No Dungeon, Axes, Gibbets, Whipping-posts, or Pillories;
No cheating Shopkeepers or Mechanicks: No Pride, Vanity or Affectation: No Fops, Bullies, Drunkards, strolling Whores, or Poxes:
No ranting, lewd, expensive Wives: No stupid, proud Pedants: No
importunate, over-bearing, quarrelsome, noisy, roaring, empty,
conceited, swearing Companions: No Scoundrels raised from the Dust
upon the Merit of their Vices; or Nobility thrown into it on account
of their Virtues: No Lords, Fidlers, Judges or Dancing-masters.[150]

This complex series is basically a list of nouns, although other,
more complicated, elements occur (including the previously-men-
tioned nested series of eight adjectives). It is possible to discern,
in the movement from nouns to modified nouns to the antithetic
pair (*Scoundrels, Nobility*) near the end, a rhythm of some power,
a drive for a high point, which is allowed to come down with what
looks like a commonplace set of four nouns at the end. But, as has
been noticed before, there is no necessary coincidence between
the formal movement and the significance of the items involved.
The tenor of the passage is evident in the long introductory list
of nouns and the whole purport is summarized in the inoffensive
sequence of four which maliciously alternates Lords and Judges,
not with criminals but with highly dispensable members of a tri-
fling society.[151] The real sting is decidedly in the tail, regardless of
the formal rhythm of the sequences, whose origin may lie in the
necessity to avoid monotony and the impulse to form seriated
elements into shapes and groups.

Much the same pattern may be seen in the series in which
Gulliver boasts about European versatility in warlike procedures
and contrivances:

[150]   *Gulliver, Works,* XI, 260-1.
[151]   Orwell (*op. cit.,* pp. 133-4, footnote), examining a series of similar
structure (quoted on p. 101, above), notes the unconscious element: "One
sees here the irresponsible violence of the powerless. The list lumps together those who break the conventional code and those who keep it . . .
the whole closing passage, in which the hatred is so authentic, and the
reason given for it so inadequate, is somehow unconvincing. One has the
feeling that personal animosity is at work." Dobree, however, citing still
another passage from the same book (*Gulliver, Works,* XI, 236), finds a
conscious purpose: "Think, for example, of the implications of lumping

And, being no Stranger to the Art of War, I gave him a Description of Cannons, Culverins, Muskets, Carabines, Pistols, Bullets, Powder, Swords, Bayonets, Sieges, Retreats, Attacks, Undermines, Counter-mines, Bombardments, Sea-fights; Ships sunk with a Thousand Men; twenty Thousand killed on each Side; dying Groans, Limbs flying in the Air: Smoak, Noise, Confusion, trampling to Death under Horses Feet: Flight, Pursuit, Victory; Fields strewed with Carcases left for Food to Dogs, and Wolves, and Birds of Prey; Plundering, Stripping, Ravishing, Burning and Destroying.[152]

The series begins with sixteen nouns which move in an orderly fashion, proceeds to a middle section containing a variety of structures, and ends with five violent verbals. Although it would be visionary to see in this conglomeration anything like a care-fully-worked out arrangement and to liken it point for point with other examples, yet it is possible to draw attention to those fea-tures which recur. These are, of course, the variation of structures, the irregularity of sequential elements, the tendency to make the center unlike both the beginning and the end of the series, and the placing of the semantic emphasis on the final element. The five items at the end of the foregoing sequence support this view.[153]

The final sequence to be presented (one of the three longest) does not conform to the hump-back scheme which has been elicited from an examination of the others, but it is nonetheless compara-ble in some respects.

They Writ, and Raillyed, and Rhymed, and Sung, and Said, and said Nothing; They Drank, and Fought, and Whor'd, and Slept, and Swore, and took Snuff: They went to new Plays on the first Night, haunted the Chocolate-Houses, beat the Watch, lay on Bulks, and got Claps: They bilkt Hackney-Coachmen, ran in Debt with Shop-keepers, and lay with their Wives: They kill'd Bayliffs, kick'd Fidlers down Stairs, eat at Locket's, loytered at Will's: They talk'd of the

---

together such activities ... he is not just laying wildly about him; he is thinking very precisely, directing his blows with an assured aim." (op. cit., p. 459). It is significant that indiscriminate lumping occurs a number of times, often enough to be called a mannerism or a technique.

[152] *Gulliver, Works*, XI, 231.

[153] Zickgraf sees the seeming disorder of this series as a list of images moving from the instruments of the "Art of War" to its techniques to its consequences, the whole comprising "The Miseries of War" (*Schrecken des Krieges*) (p. 41).

Drawing-Room and never came there, Dined with Lords they never saw; Whisper'd a Dutchess, and spoke never a Word; exposed the Scrawls of their Laundress for Billets-doux of Quality: came ever just from Court and were never seen in it; attended the Levee *sub dio*; Got a list of Peers by heart in one Company, and with great Familiarity retailed them in another.[154]

The design of this rather chaotic sequence of verbs and clauses is not unlike those previously examined. If the punctuation is ignored, there are three groups, of gradually increasing size: 1) twelve verbs, 2) twelve verbs with complements, and 3) six antithetic groups. The third of the antithetic items is imperfect, consisting of only one verb. But the verbs are seen to move in a nearly regular structure of gradually increasing size. This uncharacteristic regularity (despite its typical violation in detail) may be attributed to the type and early date of *A Tale of a Tub*, in which Swift may have been pursuing a particular parodic purpose.[155]

In the foregoing examination, a number of the patterns carrying Swift's series have been uncovered. But the significance of the attempt to find the order in what seems to be the disorder of Swift's serial practice is not in the patterns themselves. Rather it is in what these patterns and the manner of their overlapping arrangement reveal about his prose and, behind that, about his mind and personality. The irregularity, variety and subtlety of his serial patterns are but aspects of the copiousness which fathered all these lists. The copiousness of imagination which can visualize the reality it conceives of under a legion of aspects, the fertility of invention which can realize these aspects in plausible and telling detail, the energy and passion which insist that only through cumulation can its fierce disquiet be expressed – these are the progenitors of his impressive cataloguing of experience.[156] In its

[154]   *Tale of a Tub, Works,* I, 45.

[155]   According to Paulson, "The series is wholly alliterative, the implication being that all the meaning there is to the series is that some of them begin with the same letters; and this is the only principle of order in the lives of fops." (*op. cit.,* p. 69, footnote 6).

[156]   Spitzer, discussing an *Ode* of Claudel (in which long catalogues of the artifacts in the modern world are given), considers that this "chaotic enumeration" results from a fusion of the macrocosm and the microcosm. The

redundancy his cataloguing derives from the urge to control meaning, as his handling of connectives will show. In its disregard for regularity of pattern and propriety of sentence structure, it is in accord with his originality, his general suspicion of predictability.

poet is a scribe recording the plenitude of the world. The earlier list-makers (Rabelais) "respected the distinctions between the different realms of Nature" (*op. cit.,* p. 206). However, he adds that all this variety of things appears jumbled in the poem because it is blended in the imagination of the poet, who sees the world as shapeless and confusing but depicts it as such because he sees the higher order (p. 207).

V. CONNECTION

"A close reasoner and a good writer in general may be known by his pertinent use of *connectives*." [1] Although Coleridge illustrated this opinion with a reference to the seventeenth-century Whig, Samuel Johnson, it is especially applicable to Swift. His way with conjunctions and related words is a fundamental aspect of his writing.

Curme traces the history of the modern use of subordination and connection (hypotaxis) from a primitive stage of communication, in which related propositions were simply laid side by side, the relationship to be discerned by the reader (parataxis).[2] Proverbs still retain that paratactic feature: "Easy come, easy go." The intermediate stage between parataxis and full hypotaxis is one in which *and* is made to serve all kinds of connective uses, as in such dialects as Irish English, for example: "Did you not hear his reverence, and he speaking to you now?" [3] It is possible to see a remnant of this earlier syntax in the still common omission of such relatives as *which* or *that* in modern English prose; and paratactic clauses are not always considered reprehensible even in formal writing. Nonetheless, the avoidance of connectives is the exception in modern English.

Though it may be surmised that the extensive use of connectives has rendered English less direct and perhaps less colorful, there is no gainsaying that the language has increased in clarity and

---

[1] Samuel Taylor Coleridge, "Table Talk", May 15, 1833, in *Complete Works,* ed. W. G. T. Shedd (New York, 1884), VI, 467.
[2] George O. Curme, *Syntax* (Boston, 1931), p. 170.
[3] *Ibid.,* p. 172, a quotation from J. M. Synge's *The Well of the Saints.*

logical power since their emergence. But more than one writer has probably become aware of the suspicion expressed by the eighteenth-century rhetorician George Campbell: "Of all the parts of speech, the conjunctions are the most unfriendly to vivacity." [4] Perhaps as a product of these conflicting trends, there is a wide varation in the use of connectives, in such matters as choice and range of types, positioning, frequency. In this stylistic feature, it may be expected that mature writers will express a consistent preference which may be isolated by careful examination.[5]

The problem of connectives is closely related to the questions of transition and of reference. A writer articulating his thought wishes to indicate the relationship of each segment to the next and to suggest at intervals how far he has gone in the argument, as well as to set at rest any questions that may arise in the mind of the reader. The solution to this problem is in part structural, a matter of organizing the parts of the discourse into a rational and coherent order. But to do so provides only a partial solution, given the complexity of human thought and the unwillingness of many readers. Connective signposts provide the reader with the author's own key to the relation of the materials and throw the entire composition into focus. Good writers must always be concerned about the appropriateness of their connectives, as Locke suggests:

The words whereby [the mind] signifies what connexion it gives to the several affirmations and negations, that it unites in one continued reasoning or narration, are generally called *particles:* and

---

[4] *The Philosophy of Rhetoric,* p. 395.
[5] The study of individual preferences in the choice of particles is one that has had much vogue in classical scholarship. See, for example, J. D. Denniston, *The Greek Particles,* 2d ed. (Oxford, 1954), pp. lxxviii-lxxxii. Cf. Gilbert Highet, *Poets in a Landscape* (Harmondsworth, 1959): "It is possible ... to learn much about Plato by studying something apparently so insignificant as his use of particles – the little almost-meaningless words of emphasis and qualification like 'of course', 'certainly', 'at least', in which the Greek language is so rich, and which (in written prose) perform the same function as gestures, voice-tones, and facial expressions in conversation" (p. 157). *Particles* is a broader term than *connectives,* but some of the connectives considered below have only ill-defined connective functions. See also the study of *kai* previously mentioned, Ch. II, fn. 142.

it is in the right use of these that more particularly consists the clearness and beauty of a good style. To think well, it is not enough that a man has ideas clear and distinct in his thoughts, nor that he observes the agreement or disagreement of some of them; but he must think in train, and observe the dependence of his thoughts and reasonings upon one another. And to express well such methodical and rational thoughts, he must have words to show what connexion, restriction, distinction, opposition, emphasis, &c., he gives to each respective *part* of his discourse. To mistake in any of these, is to puzzle instead of informing his hearer: and therefore it is, that those words which are not truly by themselves the names of any ideas are of such constant and indispensable use in language, and do much contribute to men's well expressing themselves.[6]

A plausible place to begin the search for connectives is the beginning of a sentence. I had earlier observed that Swift seemed to have a predilection for coordinating conjunctions at the head of his sentences. A rough preliminary count was made of the first word in several hundred sentences from the works of Swift and a selection of authors whose styles had considerable reputations: Addison, Johnson, Gibbon, Macaulay, Butler, and Hemingway.[7] The predominant impressions emerging from an inspection of the results are these: Gibbon begins forty per cent of his sentences with articles, Swift only ten per cent of his, the others falling between, near the low end; conversely, only ten per cent of Gibbon's sentences begin with pronouns, whereas nearly half of Hemingway's do, Swift being second with thirty per cent; as might have been expected, Hemingway uses fewest introductory conjunctions, but the other writers, headed by Johnson and Swift, are quite uniform in this category. Gibbon and Hemingway, it seems, represent polar extremes in introductory habits; Swift and Butler are remarkably similar, except for conjunctions. The most interesting finding, however, is that Swift uses more than twice as

[6] John Locke, *An Essay Concerning Human Understanding*, ed. A. C. Fraser (Oxford, 1894), II, 98-9.

[7] The sample of Swift included material from his "signed" and his "anonymous" material and was about 1300 sentences in extent. The material for the other authors included about 400 sentences for each. The grammatical categories are the conventional ones. The evidence is not presented in any detail because no conclusions are drawn from the figures.

many coordinating conjunctions as Gibbon and Johnson, the runners-up. This count, tentative as it is, supports the observation I had made while reading *Gulliver's Travels* that Swift seemed to begin many sentences with coordinating conjunctions. A more precise count was now in order to test the accuracy of the observation with more significant data.

For this tabulation, the authors are limited to Addison, Johnson and Macaulay, in addition to Swift.[8] Only three classes of introductory words are counted: coördinating conjunctions, subordinating conjunctions, and conjunctive adverbs (and phrases).[9] The results of this test are gratifyingly conclusive.[10] Table 5.1 gives the details.

TABLE 5.1

Percentage of initial connectives in 2000-sentence samples
of Addison, Johnson, Macaulay and Swift

Connective	Addison	Johnson	Macaulay	Swift
C	5.5	5.8	7.4	20.2
S	7.1	6.2	4.1	5.4
SC	3.3	1.4	1.5	8.3
Total	15.9	13.4	13.0	33.9

Over-all, Swift's use of the connectives in these three classes is more than twice as great as that of any of the three other writers.[11] To the reader of Swift, it would appear that he begins one sentence

[8] Samples are two-thousand periods long. See Appendix I for detailed description.
[9] Examples of coordinating conjunctions (C), *and, but, or*; subordinating conjunction (S), *after, when, if*; conjunctive adverbs, or sentence-connectors (SC), *however, therefore, in the meantime, in short.*
[10] With a standard deviation of 8.8, the results are significant at the five per cent level, though there are only four sub-samples.
[11] It would be interesting to be able to compare these figures with those of some other worker. But the only possible comparison is not very instructive. Robert R. Aurner, "Caxton and the English Sentence", *Wisconsin Studies in Language and Literature,* No. 18 (1923), does not define *connective* and uses samples of 100 sentences. He finds that Addison begins 2 sentences with connectives, Macaulay 16, and Johnson 17 in the *Rambler* and 5 in the *Lives* (p. 50).

in five with a coordinating conjunction and one in three with a connective of some sort. The details of the tabulation further reveal that Swift makes unusually heavy use of *and*, *but* and *for*, half his connectives consisting of these three, the favorite being *but*.[12] This pattern of preference is surely a striking peculiarity of his style.[13] Perhaps this peculiarity is most striking because of the limitation it implies. A writer who begins one-sixth of his sentences in much the same way will seem monotonous and repetitious. Moreover, it might be difficult to imagine how he could readily adapt such a mechanism to the necessity of varying his transitions from point to point, unless he wrote always about the same subject or unless his arguments followed a rigidly similar pattern.

But limitation seems unlikely. A glance at the list of Swift's writings reveals a wide range of interests: politics, religion, economics, manners, language, history, even "Thoughts on Various Subjects", which may be taken as a symbol of his wide-ranging mind. Neither is it true that his method of argument is always the same. Some works are expository and some persuasive; some operate by *reductio ad absurdum*, some by irony, some by paradox, sarcasm (even vilification); some are satirical, some parodic, some homiletic, some narrative. In this storehouse of matters and manners one can readily detect (what no one seems inclined to deny him) a flexible and versatile mind, unlikely to be dully bound to a minute repertory of introductory devices, especially a mere triad of conjunctions.

The three coordinating conjunctions in question (*and*, *but*, *for*) may from the "notional" point of view be considered as additive, adversative, and causal. It is true that these three func-

---

[12] Of the 2000-sentence sample, Swift begins 678 with a connective and 354 with *and*, *but* or *for*.

[13] It seems to be a practice frowned on by the more puristic rhetoricians. See, for instance, James Harris, *Hermes* (London, 1751): ". . . in the modern polite Works . . . scarce such a thing as a Particle, or Conjunction is to be found." Even more particular is *The London Universal Letter-Writer* (c. 1800): "I hate particles where they are avoidable; be therefore sparing in your *fors*, your *buts*, and your *ands*." Both are quoted in *English Examined*, compiled by Susie I. Tucker, 1961, pp. 81, 146-7. See also "*And* at beginning", in Campbell, *Philosophy of Rhetoric*, pp. 441-2.

tions seem to represent the major types of links between related propositions. But it is unlikely that they would alone offer adequate subtlety of nuance for an ingenious reasoner like Swift. I speculated that in some manner these conjunctions were varied, were given a different coloring from one use to the next in order to accomplish the variety of tasks that connectives are used for. A possibility that seemed likely, on the basis of an earlier observation I had made, was the linking of the introductory word with some following word in order to produce a suitable range of compounds, such as *and* plus another connective. An examination of a number of Swift's works reveals that a coordinating conjunction is indeed often followed by another word which may classified as a connective or which has connective quality.[14]

In English it is normal to expect to find the subject (a noun or nominal) near the beginning of a sentence. When the sentence begins with a connective, it is safe to expect that the next word will be a nominal or a determiner. But a surprising number of times[15] the subject is deferred to make way for a connective or transitional word. Such collocations may be found on almost any page of Swift's works.[16] It is possible to infer, after one has gathered a sufficient number of illustrations of this procedure, that Swift does not use his introductory *and, but* or *for* in the customary way, in order to impart the logical aspect of the connection between one sentence and the next. Rather, he seems to use it as a kind of neutral connective, that is, a word which shows only that one sentence is connected with another without reference to the nature of the connection.[17]

[14] Expressions with such connective quality include, apart from conjunctive adverbs, a number of adverbs, such as *perhaps, then, surely,* and phrases like *of course, to be sure, on the other hand.*
[15] On the basis of a rough count without statistical pretensions, I would say between a quarter and a third of the time.
[16] In *Works,* III, the following examples were found: "But, although" (58), "And first" (58), "But then" (59), "But, at present" (59), "But, by the Way" (60), "And for that Reason" (61), "And indeed" (63), "But as" (63), "And, not to mention more" (65), "But however" (65), "Or else" (66), "But beside" (67), "And so" (69), "But after all" (71), "For where" (75). Doubtless, more varied examples could be found in a wider area of search.
[17] It is possible to observe a similar use in the King James version of the

Despite Swift's considerable dependence on a limited number of coordinating conjunctions, his use of connectives of all types is less limited than his contemporaries'. This hypothesis was tested by counting the number of connective types that appear in consecutive 1000-word samples of Addison, Johnson, Gibbon and Swift. The results, which are merely indicative, are given in Table 5.2.

TABLE 5.2

Number of different connective types in two 1000-word samples of Addison, Johnson, Gibbon and Swift

	Addison	Johnson	Gibbon	Swift
Types	20,20	12,21	19,12	22,25

In a thorough study of Swift's vocabulary, we should expect to find a large number of the standard connectives, a number of words used as connectives which are not primarily connectives (*now, then, again*) and a variety of phrases serving as connectives (*'tis true, for these reasons*). This range of variety together with his predilection for introductory connectives and his dependence on a favorite triad of conjunctions implies a pattern of use which is quite consistent, both with itself and with as much of his personality as it may be relevant to refer to.

The classification of connectives into grammatical types on the basis of their function is a well-established practice, both in traditional grammars and in modern works. The logical or "notional" classification has been set aside, however, with much of the terminology of traditional rhetoric.[18] It is perhaps that readers and

---

Bible and in some other seventeenth-century stylists. Swift was, it must be recalled, thirty-three before the century ended and it is not unreasonable to suppose that he was subject to the same influences as affected the other writers of his time. That is, if he uses introductory conjunctions in the same way as the King James version, it need not be because he imitated the Biblical style, though he was doubtless subject to its influences. It is more probable that he responded to the challenge of connection in the same way as the translators of the Bible did.

[18]   Both classifications are used in two such different books as George

especially writers realized that such notional concepts as "causal", "concessive", "adversative", "alternative" and the like did not say enough about the types of relationships possible between propositions. Connectives themselves are mere shorthand means to that end. Obviously, complicated relationships require more than a mere *but* or *however* can provide. Such connections must be outlined with all the logical facilities inherent in discursive prose. But for the purpose of moving the reader's attention in the direction of a certain type of expectation or disappointment, these *buts, fors* and their more elaborate brethren have their use. Curiously enough, the most sophisticated writers have sometimes sedulously avoided making use of any more of these than the inevitable *and*, suggesting in this way what their subtlety of thought transcended mechanical means of showing relationships or perhaps that the relation was so inescapable that marking it would be anti-climactic. Conversely, it is possible to use connective words without reference to their notional significance. It is this that Swift does quite frequently with his *ands, buts* and *fors*, as well as with some others.

Normally, when a sentence begins with *for* (in itself rather uncommon), it is expected that the relationship between the previous sentence and the present one will be causal or resultative or the like, "Introducing the ground or reason of something previously said." [19] Swift, however, begins a sentence with *for* which opens a paragraph containing an announced digression from the main line of narrative:

But all would not suffice, and the Ladies aforesaid continued still inflexible: To clear up which Difficulty, I must with the Reader's good Leave and Patience, have recourse to some Points of Weight, which the Authors of that Age have not sufficiently illustrated.

For, about this Time it happened a Sect arose, whose Tenents obtained and spread very far . . .[20]

It is evident that the purpose of this *for* is merely to supply a con-

O. Curme, *English Grammar* (New York, 1947), and Harold Whitehall, *Structural Essentials of English* (New York, 1956).
[19]   *Oxford English Dictionary,* s.v. *For,* conj.
[20]   *Tale of a Tub, Works,* I, 45-6.

nection between the matter being dwelt on and the matter now introduced as illustrative of it. The conjunction *for* in that location might very readily be replaced by *thus* or *so* or even the bare indefinite article ("A sect arose . . ."), and in the prose of another writer might well have been, but Swift prefers to suggest a specious causality as a means of directing his reader.

In the same way, Swift uses the conjunction *nor* in the first paragraph of Section IX of *A Tale of a Tub* ("A Digression concerning Madness"): "nor shall it any ways detract from the just Reputation of this famous Sect, that its Rise and Institution are owing to such an Author as I have described Jack to be." [21] The promise made by that initial *nor* is that the writer will continue to give reasons why the Aeolists' ("this famous Sect") reputation should not be attacked. In fact, in the previous section Swift has introduced the Aeolists and ironically proposed to do them justice but has not given any reasons for the depreciation of their reputation. Instances of this sort, where the notional aspect of the connective is either wholly disregarded or distorted or made use of for the purpose of suggesting a relationship which has not been presented, are very frequent. To this might be added those uses of connectives which exaggerate or intensify beyond what seems reasonable the relationship between the current statement and a previous or remote one.

As an illustration, the two paragraphs which follow may be cited:

Lord Peter was also held the Original Author of Puppets and Raree-Shows; the great Usefulness whereof being so generally known, I shall not enlarge farther upon this Particular.

But, another Discovery for which he was much renowned, was his famous Universal Pickle. *For* having remark'd how your Common Pickle in use among Huswives, was of no farther Benefit than to preserve dead Flesh, and certain kinds of Vegetables; Peter, with great Cost as well as Art, had contrived a Pickle proper for Houses, Gardens, Towns, Men, Women, Children, and Cattle; wherein he could preserve them as Sound as Insects in Amber. *Now*, this Pickle to the Taste, the Smell, and the Sight, appeared exactly the same, with what is in common Service for Beef, and Butter, and Herrings

[21]   *Works*, I, 102.

(and has been often that way applied with great Success) *but* for its many Sovereign Virtues was a quite different Thing. *For* Peter would put in a certain Quantity of his Powder Pimperlim pimp, after which it never failed of Success.[22]

In this passage, five connectives are italicized, of which four might very easily be spared as guides to the notional relationship between the elements they govern. This is not to say that they might altogether be spared, because they perform a function of a special nature, unlike the interior *but* whose function is precisely adversative, opposing the sovereign virtue of the pickle with its common appearance. However, the initial *but* implies that the discovery of the pickle will be enlarged on, unlike that of Puppets and Raree-shows which will not, but it actually opposes the dismissal of further discussion about the two items with another discovery for which Peter is renowned. Although this appears to be a mere rhetorical error, it is wholly in the spirit of Swift's irregular use of these introductory particles. This is fully shown by the initial *for* which follows the antecedent *but*. Its value seems closest to *thus* or other illustrative connective, fulfilling a function designed to display a stage or point in the argument, like the *now* which follows it, and whose notional value is approximately null. The final *for* possesses a hint of indispensability, as it pretends to connect the unexpected sovereign virtue of the pickle with an explanation of its operation. Nonetheless, its presence is supererogatory, as can be demonstrated by a re-writing of the passage without the four dispensable connectives:

Lord Peter was also held the Original Author of Puppets and Raree-Shows; the great Usefulness whereof being so generally known, I shall not enlarge farther upon this Particular.
   Another Discovery for which he was much renowned, was his famous Universal Pickle. Having remark'd how your Common Pickle in use among Huswives, was of no farther Benefit than to preserve dead Flesh, and certain kinds of Vegetables; Peter, with great Cost as well as Art, had contrived a Pickle proper for Houses, Gardens, Towns, Men, Women, Children and Cattle; wherein he could preserve them as Sound as Insects in Amber. This Pickle to the Taste, the Smell, and the Sight, appeared exactly the same, with what is in com-

[22]   *A Tale of a Tub, Works*, I, 67-8, italics supplied.

mon Service for Beef, and Butter, and Herrings, (and has been often that way applied with great Success) but for its many Sovereign Virtues was quite a different Thing. Peter would put in a certain Quantity of his Powder Pimperlim pimp, after which it never failed of Success.

This passage in the revised version can be understood as readily as the original and is perhaps a little more compact. The change that took place points to the unorthodox use of these connectives. The omission of two *fors*, a *but* and a *now* does not so much obscure the relationship of the parts, which is obvious enough, as it removes the emphasis, the continuity, what might be called the entrainment of the passage. Such use of more words than are strictly necessary, however it may resemble pleonasm, because it is directed toward the more accurate reception of the message, is in the spirit of the redundancy valued by communications engineers.[23]

A similar pseudo-pleonastic use of connectives is found where two are used instead of one. Usually these combinations consist of a coordinating conjunction followed by a conjunctive adverb. The most common, one for which eighteenth-century rhetoricians and lexicographers castigated Swift, is *but however*,[24] as in, "But however, such great Frenzies being artificially raised . . ." [25] Other adversative combinations present *but* with a phrase, as in "But on the other side, whoever should mistake the Nature of things so far . . ." [26] Additive pleonasms are common with *and*: "and, indeed, if the former Danger . . ."; [27] "And besides there was already in the Town . . ."; [28] "And likewise because too great an Affectation of Secrecy . . ."[29] Other combinations may be found of varying rarity: "But still, there is in this Project a greater Mischief . . ."; [30] "Or perhaps they scare us . . ." [31] A cursory examina-

[23] The purpose of safeguarding the message need not be conscious, however.

[24] Sterling A. Leonard, *The Doctrine of Correctness in English Usage 1700-1800* (Madison, 1929), p. 280.

[25] *Examiner, Works,* III, 65.

[26] *A Tale of a Tub, Works,* I, 31.

[27] *Examiner, Works,* III, 63.

[28] *History of the Four Last Years of the Queen, Works,* VII, 142.

[29] *Free Thoughts, Works,* VIII, 81.

[30] *Argument, Works,* II, 30.

[31] *Examiner, Works,* III, 17.

tion reveals that of the cited pairs either word alone would suffice. That Swift uses both should lead us to wonder whether he intends the particular effect or whether the mechanism and the resultant effect were beyond the reach of Swift's consciousness.

Another type of connective use may help to elucidate this question. It has been shown that introductory connectives (usually coordinating conjunctions) are used as mere links or joints in the syntactic architecture of Swift's prose. The actual task of specifying a notional relationship is handed over to a pleonastic or redundant pair. More often, however, the introductory group of connectives is made up of two or more from different national classes. These usually consist of *and, but, for* followed by a conjunctive adverb or a subordinating conjunction, though others appear as well.

The most common combination is the one beginning with *and*, which is found with a very wide variety of companions: *and after all, and although, and as, and if, and therefore, and thus.* Some more elaborate examples may be unearthed: *and indeed if,*[32] *and likewise because,*[33] *and therefore as,*[34] *and therefore when,*[35] and perhaps most interesting, *and therefore if notwithstanding!* [36] There is a large number of *but if, but though, but when, but whether,* and *but while* combinations, not to mention all the derivatives of *for, or, nor, so, neither, yet.*

If it is recalled that these groupings occur at the head of sentences, it may be inferred that Swift is availing himself of two rhetorical opportunities. He is modifying the plain and rather bare character of the unadorned connective, especially the favored triad, and presenting it in such a variety of guises that his prose achieves a highly diversified appearance, far more so than could be guessed by the frequency with which these particular three recur. Moreover, he presents his reader, at the beginning of each sentence headed by this kind of grouping, with a set of guides to the relationships involved in the thought which is often contra-

[32]   *Examiner, Works,* III, 63.
[33]   *Free Thoughts, Works,* VIII, 81.
[34]   *Freemen of Dublin, Works,* XIII, 85.
[35]   *Hatred of Clergy, Works,* XIII, 124.
[36]   *Argument, Works,* II, 37.

dictory, for example, *for although* in "For although he were at last undeceived and reconciled to her, yet I lost all Credit with him".[37] The combination of causal with concessive, pretending to adduce a result of some antecedent happening but diluting it with a concession or diminution of the explanation, is confusing if not contradictory. But in the sentence cited it may be seen that both *for* and *yet* do not function except for emphasis. The sentence makes perfect sense without them. They are not confusing because they are here as in the earlier-cited examples merely emphatic or redundant.[38]

A concatenation such as *and therefore if notwithstanding,* which consists of three essential elements, each one promising the later introduction of a relevant clause, would burden the reader's mind with an excess of difficulty before permitting him to proceed with the argument. Actually, the sentence in which that grouping occurs, even out of context and without punctuation is not difficult to understand:

and therefore if notwithstanding all I have said it shall still be thought necessary to have a bill brought in for repealing Christianity I would humbly offer an amendment that instead of the word Christianity may be put religion in general which I conceive will much better answer all the good ends proposed by the projectors of it.[39]

To say that something is not difficult to understand is not to say that it is especially clear. The clarity with which Swift has al-

Gulliver, Works, XI, 50.
[38] This closely resembles what Denniston, *op. cit.,* p. xli, calls the "corresponsive use of particles" in Greek: "Coherence of thought is adequately secured by the presence of a backward-pointing particle. The reader or listener, when he has reached a certain point, meets a particle which looks back to the road he has traversed, and beckons him on in a certain direction. But greater coherence is attained if in addition a forward-pointing particle warns him in advance what path he will soon have to travel, the connexion being expressed reciprocally, from rear to van and from van to rear."
[39] The original, punctuated, version follows: "And therefore, if, notwithstanding all I have said, it shall still be thought necessary to have a Bill brought in for repealing Christianity; I would humbly offer an Amendment, that instead of the Word *Christianity,* may be put Religion in general; which I conceive, will much better answer all the good Ends proposed by the Projectors of it" (*Argument, Works,* II, 37).

ways been credited is not helped by this proceeding. It is well-known that Swift favored clarity as a characteristic of style, and it seems therefore likely that he would have eschewed what in his writing might be inimical to it. It can hardly be supposed that he would think the multiplication of non-essential connectives at the beginning of sentences a help to clarity. The conclusion cannot be escaped that Swift was not aware of the extensiveness or the idiosyncrasy of his practice in this regard. Even his manuscript corrections and textual variants do not show any curbing of this trait, but rather a juggling of *yets* and *fors*.[40] He revised the surface but could not modify the fundamental structure. One of his recent editors, commenting on the ineffectiveness of Swift's revisions, specifies it accurately: "He was struggling against a tendency to write in just the way he disliked." [41] This observation is supported by the constant gap between Swift's ideals of style and his practice.

A prose which is as extensively connected as Swift's has been shown to be cannot fail to impress the reader. His attention is inevitably called to the connective tissue between sentences, although the effect must be to a great extent below the threshold of consciousness, judging by the lack of comment about this feature of Swift's writing. Nonetheless, the connectives must diffuse an appearance of great logic, convey the picture of a writer whose material is so ready to his mind that he distributes concessions, hypotheses, causes, results with such freedom that he can scarcely fit them all into his sentences. But, in spite of the forbidding aspect of some of these mounds of connectives, the reader has no difficulty in understanding; in fact, he is not at all put off by the complex web of inter-relationships. Because he does not realize that his understanding is due to the redundant nature of the connective guides, he reaches the conclusion that the writer is eminently logical, transpicuously clear, and economical with words to the point of terseness.

[40] E.g., the textual notes to *Gulliver's Travels* in *Works*, XI.
[41] Jonathan Swift, *An Enquiry into the Behavior of the Queen's Last Ministry*, ed. Irvin Ehrenpreis (Bloomington, 1956), p. xxxi. Ehrenpreis notes a number of amplifications serving to introduce smoothness by means of additional introductory conjunctions.

Clarity of language, it has often been said, results when clarity of thought is adequately translated into words. That this is an inadequate concept scarcely needs documentation. Swift's reader is permitted to glimpse the complexity of a question or event and given a succession of interrelated data providing a semblance of inevitability, in a manner exuding vigor and confidence. Because the randomness of events has been given form, the reader feels enlightened by order and clarity.

But it is persuasiveness, not clarity, which results from Swift's use of connectives.[42] The enchainment of sentences by means of connectives carries the reader along with great mobility and induces him to believe in the clarity and simplicity of what he has read.[43] He has been moved rapidly through Swift's line of argument, has become persuaded by it and has emerged feeling that everything is clear. And Swift's handling of connectives is an important factor in that success.

Redundancy then, in the sense both of copiousness and of control of meaning, is an integral feature of Swift's style and contributes an important share to his achievement. Though it would be absurd to contend that Swift manipulated series and connectives without conscious art, it is not beyond probability to suggest that the great disparity between his expressed ideals and his practice was due to the unconscious factor in composition, a factor to which he was perhaps unusually susceptible. The matter, in any case, needs no debate, as we turn our attention now to the microscopic aspect of style, to which no deliberate contribution is possible and in which words have no lexical meaning.

[42] Johnson well says: "it will not be easy to find ... any inconsequence in his connections, or abruptness in his transitions." *Lives of the Poets,* ed. Hill, III, 52.
[43] To discover how successfully, see Johnson's famous comment on Swift's pamphlet, "The Conduct of the Allies", in *Boswell's Life of Johnson,* ed. Hill-Powell, II, 65: "He had to count ten, and he has counted it right."

VI. WORDS WITHOUT MEANING

> [he had] made the strictest Computation of the general
> Proportion there is in Books between the Numbers of
> Particles, Nouns, and Verbs, and other Parts of Speech.
> *Gulliver's Travels,* Ch. V [1]

Euclid loftily gave a drachma to a student who had asked what
geometry was good for. This characteristic Greek contempt for
pragmata is too often shared by students of literature. They make
a virtue of the immediately unpractical nature of their knowledge
and deplore studies with a merely pragmatic intention. Hence
bibliography, lexicography, and editorial drudgery are accorded
only qualified praise, the most generous compliments being reserved for the inventive analysis of the critic. Such a division of
praise is ultimately just, but only if the critic brings to his work
patient and responsible concern with detail and a clear sense of
purpose.

Thus is it in the study of style. If its purpose is left unstated, no
means exist to check the repetition of error or to verify results.
Almost anything may be said because hardly any way can be
found to argue with evidence presented with no specific end in
view. Errors are made, borrowed, repeated, embroidered and become part of the canon, because they have never been tested. The
history of criticism offers ample documentation for this view.[2]

But if every critic kept in mind that a possible use of his description of an author's style might be to try to identify that author's
writing, he would be held to a moderate use of impressionistic

---

[1]   Swift, *Works,* XI, 168.
[2]   The whole question is treated in some detail in Chapter I.

description. He would perhaps rely less on traditional adjectives[3] and more on observed linguistic peculiarities supported by some sort of quantitative evidence. His objectivity would increase and the study of style would become respectable and authoritative.

The earlier procedure of this study, it may be recalled, involved the reading of the relevant texts, the observing of some notable peculiarities and the comparative and systematic search for the presence and frequency of these features in the work of Swift and others writers of comparable distinction. The results of that examination were then used as the basis of some speculations about the significance of these peculiarities in the prose of Swift. The limitations of the procedure are specifically the necessity of comparing roughly similar kinds of writing (because of the influence of the subject-matter), and the problem of human error or bias. Obviously these limitations are not sufficient to invalidate the results achieved, but they constitute a boundary to their usefulness in identifying unknown texts. How the limitations operate requires a moment's digression.

The first of these limitations (the subject-matter) tends to raise the whole issue of diction as a part of style. Since this matter has been previously gone into,[4] the arguments will not be rehearsed here. It was concluded, however, that the vocabulary was a relatively unstable aspect of a writer's prose.[5] This conclusion rests on several bases. For one thing, the vocabulary is strongly affected by the type and subject matter of a piece of writing. Two sermons by different writers may have more words in common than a sermon and a romance by the same writer. It follows that the study of a writer's vocabulary, though it may be informative about his reading (for instance), is likely to be useless as a criterion of identification. It is, of course, possible to find works to compare which are similar in type and subject matter,[6] but that is a risky undertaking, always dependent on the hazard of finding a compa-

---

[3] Swift's "masculine" or "nervous" style, for example. See Ch. I, above.
[4] See Chapter III, above.
[5] Taken as individual words and not as an abstract total.
[6] By necessity, this procedure was, of course, adopted in Chapters IV and V, but not to the extent that any doubt was reflected on the integrity of the results.

rable work. Techniques which depend on such similarities involve the researcher in the necessity of making allowances for the differences he finds in the fact that the works he compares are not strictly comparable.[7] Such a necessity must lead to frighteningly subjective decisions and to results of uncertain applicability.

Vocabulary is not only sensitive to changing subject matter; it is also susceptible to the writer's voluntary choice. Everyone concedes to the writer the option of selecting the word he prefers, whether *paternal* or *fatherly, say, assert* or *asseverate,* and the like. Why then should this unquestioned right be considered a handicap in the analysis of style? The answer is bound up with the *consciousness* of the choice. If a writer deliberately sets out to limit himself to short Anglo-Saxon nouns, or to a particular set of words, he is creating an imitable style, which defeats the purpose of text identification. A clever imitator could perhaps duplicate the imitable features of the vocabulary and thus render worthless the lexical criteria of style description and identification.

To what extent a person's whole vocabulary is modifiable is a dubious question. We know that the child's grows at a standard rate,[8] but there is not much evidence about its growth in adulthood. It seems probable (despite the claims of commercial experts) that the adult reader's vocabulary is relatively static, except when he makes a deliberate effort to acquire the language of a trade or specialty. This stasis might seem to favor the use of a criterion based on favorite vocabulary items. But such a criterion has not proved to have any ability to discriminate between authors,[9] partly because such items cannot be relied on to appear except in certain contexts. What is needed is a criterion stable enough to offer predictive power yet safe from imitation, conscious modifica-

---

[7] Such compensation is a feature of the work of G. U. Yule, *The Statistical Study of the Literary Vocabulary* (Cambridge, 1944), pp. 122-3 and of S. Krishnamurti, "Vocabulary Tests Applied to (Dr. Johnson's) Authorship of the 'Misargyrus' Papers in the Adventurer", *Journal of the University of Bombay,* XXI (Sept. 1952), 54.

[8] See Margaret Nice, "On the Size of Vocabularies", *American Speech,* II (1926), 3-4, and Irene Gansl, *Vocabulary: Its Measurement and Growth* (New York, 1939), pp. 46-7.

[9] E.g., Teerink's approach to the identification of *The History of John Bull,* discussed above, pp. 34 ff.

tion and the variability of subject matter. If such a criterion cannot be found in the words of the text, in the vocabulary, where is it to be found?

It is not in the words but in the structure that the stability of an author's style resides. The words must be taken as carriers not of lexical but of grammatical content, that is, from the point of view of their primary syntactic function.[10]

It seems a legitimate extension of the conclusions reached about the vocabulary to expect that elements of the writing further removed from the possibility of deliberate tampering would be found to be more consistent and less sensitive to variation in subject matter. If the grammatical structure is examined in some relatively simple way, something like parsing,[11] an adequate analysis of the text would be made available for quantitative treatment, provided suitable refinements were incorporated into the analytical instrument.

To be sure, such analysis tends to blur certain distinctions, as an example will demonstrate. "Apples and pears taste good" consists of a noun, a coordinating conjunction, another noun, equational verb and an adjective, a description which also applies to the fancier "Pomegranates and honeydews appear magnificent". The sacrifice of literary quality is even more evident when Gibbon's "I have described the triumph of barbarism and religion"[12] is equated with "I have taken the road to Hoboken or Newark". The choice of word is important, there is no denying, but it is not measurable and as such is sacrificed to the greater certainty to be obtained by more abstract methods.

Part of the usefulness of a grammatical criterion of style is its remoteness from the conscious activity and interest of the writer, who handles words rather than grammatical entities.

[10] Syntax is here limited to placing the words of the text into part of speech word-classes. It is realized that such syntax is not the sole grammatical element of utterances, but inflection does not offer a wide range of implication and word order is not very readily classified. It has in any case been in part dealt with in Chapters IV and V.
[11] Only the analysis into parts of speech, not the particulars of dependency, modification, government, and agreement, is meant.
[12] Cited by J. B. Bury, "Introduction", *The Decline and Fall of the Roman Empire* (London, 1900), I, xxxviii.

Though he may bite his pen while deciding whether to use *honeydew* or *melon*, he is unlikely to consider often whether he wants a subordinating conjunction or a relative adverb, a conjunction or a conjunctive adverb. He is doubtless aware of the grammatical values of the words he employs – he could hardly write otherwise – but the awareness is not immediate or tangible.[13] It is a subterranean undercurrent running parallel to his consciousness of the lexical meanings of the words. It seems probable, then, that a writer's consistency in the use of certain word-classes would be higher than his consistency in the use of any vocabulary items.

Furthermore, it is unlikely that such a classification would be highly sensitive to the genre or the subject matter of the text. Doubtless more pronouns are used in a first-person narrative than in a philosophical essay, but it is not obvious that all word-classes should be affected.

Finally, the consistency of an individual writer's style within the body of his own works can be better shown in his grammar than in his vocabulary, not only because the grammar is for the most part beyond his conscious reach, but because it tends, even more than the vocabulary, to remain static in adult writers. A writer of any experience is aware how often he slips into certain familiar structures, especially at the beginnings of sentences. In writing letters, conscious effort is required to keep each sentence (or paragraph) from beginning with "I". That by conscious effort the writer should be able to control some aspect of his grammar [14] does not invalidate the contention that his grammatical choices are mainly unconscious or beyond the reach of systematic or large-scale tampering. Rather it suggests that there must be many other aspects of structure which are not open to casual inspection

[13] "... it is a plain mistake to assume that conscious knowledge of the grammatical system is necessary to good writing. Some of our best writers know very little about grammatical analysis. Not only that, but writers who do understand the system do not apply this knowledge when they write ... as I write these lines, I have no awareness at all of the particular structures that fall – which are subjects, which adverbs, which relative clauses." Paul Roberts, *English Sentences: Teacher's Manual* (New York, 1962), p. 2.
[14] By "grammar" is only meant here the syntactical word-class substructure, defined at length hereunder.

and which even the most intense scrutiny will not lay bare without the appropriate method and instruments.

I am speaking of certain configurations of word-classes which only a high-speed electronic computer has the leisure to observe and to quantify. The use of such an aid may be considered essential to reach those levels of composition of which the writer is not aware. The computer, in this sense, is like a high-powered microscope, with which the cellular structure of a body may be examined. No amount of peering with the naked eye can ever resolve the distance between the observer and the mystery.

The electronic computer, moreover, aids in removing the other limitation previously mentioned, the bias or error of the observer. The wish is frequently father to the thought, and experimenters in the sciences have often found it necessary to circumvent their own desire to find the sought-for effect in samples in which it is to be expected. Similarly, in such a project as this it is a comfort to the experimenter to realize that the machine will count impartially both what is favorable and what is unfavorable to his hypothesis and so free him from the possible guilt of collusion, even if unconscious. Electronic equipment is also less apt to make small counting errors, which may add up to results that are a few percentage points away from the truth. Of course, computers are themselves liable to error, but small errors can be easily circumvented by automatic checking routines and large errors regularly produce figures of such gross implausibility as to require investigation.

But the tendency of computers to err is a very tiny hazard indeed, if they have been properly instructed or "programmed". The program supplied to a computer consists of a set of detailed and unambiguous instructions as to what must be done to the data which it is to process. The computer's electronic intelligence is, unlike the human mind, inflexible. It requires precise criteria and precise instructions. If it is programmed to count all the modifiers known as "articles" in a set of data, it must be informed how to identify an article in wholly unambiguous terms. Thus, assuming that a program contains the information that all words spelled *a*, *an*, or *the* are to be counted as articles, it will do so even if the context does not justify such an interpretation, as in "John A. Brown" or "the more, the merrier". The ambiguity can be guarded against by defining articles more precisely, listing all the possible contexts in which they appear, but only at the cost of increasing the complexity of the program to the point where it would no longer be economical to use a computer.[15]

To simplify the process and make only such use of the computer as might be efficient, I decided to analyze the texts into word-classes "manually". The alternative – programming a computer to analyze the syntax of the texts – is beyond the present ability of both programmers and computers. Each word of the texts (63,000 words) was individually classified, the word-class translated into its numerical equivalent, each sentence thus being reduced to a series of significant numbers. The data obtained were then punched onto IBM cards, each of the prose samples recorded in this manner on a sequence of cards making up a data deck.

Although this procedure sounds quite simple, it involves the resolution of a number of difficulties raised by the need for a suitable system of word-classes. The usual set of eight to ten parts of speech, a system of considerable age and ubiquity, has recently come under heavy attack on account of its ambiguous criteria for classifying words, some by function, some by position, some by inflection, and some by vague, even mystical aspects.[16] The alternative suggested by one of the foremost modern grammarians and a critic of the old system, Charles C. Fries, consists of a division into two sets of classes: Parts of Speech proper (words which bear

---

[15] Machine translation depends on the ability of a program to analyze sentence structure mechanically, something which has not yet been achieved and which if it is will probably make Machine Translation more expensive than manual. See W. N. Locke and A. D. Booth, *Machine Translation of Languages* (New York, 1955), for advocacy. Anthony G. Oettinger, "Automatic (Transference, Translation, Remittance, Shunting)", in *On Translation*, ed. Reuben A. Brower (Cambridge, Mass., 1959), pp. 240-267, gives a clear explanation. For reservations and criticisms, see Mortimer Taube, *Computers and Common Sense* (New York, 1961), Chapter III.

[16] By "recently" is meant in this century. A concise statement of the objections to the standard system may be found in Charles C. Fries, *The Structure of English* (New York, 1952), pp. 65-72. The presentation of his revision occurs in the same book, Chapters V and VI in particular.

the major lexical burden of the sentence), and Function Words (words which constitute one of the major means of conveying grammatical information in English).

Because of its clear theoretical superiority, Fries's division into two types of word-classes has been adopted, but the word-classes themselves have been modified. His four classes of Parts of Speech (numbered from one to four) are roughly equivalent to nouns, verbs, descriptive adjectives and adverbs, but are classified in terms of their function, not of their appearance or customary use. Thus they are not exactly equivalent to conventional nouns, verbs, adjectives and adverbs. The system I have devised includes under Parts of Speech these four classes [17] and an additional four. The purpose of diverging from Fries's system here is not to assert a doctrinal difference of opinion but to secure greater analytical refinement. My Classes Five, Six and Seven comprise infinitives, participles and gerunds, respectively, which Fries classifies variously depending on the function they perform. In spite of the uniformity sacrificed by diverging from Fries's system, I anticipate some benefit from a precise count of verbals, which some earlier tests have led me to believe might be significant. Though it is true that this divergence introduces some theoretical ambiguity in the criteria of identification, in practice the verbals are readily enough distinguished.[18] The eighth class includes foreign words, quotations, titles and other miscellaneous substantive expressions.

The fifteen categories of Function Words provided by Fries do not prove as satisfactory as the Parts of Speech classes and have therefore been considerably revised. In order to provide opportunity for certain peculiarities to manifest themselves, classes of function words are devised for which Fries had no provision. It would be tedious to criticize in detail each of his fifteen groups and

[17]   Because of the limitations of the IBM equipment all the word-classes receive two-digit class designators. Fries's Classes One, Two, Three and Four thus become Classes 01, 02, 03 and 04.

[18]   Participles normally serving the function of verbals (verbs of infinite predication) are classed 06: for example, "*Hanging* on the vine, the grapes looked sour". But they are classed 03 (adjectives) when they are in attributive position: "the *hanging* gardens of Babylon". Appendix A gives a full list of classes and illustrations.

compare item for item with the sixteen with which I replaced them. Instead a summary description of my classes will be provided.

The major difficulty lies in defining the concept of Function Word, a necessity that Fries avoids until he has first dealt with the Parts of Speech and then classified the words which are left over. These he tentatively delimits as words that operate in "positions" other than those of the Parts of Speech.[19] This delimitation provides a single unambiguous criterion, but difficulties develop as soon as it is compared with the inductive criteria that he finds all the classes of Function Words seem to have in common. These are three: (1) each class has only a limited number of members; [20] (2) the words have a preponderance of structural over lexical meaning; (3) speakers of the language must learn these words as individual items because they are not distinguished by formal features, as are the Parts of Speech.[21]

Although Fries does not present these points in common as a definition of Function Word, they constitute one which is at odds with his procedure. For example, personal pronouns in Fries's system are classified as Class One because they will fit in the same test frames as nouns.[22] Yet they are very like Function Words in that there is a limited number of them, which is unlikely to expand; they have as much structural as lexical meaning; and their formal features are highly unreliable. The precedence of criteria is involved. There seems to be no reason to prefer the test-frame criterion to the others and therefore in my system pronouns are classified as Function Words.[23]

[19] *Structure*, p. 88. "Positions" refers to the test frames that Fries uses to isolate the words of his Classes One to Four. For example, a word that fits in the test frame "(the) ———— is/are good" is Class One. "Fits" may be defined as "may be placed and will be recognized as making grammatical if not semantic sense by a native speaker of English".

[20] Fries counted 154 in all (p. 104).

[21] *Structure*, pp. 104-109.

[22] In such a test frame of Fries's as "(The) ———— is/are good", it is clear that the pronouns *he, they, some* and others will fit. But what of *I*? And how many pronouns will fit in the frame "(the) green ———— is/are good"?

[23] I am fortified in this stand by a comment of H. A. Gleason, *An Introduction to Descriptive Linguistics*, rev. ed. (New York, 1961): "These 'small words' are commonly grouped as function words. The term is use-

The sixteen classes of Function Words which I devised may be grouped into nine types, each one characterized by some functional attribute. The first type contains the single class (11) of those pronouns which can serve a "nominal" function, for example, *I, we, some, this, anybody*,[24] but specifically excluding relative pronouns, limiting adjectives and interrogatives, which belong to three other classes.

Auxiliary verbs and all parts of the verb *to be* constitute the single class of the second type (21), which includes such items as *shall, have*,[25] *must, ought, will, be, is, would*. This class probably causes less uncertainty than any other.

The third type includes all modifiers which are not descriptive, as 03 and 04 are, and is divided into four classes. The first one (31) includes all the words which modify Class 01 words, such as *a, the, this, any, both, such, every, our, his, most*, roughly, that is, the limiting adjectives.[26] The other three classes of this type are words that perform adverbial modifying functions. Class 32 comprises prepositions (so-called postpositions) which modify verbs, on the model of German verbs with separable prefixes: "look *out* for oneself", "get *up* in the morning", "move *around* with ease". Intensifiers like *very, so, more* and the unique *not* make up Class 33. The last class (34) of this type is, it must be admitted, somewhat miscellaneous. It includes all the function adverbs which

---

ful, but the concept is very difficult to define. There is a complete intergradation from items which are almost purely structural markers, to ones which have considerable lexical meaning and for which the function of marking structure is incidental. A function word is any word near one end of this continuum. How purely a structural signal it must be to qualify cannot be specified, and the limit of the group must be somewhat vague, and a matter of each linguist's opinion and convenience" (p. 156). W. Nelson Francis, *The Structure of American English* (New York, 1958), hedges and calls pronouns "function nouns" (p. 244). James Sledd, *A Short Introduction to English Grammar* (Chicago, 1959), divides them into Nominals and Function Words (pp. 96-111). Ralph B. Long, *The Sentence and Its Parts* (Chicago, 1961), creates a new non-function word class for them (pp. 45-46). Obviously the matter is open to interpretation.

[24]   The pronouns included are those usually called personal, reflexive, reciprocal, indefinite, demonstrative.

[25]   When *have* functions as an independent verb and not as an auxiliary, it is of course classified 02.

[26]   Called "determiners" by some modern grammarians, e.g., Sledd, p. 209.

could not be fitted into any of the other classes. These are for the most part adverbs of place (*here, thence*), time (*now, never, seldom, always*), and possibility (*perhaps, only*).

The fourth type includes five classes of connectives of perfectly standard character. Coordinating conjunctions (*and, but, or*) are in the first class (41). Subordinating conjunctions (*sice, although, because*) are in the second (42). All the relatives are grouped in the third class (43): *who, which, what*. Interrogatives constitute the fourth class (44): *who, when, which, how;* and correlative conjunctions (*either . . . or*) the fifth and last (45).

True prepositions make up the single class of the fifth type (51), a large number. By contrast, a mere three words constitute the sixth type (61): *there, it* and *to*, in certain very specialized uses. These words may be lumped as pattern-markers.[27] In traditional grammar, the first two are variously called anticipatory words or expletives.[28] Even grammars with modern orientation [29] take up *there* and *it* together. Although the function performed by *to*, which is not really indispensable for identifying the infinitive, makes it only metaphorically similar to those of the expletives *there* and *it*, it seemed expedient to bring these words together.[03]

The seventh type (Class 71) is a combination of several groups devised by Fries [31] to handle such words as appear at the beginning of sentences but have little grammatical relation with them: *Well, Yes, Listen, John!* All such terms were combined into this one class.

The eighth type (Class 81) comprises the numerals, which

[27] A term derived from Sumner Ives, *A New Handbook for Writers* (New York, 1960), who calls them "pattern words" (pp. 141-2).
[28] Fries has a place for *there* – Group H (p. 97) – but none for *it*.
[29] Such as Paul Roberts, *Understanding Grammar* (New York, 1954), pp. 252-4.
[30] *There* and *it* as expletives signal that a grammatical inversion has taken place. E.g., "there is a man outside" can be converted to "a man is outside". *There* indicates the delay in announcement of the subject, and tells something about the syntax of the sentence. In the same way *to* signals the infinitive. This explanation is not wholly satisfactory because *to* may be followed by an article, adjective, noun or pronoun. The decision to group these may not have been wise: the problem was what to do with *to*.
[31] Group K (*Well, oh,* interjections); Group L (*Yes, No*); Group M (*Say, Listen*); Group N (*Please*); *Structure*, pp. 101-103.

seem to be treated inconsistently by Fries. A word like *eighth*,[32] he
considers a Part of Speech structurally identical with an adjective
(Class Three). But the word *eighteen*[33] is classified as a Function
Word of Group A (my Class 31). Furthermore, *eighteen* may
also serve as a Class One word. I am treating numerals as a single
class. It is true that Fries might find it possible to justify his classification on the basis of the performance of these words in his
test frames, but this requires ignoring his other criteria for Function Words. The numerals as a class are a finite, smallish group
(though in combination they are of course unbounded) to which
it is difficult to make any addition.[34] Further, they have no semantic
content: *eighth* only has meaning with reference to *seventh* and
ninth. In a continuous series, *eighth* could be any item, depending
on the starting point. It has merely a "structural" meaning. But
some confusion arises from its position in more than one symbolic
system. A number is a member of the class of numerals and its
literal representation makes it a word at second hand. Therefore
the position of numbers as words is ambiguous and their distinctiveness ought to be recognized by assigning them to a distinctive
class. They must also be learned as items, for their formal
features do not help to identify them. Obviously there is warrant
for collecting all the numbers into one function class, especially
if it is postulated that the use of numbers by a writer may be
stylistically important.

The final group (91) consists of what Roberts calls "sentence-
connectors",[35] such words as *however, nevertheless, therefore*.
Fries finds no place for these words in his system at all, referring
to them as "so-called conjunctions".[36] Although he recognizes
them as similar to function words, he labels them "sequence
signals" and notes the difficulty that dictionary editors have had
in deciding whether they were conjunctions or adverbs. It seems

[32]   P. 83, fn. 15. No example is given but the test frame reads "The
eighth ——— is good."
[33]   P. 89. The test frame: "Eighteen ———s are good."
[34]   The nephew of the mathematician E. Kasner is one of the few people
credited with coining the name of a new number: *googol*, 10^{100}.
[35]   Paul Roberts, *Understanding English* (New York, 1958), pp. 230 ff.
[36]   *Structure*, p. 250.

right to acknowledge their special status by placing them in a special class.

The system just outlined I do not claim to be superior to Fries's. It is simply more precisely suited to the requirements of literary style analysis.[37] With this system in hand, it becomes possible to convert the selected texts from their normal form into the numerical equivalents required for convenient machine processing. One more decision, however, remains to be made: the definition of *word*. Throughout this discussion I have used *word* as if it were possible to define the term exactly and as if everyone agreed about a definition. The fact is that this question has been extensively discussed by linguists and grammarians and to some extent left undecided.[38] Unlike their predecessors, they can no longer postulate the equation: one word equals one concept. Nor is the typographical description – letters surrounded by spaces – theoretically adequate for a systematic definition, though it may serve here for a starting point.

Because we are dealing here not with recorded speech but with written language,[39] most words [40] are adequately described by the typographical definition. But in connection with the definition

[37] Fries collected his material from miscellaneous correspondence received by a government office and from recorded telephone conversations. In neither of these contexts would certain literary forms appear.

[38] For an idea of the dimensions of this disagreement, see Edward Sapir, *Language* (New York, 1921), pp. 32 ff.; Leonard Bloomfield, *Language* (New York, 1933), pp. 178 ff. Sapir and Bloomfield use the same illustration – the ability or absence of ability of native speakers to make word divisions – to support their contradictory views on the "naturalness" of the word-concept. More elaborate though not final treatments of the question may be found in W. Nelson Francis, *The Structure of American English* (New York, 1958), pp. 200-208 and Charles F. Hockett, *A Course in Modern Linguistics* (New York, 1958), pp. 166-173. Useful techniques for setting word boundaries are the insertion method described by Joseph H. Greenberg, *Essays in Linguistics* (Chicago, 1957), pp. 30-31 and the similar concept of interruptibility suggested by Kenneth L. Pike, *Language,* Part III (Glendale, Calif., 1960), p. 4.

[39] There is no longer any way to tell whether Swift pronounced words written as compounds (with or without hyphen) as one word or two. In this and other cases, recourse to phonology was avoided on the ground that it was not certainly applicable, and that it would not solve enough problems to be worth the trouble.

[40] Probably about 95 per cent.

of *word*, questions of grammar, not of phonology, produce the thorniest cruxes. For example, correlative conjunctions are cited in pairs in dictionaries, as if together they constituted a unit. If we are encouraged to count "as . . . so" and "neither . . . nor" as single words, we risk perplexity when such a distortion of the usual pattern occurs as "neither . . . neither . . . nor" or "as . . . and as . . . so." If the correlative pair is one word, what of the expanded form? Further what of such pairs as "Not only . . . but also"? The simplest solution seems to be to count each element of a correlative pair as one word, whether it consists of one (*as*) or two (*not only*) items. Because the number of items involved is relatively small and the decision, once made, can easily be extended to all the members of the set, the correlatives do not cause a maximum of difficulty. But they illustrate the type of problem raised by the necessity of pragmatically settling word-definitions falling outside the typographical description.

A larger source of delay and hand-wringing lies in the idioms and phrases which are so prominent a feature of Swift's language. Introductory phrases, similar in function and meaning to words like *however* (Class 91) provide an inkling of the difficulty. If *nevertheless* – itself patently a former phrase – is counted as one word, then *on the other hand* should also be counted as one, being similar in the meaning (and syntactically equivalent) to words like *contrariwise, conversely, however*. In addition, this phrase has the characteristic feature of idioms: it is unanalyzable – the components cannot be explained literally. Most prepositional phrases are considered unitary if they meet two criteria: one, if they can be replaced by a single word of approximately the same semantic and syntactic value, and, two, if they have an arbitrary meaning transcending the sum of the parts.

Still more perplexing are those grammatical idioms which abound in Swift and whose peculiar character resists analysis. The word *own*, for example, except as a verb, never appears by itself: it always shadows a personal pronoun or limiting adjective: [41] "his

---

[41] A possible exception is the unusual "my very own". See the *Oxford English Dictionary* and *Webster's Third New International Dictionary*, both s.v. *own*.

own countrymen", "as to our own".[42] For simplicity's sake, such combinations are merely considered emphatic forms of the respective pronouns and adjectives. To treat them as independent limiting adjectives might give a false representation of the number of true limiting adjectives a writer used. This solution, such as it is, unfortunately furnishes no guide to the handling of the problems posed by such other compounds as "together with" and "as well as". The usual authorities [43] are evasive or in disagreement in the matter. Only arbitrary decision will cut through the knot.

But what is to be done with such constructions as those italicized in the following: "no occasion *in the least* had been given", "cannot *but have* heard", "Hath been a *great deal* worse", "were *so far* from returning respect *that*".[44] or such transitional forms as "not exceeding" and "provided", which may still be participles (06) or may already have become Function Words.[45] All these cases, of which there are in the aggregate less than one percent, have been resolved by *ad hoc* decision. The possible source of error is mitigated by the small number of such cases in the total context and by the fact that one person makes all the decisions and, if he errs, probably always errs in the same direction.[46]

The procedure followed in transcribing the texts by the system just outlined may be illustrated by an example: [47]

[42]   Swift, *Works*, III, 110, 99.

[43]   *Webster's New International Dictionary,* Second Edition, *Webster's Third* and the *Oxford English Dictionary* agree in that they cite "together with" as a functional unit but none of them labels it with a part of speech: it is merely given under *together* (adv.). "As well as" is not given in Webster's Second, cited as a preposition in Webster's Third, as an adverb in the Oxford, and a conjunction by George Curme, *Syntax* (Boston, 1931), p. 163.

[44]   All from Swift, *Works,* III, 93.

[45]   "Provided they continue long enough in power", *Works*, III, 29, where *provided* is construed as a subordinating conjunction (42); "Lads and Maidens, not *exceeding* fourteen Years of Age, nor under twelve", *Works,* XII, 113, where *exceeding* is construed as a preposition on the analogy of *under*.

[46]   An estimate of the error may be obtained from the two analyses of *A Modest Proposal,* for which see Appendix B.

[47]   The symbols preceding and following the sequence of word-class nu-

‡‡42 11   02   61 05 31   01   51 31   07   31   01
Before I proceed to give an Account of my leaving this Kingdom,
61 21 21   03   61   05   31   01   51 31   03   01
it may be proper to inform the Reader of a private Intrigue
43   21   21 51 81   01   02   51   11‡‡
which had been for two Months forming against me.

The texts, reduced to the two-digit word-class designators and sentence-separators, are inscribed (key-punched) consecutively on a series of IBM cards. Although each card has room for 80 digits, only the first 72 places are used for the text, the remaining 8 serving to identify the sample and the card itself. Since 72 digits accommodate 36 words, a "deck" of 100 cards would have room for 3600 words of text. Deducting the space needed by the record marks serving as end punctuation – about one hundred in the average text –, we have left in each deck of 100 cards space for 3500 words of text.[48] This convenient sample size represents about ten octavo pages, ten cards to the page.[49]

The samples themselves,[50] of which there are eighteen, are distributed and selected as follows: eight from Swift's work, two each from Addison, Johnson, Gibbon and Macaulay, and two from a work attributed to Swift, about which there has been some controversy.[51] Of the eight Swift samples, one is considered a "signed" work and therefore atypical.[52] It is used chiefly for comparison. The remainder stretch chronologically through Swift's writing career, beginning with *A Tale of a Tub* (Sample

---

merals are called record marks: ‡ ‡. Their function is to signal breaks between sentences. Only end punctuation is taken account of. A sentence is considered ended when a period, exclamation point or mark of interrogation is followed by a capital letter. The selection is taken from *Gulliver's Travels, Works*, XI, 51.

[48] The amount varies because the sample is always taken to the end of the last full sentence in it.

[49] See discussion of sample size, below, p. 280.

[50] See detailed table in Appendix C, below.

[51] *A Letter to a Young Poet*. For the background of the controversy, see pp. 35 ff., above. The unknown is mentioned here but will not be discussed with the other samples.

[52] *History of the Four Last Years of the Queen*. A "signed" work differs from other writings of Swift in that it appeared with his name on the title page or, as in this case, posthumously. See above, p. 80.

10) and ending with *A Modest Proposal* (Sample 29).[53] Sample 10 was chosen by a random number method.[54] *The Examiner* is represented by two samples, both random and with no common pages (Samples 12 and 13). Sample 20 is a mixed group of works from volumes not otherwise drawn on. *Gulliver's Travels* appears in two samples chosen by different methods: Sample 26 is a random sample, sample 25 a stratified or spread sample.[55] The whole of *A Modest Proposal*[56] constitutes Sample 29, though it falls a trifle short of the standard sample length (3324 instead of 3500 words). The Swift samples thus adequately cover the range of Swift's best-known work and their sequence provides opportunity for the discovery of changes in his style with time.

The control samples are all chosen by the same random method, one page at a time. There are two samples for each author, to reduce the effect of random variation. Except for Macaulay, the second sample in each pair is later than the first. Except for Johnson, the genre is the same throughout: *Rasselas* is philosophy, but it is also fiction. The following list gives the details more plainly:

Sample	Author	Work	Date	Short Title
61	Macaulay[57]	*Literary Essays*	1825–1843	*Macaulay-L*
62	„	*Historical Essays*	1823–1844	*Macaulay-H*
65	Addison[58]	*Tatler*	1709–10	*Tatler*
66	„	*Spectator*	1711–12	*Spectator*
71	Gibbon[59]	*Decline* (Chs. 1-38)	1776–1781	*Decline A*
72	„	„ (Chs. 39-71)	1788	*Decline B*
75	Johnson[60]	*Rasselas*	1759	*Rasselas*
76	„	*Lives of the Poets*	1781	*Lives*

[53] It may be noticed that the Swift samples (with the exception of 20) are for convenience numbered according to their dates of publication in the eighteenth century. The exact constitution of each sample may be examined in Appendix C, below.
[54] This is explained below, p. 280.
[55] The idea is borrowed from Yule, *The Statistical Study of Literary Vocabulary*, pp. 39-41. The procedure consists in taking the first complete sentence from consecutive pages until the desired total is reached. This method tends to sample the whole book more representatively.
[56] This is the second time that this work has been analyzed. For an account of the results of the first (manual) analysis and the amount of divergence, see Appendix B, below.
[57] Lord Macaulay, *Literary and Historical Essays*, 2 vols. (London, 1923).

THE CONSISTENCY OF SWIFT'S STYLE

The hypothesis that I had tentatively formulated – that a writer's mental bent impresses itself indelibly and despite himself on all [61] his writing in such a way that it may be revealed by suitable means – required that the first concern of this part of the study be a demonstration of the consistency of Swift's own writing. If Swift's writing showed demonstrable quantitative consistency, there would be ground for assuming that the hypothesis was tenable [62] and for proceeding to the next part of the analysis, a comparison of Swift with the controls. If Swift did not differ from the controls, then even his own consistency would be without meaning, perhaps merely a reflection of certain central tendencies of the English language itself. Although the details of this type of agreement might be valuable in themselves, the event would preclude any further optimism for a quantitative formulation of individual style differences by means of word-class analysis. If, however, Swift's style showed uniformity and differed meaningfully from the controls, there would be a basis for considering the hypothesis demonstrable.

The distribution of the word-classes offered a jumping-off place for the search for consistency in Swift. Each sample was counted and tabulated by the computer and the results were compared. These results were in the form of an actual count of occurrences in each word-class and a number representing the percentage of the total sample. If the figures in Table 6.1 are simply inspected even without recourse to any external point of reference, some observations may be made. The most frequent word-class is 01 (nouns), constituting one-fifth of the total, a figure which may

---

[58]   *The Works of the Late Right Honorable Joseph Addison, Esq.,* 4 vols. (Birmingham, 1761).

[59]   Edward Gibbon, *The Decline and Fall of the Roman Empire,* ed. J. B. Bury, 7 vols. (London, 1896-1900).

[60]   Samuel Johnson, *The History of Rasselas,* ed. by R. W. Chapman (Oxford, 1927); *The Lives of the Poets,* 4 vols. (London, 1781).

[61]   "All" is to be taken at the value explained above, pp. 80 ff.

[62]   The consistency of each pair of control samples was not examined because two samples are not enough for determining consistency.

be common to much English prose. Next come the limiting adjectives (31), of which a large part are articles. It seems that a quarter of the nouns in *A Tale of a Tub* [63] somehow escape the use of an article or other determiner. It is not surprising that prepositions should come third, as the prepositional phrase is the most common short structure in the language.[64] These three word-classes stand out at the summit of the scale. The base is also of

TABLE 6.1*

Distribution of the words of a c. 3500-word text (Swift's Tale) into word-classes, according to actual count and percentage

Class	Count	Percentage
01	756	21.61
02	234	6.69
03	239	6.83
04	19	0.54
05	85	2.43
06	35	1.00
07	16	0.46
08	10	0.29
11	201	5.74
21	248	7.09
31	547	15.63
32	17	0.49
33	82	2.34
34	64	1.83
41	186	5.32
42	94	2.69
43	75	2.14
44	0	0.00
45	12	0.34
51	438	12.52
61	96	2.74
71	2	0.06
81	20	0.57
91	23	0.66

* See folding table, below, for key to sample numbers and word-class codes.

interest. For instance, there are no interrogatives (44), and only a trace of appellatives (71). Quotations (08) and correlative con-

[63] Strictly speaking, this sentence applies only to Sample 10. The assumptions of the sampling technique imply that it is correct about *A Tale of a Tub* as a whole.
[64] The evidence for this statement may be found below, p. 210.

junctions (45) are also very sparsely used. In the middle range of frequencies, we see that verbs (02) and adjectives (03) are about equal and that there are about as many auxiliaries (21) as finite verbs. There are about one-fourth as many pronouns (11) as nouns (01). And there are almost as many coördinating conjunctions (41) as pronouns (11). The remaining classes, without points of comparison, do not reveal anything.[65] Unless we can compare the frequency distribution of one sample with another, we shall have no measure of the stability of the word-classes. It is appropriate therefore to examine two samples from the same author, in fact, from the same work.[66]

Inasmuch as Table 6.2 presents two samples of different sets of pages from the same work,[67] we should expect a noticeable cor-

[65] These figures may be compared with those of N. R. French, C. W. Carter and W. Koenig, "The Words and Sounds of Telephone Conversations", *Bell System Technical Journal,* IX (1930), 290-324, as cited by George A. Miller, *Language and Communication* (New York, 1951), p. 94. Their figures, reduced to percentages (from a sample of 79,390 words) are:

Word-class	Telephone Users	Swift (Sample 10)
Nouns (01)	14.6	21.6
Adj. and Adv. (03, 04, 33, 34)	12.5	11.4
Verbs (02, 05, 06, 07)	15.7	10.6
Auxiliary verbs (21)	11.8	7.1
Prep. and Conj. (32, 41, 42, 51, 91)	15.5	21.7
Pronouns (11, 43)	22.5	7.8
Articles (31 less some)	7.0	15.6 less some

The factors which affect the comparison include the two-century gap, spoken vs. written language, American vs. English, among others, including incompatible grammatical classes. Still, it is clear that there is a certain correspondence, which is affected by the telephone user's reliance on pronouns and consequent avoidance of nouns. He is also more dependent on verbs and uses fewer connectives, probably because his sentences are shorter and simpler. What emerges from this comparison is a hint (no more) that some constants of written prose may be found if the variable factors can be kept in check.

[66] Samples 12 and 13 are two random samples from Swift's contributions to *The Examiner.* The samples are mutually exclusive (have no pages in common). Table 6.2 shows only the percentages, rounded to one decimal place.

[67] Pages 110, 93, 29-30, 99, 159, 64, 36, 145, 79 of *Works,* III, for Sample 12; pages 49, 60, 165, 124, 115, 39, 24, 151, 149, 139 for Sample 13. The page numbers are given in the order drawn by the random number table.

TABLE 6.2

Comparison of the percentages of word-class frequency between two random samples of the same work of Swift (Examiner)

Class	Sample 12	Sample 13	Difference
01	19.3	19.2	−.1
02	7.2	7.4	.2
03	6.3	5.2	−1.1
04	.9	.6	−.3
05	2.6	2.7	.1
06	.6	.8	.2
07	1.0	.6	−.4
08	.1	.1	.0
11	7.5	6.9	−.6
21	7.5	8.2	.7
31	14.7	15.6	.9
32	.6	1.0	.4
33	2.3	2.6	.3
34	2.6	2.1	−.5
41	5.0	4.6	−.4
42	2.8	2.6	−.2
43	2.0	2.7	.7
44	.1	.1	.0
45	.3	.5	.2
51	12.7	12.4	−.3
61	3.0	3.0	.0
71	.0	.0	.0
81	.5	.7	.2
91	.5	.3	−.2

respondence between them. A cursory inspection reveals that they are in very good agreement [68] in some classes and in a disagreement reaching 1.1 per cent in the class of adjectives (03). It may be observed that in this particular comparison more agreement is found among the Parts of Speech than the Function Words.[69] In general, the extent of the agreement is a good indication of the soundness of the initial assumptions. But very little can be said about the meaning of the agreement until criteria

[68]   Half are less than three-tenths of one percent apart.
[69]   I had expected that Function Words would be stabler than Parts of Speech, an expectation shared by the Harvard investigators of the *Federalist* Papers; see p. 71, n. 8, above and Appendix D, below.

TABLE 6.3

*Comparison of percentages of word-class frequency between two
samples drawn from the same work of Swift* (Gulliver) *by
different sampling methods*

Class	Sample 25	Sample 26	Difference
01	21.1	19.8	−1.3
02	7.8	8.4	.6
03	6.4	5.1	−1.3
04	.6	.7	.1
05	1.9	1.9	.0
06	1.3	1.3	.0
07	.3	.6	.3
08	.0	.0	.0
11	8.5	9.3	.8
21	5.7	6.0	.3
31	15.9	16.3	.4
32	.5	.7	.2
33	2.2	2.0	−.2
34	1.7	2.2	.5
41	4.9	4.8	−.1
42	3.1	2.9	−.2
43	2.0	1.9	−.1
44	.0	.0	.0
45	.4	.2	−.2
51	12.4	12.6	.2
61	2.3	2.1	−.2
71	.0	.0	.0
81	1.0	.9	−.1
91	.4	.3	−.1

are formulated for determining the permissible limits of divergence.

If the other paired samples (25 and 26: *Gulliver*) are also examined, in Table 6.3, some variation is again perceptible, two large classes varying as much as 1.3 percent and a number of others remaining close and even stable. A juxtaposition, as in Table 6.4, of the differences between pairs of samples is illuminating.[70] The status of Class 03 (descriptive adjectives), for example, suggests that adjectives are an unreliable measure of authorship and that a writer will use adjectives more freely in one set of

[70] Note that the differences are shown without plus or minus sign.

TABLE 6.4

Comparison of the differences in word-class percentage between two
pairs of samples of Swift, each pair representing a different work

Class	12-13	25-26
01	.1	1.3
02	.2	.6
03	1.1	1.3
04	.3	.1
05	.1	.0
06	.2	.0
07	.4	.3
08	.0	.0
11	.6	.8
21	.7	.3
31	.9	.4
32	.4	.2
33	.3	.2
34	.5	.5
41	.4	.1
42	.2	.2
43	.7	.1
44	.0	.0
45	.2	.2
51	.3	.2
61	.0	.2
71	.0	.0
81	.2	.1
91	.2	.1

pages than in another, will seem to vary widely in his use of
these words.[71] Nouns, (Class 01), however, show a fine consistency in *The Examiner* but very little in *Gulliver*. A number of
important [72] classes show good agreement: verbs and verbals, conjunctions and prepositions. Because the two pairs of samples
differ in method of selection,[73] it may be appropriate to attribute
some of the lack of agreement to that cause. Because the two
Examiner samples were selected by the same random-number

[71] This observation is naturally at odds with impressionistic comments
about Swift's use of adjectives. See Chapter I, above.
[72] They are important because they are large enough to be reliable and
because they can be accounted for within the limits of the hypothesis.
[73] This is the only known variable, the identity of the works apart.

technique, any variation between them must be credited to natural causes, such as random variation or failure of the hypothesis. If the hypothesis should be incorrect – if there is no consistency in the word-class frequency distribution of an author – the variation is of course easily accounted for. But if random variation is taken into account, there is no need to reject the hypothesis.

Random variation results from the fact that a sample of a given population does not always reproduce all the characteristics of the population. For instance, each of the four bridge hands (of thirteen cards apiece) dealt from a well-shuffled pack, will usually contain three cards in each suit (more or less). But as any bridge player knows, such regular distributions, though frequent, are not invariable and distributional freaks occur (of which the one-suited hand is the extreme). Yet every player may expect an equitable distribution of cards from each suit and of high cards, if the game goes on long enough (the sample taken is large enough).[74] Similarly, two 3500-word samples from the same work, though doubtless very similar, cannot be expected to be identical. The similarity, as might be expected, varies with the size of the sample. The bigger a proportion of the population the sample includes, the more closely the sample will approximate the population, until the sample and the population become identical. To observe this process, let us compare two pairs of samples, one-tenth the size of the full samples.[75]

Two things are at once obvious from the comparison in Table 6.5. Classes which showed some stability in the comparison of full samples no longer do (for example, 02, 05, 51). The range of variation for each wordclass among the four sub-samples (which, it must be remembered, are all from the same work), is so great as to threaten to swamp differences between individuals. The size of the differences, at any rate, is much greater, as can be observed from a juxtaposition of differences between full samples and be-

---

[74]   During the Culbertson-Lenz match of the late twenties, games were played all day for a month. At the end of that time, the distribution of aces, kings, etc. . . . came "within an ace" of being perfect.

[75]   Sub-samples 12_1 and 12_2, 13_1 and 13_2, all representing Swift's *Examiner*, specifically pages 110, 93, 49 and 60, respectively, *Works*, III.

TABLE 6.5

Comparison of word-class frequency distributions between two sets of one-tenth samples (350 words) of Swift's Examiner

Class	12_1	12_2	Difference	13_1	13_2	Difference
01	17.7	19.9	2.2	23.0	21.2	−1.8
02	5.1	7.4	2.3	6.6	6.6	.0
03	7.7	5.7	−2.0	4.3	6.0	1.7
04	2.0	.6	−1.4	.3	.0	−.3
05	4.3	1.7	−2.6	3.4	2.3	−1.1
06	.9	.6	−.3	1.4	.0	−1.4
07	.9	1.4	.5	.9	1.4	.5
08	.3	.0	−.3	.6	.0	−.6
11	5.4	6.6	1.2	4.8	4.9	.1
21	9.1	8.3	−.8	8.0	6.6	−1.4
31	15.7	14.8	−.9	18.2	18.3	.1
32	.3	.6	.3	.0	.6	.6
33	2.0	1.4	−.6	.9	2.0	1.1
34	3.7	2.6	−1.1	1.7	1.7	.0
41	3.4	5.7	2.3	5.4	6.0	.6
42	3.7	2.3	−1.4	2.8	2.0	−.8
43	1.7	3.1	1.4	1.7	3.4	1.7
44	.3	.0	−.3	.0	.9	.9
45	.0	.6	.6	.6	.0	−.6
51	9.7	13.1	3.4	12.5	12.3	−.2
61	5.7	1.7	−4.0	3.1	3.2	.1
71	.0	.0	.0	.0	.0	.0
81	.3	.6	.3	.0	.3	.3
91	.0	1.4	1.4	.0	.3	.3

tween tenths in Table 6.6. The much greater variability of the sub-sample is clearly in evidence. Only three of the full-sample differences exceed one per cent. Among the sub-samples, however, there are twenty which do, one reaching four per cent. Moreover, the differences between the members of one pair have no relation to the differences between those of the other. Classes 02, 51 and 61 are most striking in this respect. What may be concluded, then, is that the variability of the sub-samples is indeed far greater and more capricious than that of the full samples.[76]

How does this help to answer the question posed about criteria of permissible differences between members of the same popula-

[76] But compare the Stability test made below, p. 187.

TABLE 6.6

Comparison of absolute differences resulting from the comparison of two pairs of whole samples of Swift and two pairs of one-tenth samples from Examiner

Class	12-13	25-26	12_1-12_2	13_1-13_2
01	.1	1.3	2.2	1.8
02	.2	.6	2.3	.0
03	1.1	1.3	2.0	1.7
04	.3	.1	1.4	.3
05	.1	.0	2.6	1.1
06	.2	.0	.3	1.4
07	.4	.3	.5	.5
08	.0	.0	.3	.6
11	.6	.8	1.2	.1
21	.7	.3	.8	1.4
31	.9	.4	.9	.1
32	.4	.2	.3	.6
33	.3	.2	.6	1.1
34	.5	.5	1.1	.0
41	.4	.1	2.3	.6
42	.2	.2	1.4	.8
43	.7	.1	1.4	1.7
44	.0	.0	.3	.9
45	.2	.2	.6	.6
51	.3	.2	3.4	.2
61	.0	.2	4.0	.1
71	.0	.0	.0	.0
81	.2	.1	.3	.3
91	.2	.1	1.4	.3

tion? That is, how large may the differences for a given size of sample be and still permit the belief that they represent the same population? This question must be answered before it is possible to evaluate the consistency of the Swift figures. Inasmuch as no previous researcher's figures are available for comparison, an informal procedure may be devised for the purpose. I have claimed that the characteristics of Swift's style would be revealed by examining his frequency distribution of word-classes. If the contention is incorrect, any set of samples from any author or group of authors would be as consistent (or inconsistent) as the Swift samples. Therefore, if the seven samples from Swift's work are

TABLE 6.7

Word-class frequency distribution of all the whole samples of Swift, with computed arithmetic mean

Class	10	12	13	20	25	26	29	$\bar{x}$
01	21.6	19.3	19.2	20.2	21.1	19.8	20.9	20.3
02	6.7	7.2	7.4	6.9	7.8	8.4	6.0	7.2
03	6.8	6.3	5.2	5.6	6.4	5.1	6.9	6.0
04	.5	.9	.6	1.2	.6	.7	1.0	.8
05	2.4	2.6	2.7	2.7	1.9	1.9	1.8	2.3
06	1.0	.6	.8	.8	1.3	1.3	1.5	1.0
07	.5	1.0	.6	.9	.3	.6	1.0	.7
08	.3	.1	.1	.1	.0	.0	.0	.1
11	5.7	7.5	6.9	6.7	8.5	9.3	5.1	7.1
21	7.1	7.5	8.2	8.1	5.7	6.0	7.8	7.2
31	15.6	14.7	15.6	14.9	15.9	16.3	14.4	15.3
32	.5	.6	1.0	.5	.5	.7	.4	.6
33	2.3	2.3	2.6	2.5	2.2	2.0	3.0	2.4
34	1.8	2.6	2.1	1.7	1.7	2.2	2.1	2.0
41	5.3	5.0	4.6	4.6	4.9	4.8	4.9	4.9
42	2.7	2.8	2.6	2.6	3.1	2.9	2.5	2.7
43	2.1	2.0	2.7	2.1	2.0	1.9	1.9	2.1
44	.0	.1	.1	.3	.0	.0	.1	.1
45	.3	.3	.5	.3	.4	.2	.5	.4
51	12.5	12.7	12.4	12.5	12.4	12.6	13.3	12.6
61	2.7	3.0	3.0	3.4	2.3	2.1	2.3	2.7
71	.1	.0	.0	.0	.0	.0	.0	.0
81	.6	.5	.7	.7	1.0	.9	1.8	.9
91	.7	.5	.3	.7	.4	.3	.9	.5

compared with a population composed of the four control authors' eight samples, the consistency can be simply measured by means of the standard deviation for each word-class.[77]

[77] The standard deviation is a measure of the dispersion (or scatter) of a set of data around the mean. Sets of figures may have the same mean yet be so scattered that the mean tells almost nothing about their cohesiveness. This is especially true of small samples. But the standard deviation reveals the scatter. The larger it is, the more widely the figures are scattered around the mean. Roughly speaking, more consistency equals smaller standard deviations. To illustrate, the three sets of figures below have all the same mean (35) but their standard deviations vary widely:

A. 15, 25, 65 – standard deviation: 26.5
B. 29, 35, 41 –   „   „   6.0
C. 34, 34, 37 –   „   „   1.7.

More inspection of the distribution of word-class frequencies given in Table 6.7 for the seven Swift samples shows a considerable patterning. The large classes (01, 31, 51) are very similar and certain intermediate classes (41) are noticeably consistent. But the smallest classes exhibit a good deal of fluctuation (04, 81). Scarcely more than juxtaposition, however, is required to bring out the extent to which the fluctuation (variability) is greater in the control population shown in Table 6.8. The consistency of each author pair is noticeable and results in a large range of variation in each word-class. If the means and standard deviations are computed and placed side by side, the higher con-

TABLE 6.8

Word-class frequency distribution of whole samples of the four control authors, with computed mean of the total

Class	61	62	65	66	71	72	75	76	x̄
01	22.4	24.6	21.3	20.9	25.1	28.9	21.4	23.1	23.4
02	7.4	7.2	7.7	8.2	7.2	7.0	10.5	8.2	7.9
03	7.9	7.8	6.9	7.0	8.8	7.3	4.5	6.2	7.1
04	1.2	.9	.3	.4	.8	.5	.3	.7	.6
05	1.4	1.6	1.7	1.5	1.3	1.0	2.6	1.6	1.6
06	.7	.8	.4	.4	.4	.3	.8	.7	.6
07	.6	.5	.6	.7	.2	.3	.3	.6	.5
08	.1	.1	.0	.0	.0	.1	.0	.1	.0
11	6.2	4.2	7.7	7.5	2.5	2.0	8.1	6.4	5.6
21	8.2	7.2	7.1	6.8	5.7	5.1	7.6	7.9	7.0
31	14.9	16.4	16.1	15.5	19.3	19.4	14.7	14.4	16.3
32	.2	.4	.9	.6	.1	.0	.4	.2	.4
33	2.9	1.5	2.4	2.6	1.4	.7	1.4	2.2	1.9
34	1.5	2.0	1.4	1.6	.9	1.0	2.0	1.8	1.5
41	4.5	4.0	4.1	4.6	5.3	6.6	5.0	4.8	4.9
42	2.3	1.7	2.6	2.7	1.7	1.1	2.3	2.6	2.1
43	2.1	1.8	2.4	2.8	2.2	1.0	2.3	2.4	2.1
44	.0	.0	.0	.0	.0	.0	.1	.0	.0
45	.4	.1	.2	.4	.3	.2	.5	.4	.3
51	12.7	14.5	13.6	13.3	15.0	16.3	12.2	12.8	13.8
61	2.0	2.2	2.2	1.9	1.6	1.1	2.6	2.2	2.0
71	.0	.0	.0	.0	.0	.0	.1	.0	.0
81	.3	.4	.3	.3	.5	.7	.2	.3	.4
91	.3	.2	.2	.2	.1	.0	.1	.5	.2

sistency of the Swift population may be easily observed, in Table 6.9. Even in cases where the means are identical (41), the standard deviation reveals the greater inner consistency of the Swift population.[78]

If Table 6.9 is carefully examined, it will be seen that in all but two classes [79] the standard deviation of the Swift group is lower than that of the controls; that is, the dispersion is less and the consistency higher. These figures definitely permit the conclusion that the Swift samples are members of the same family of numbers, constitute a coherent population, one with certain denumerable characteristics, rather than a casual heap of numbers. The controls group reveals its varied constitution by its higher diversity. But how to account for the two classes in which the controls group was equal or lower, in which, that is, the Swift samples showed as much or less uniformity than a heterogeneous group?

The two classes involved are 34 and 61. Both of these are more miscellaneous in character than the other classes.[80] The former contains a variety of non-descriptive adverbs. The other contains the three words called "pattern-markers". It may be that these classes show less consistency than the others because the organizing principle is not strict or functional enough. It is also possible that these classes represent linguistic constants rather than a field for personal choice. The numerial difference between the standard deviations is so slight that they may be considered identical. Perhaps then all writers use the words of these classes with more or less the same frequency or at a rate which has nothing individual about it.

[78] The standard deviation decreases as the uniformity of samples increases. Therefore the standard deviations may be compared horizontally. But they cannot be compared vertically because they tend to increase as the size of the unit numbers increases. For example, 10, 12, 14 and 16 and 1.0, 1.2, 1.4, 1.6 have the same relative dispersion, but their respective standard deviations are 2.58 and .258.

[79] No standard deviations were computed for classes whose arithmetic mean was lower than 1.0 because such values could not be considered part of any Normal distribution. There are nine of these classes for Swift and ten for the controls: 04, 07, 08, 32, 44, 45, 71, 81, 91; 04, 06, 07, 08, 32, 44, 45, 71, 81, 91.

[80] This point was brought out in the original discussion, pp. 146-147, above.

TABLE 6.9

Means and standard deviations of the Swift samples and the control samples, each taken as a separate population

Class	SWIFT		CONTROLS	
	$\bar{x}$	S.D.	$\bar{x}$	S.D.
01	20.3	.93	23.4	2.60
02	7.2	.78	7.9	1.14
03	6.0	.74	7.1	1.30
04	.8		.6	
05	2.3	.35	1.6	.47
06	1.0	.33	.6	
07	.7		.5	
08	.1		.0	
11	7.1	1.48	5.6	2.40
21	7.2	.99	7.0	1.10
31	15.3	.69	16.3	1.98
32	.6		.4	
33	2.4	.32	1.9	.75
34	2.0	.41	1.5	.41
41	4.9	.24	4.9	.82
42	2.7	.20	2.1	.57
43	2.1	.28	2.1	.54
44	.1		.0	
45	.4		.3	
51	12.6	.32	13.8	1.37
61	2.7	.47	2.0	.46
71	.0		.0	
81	.9		.4	
91	.5		.2	

Note: Values less than one per cent are considered insignificant.

QUANTITATIVE FEATURES OF SWIFT'S STYLE: GROUPED WORD-CLASSES

It becomes clear, after one has become familiar with the figures resulting from the kind of analysis which is made here, that it is futile to look for distinguishing peculiarities in every quantitative aspect of style description. The conclusion emerges that there is an ordering of the linguistic materials which must be characteristic of a whole language. It is improbable, for example, that any writer of English could avoid completely the use of verbs.

It is even more unlikely that any amount of ingenuity could produce a frequency distribution empty of nouns and half-full of prepositions. The English language has certain requirements which dictate that the number of nouns in any text must be superior to the number of prepositions and that the number of noun determiners should not be too far below that of nouns. Although the author's choice in any given sentence seems to be quite free, in the aggregate he is hemmed in by a combination of forces which adds up to a linguistic-statistical determinism.[81] In normal literary writing in English, nouns are used about one-fifth of the time, but individual variation creates a range perhaps between ten and thirty per cent.[82] Although very few data are available, we learn from one source [83] that the French use is nearer to twenty-five per cent and the Spanish to thirty-three. Similarly fewer adverbs are usual in Spanish than in French and fewer in French than in English. If individual variation is to express itself it must be within the exterior bounds imposed by the language. When these are too narrow to permit a range of individual expression, the resulting figures may be considered as linguistic constants, characteristics of the English language as a whole.

Such linguistic constants are not without interest – especially as primitive strokes with which to sketch the statistical profile of the English language. As such, they will be given a place later.[84] But less general factors are in view at the moment. For, having established the statistical cohesiveness of Swift's use of various word-classes, I must now show in more detail the quantitative characteristics of Swift's style and bring out the contrast between his work and that of the controls.

[81] On this point see G. Herdan, *Language as Choice and Chance* (Groningen, 1956), Chapter I, passim.
[82] No figures permitting a confident statement are available but those which are at hand range from 14.6 for the telephone conversations (see p. 156, fn. 65, above) to 27.1 for Aldous Huxley (Gilbert Barth, *Recherches sur la Fréquence et la Valeur des Parties du Discours en Français, en Anglais et en Espagnol,* Paris, 1961, p. 109). or 28.6 for Gibbon, *Decline* B.
[83] Barth, pp. 109-113. Barth's parts of speech are not wholly compatible with mine but an illuminating comparison is possible. See Appendix E, below.
[84] See "Conclusion", below.

It must be remembered that the method used to show Swift's consistency required comparing the seven samples of his work with the eight samples of the controls, as if these latter constituted a population. This procedure was justified as a method of showing that Swift's figures had the cohesion characteristic of a set of related phenomena. That Swift's word-class frequency distributions showed less dispersion than that of the control population allows nothing more to be inferred, however. In order to show that Swift's figures in any word-class are peculiar to him and can be used as criteria of identification, it will be necessary to show that the individual controls vary enough from the Swift figures so that no confusion can exist. If Table 6.7 is referred to, the first line shows that Swift's use of Class 01 words ranges from 19.2 to 21.6 per cent. Table 6.8 shows us that both Addison samples are included within this range: 21.3 and 20.9 per cent. Macaulay is above it and Gibbon well above it, whereas Johnson has one foot in and one above. In other words, if the Class 01 distribution were being counted on to help distinguish the work of Swift from that of Addison, success would not be possible.[85] A close scrutiny of Tables 6.7 and 6.8 reveals that much the same is true for the other word-classes as well. Individually they will not serve to differentiate between Swift and *all* the controls.

For this to be possible, Swift and all the controls must show different values of any word-class in which they are compared. It is naturally possible for their use of nouns to differ in quality though not in quantity. However, such a difference would not be perceived be this measurement, which has reduced all differences to a matter of relative frequency of occurrence. To distinguish between Swift and the controls in the use of nouns, it would be necessary that their individual frequencies (percentages) happen to be spaced wide enough apart to permit distinction. Swift's and Addison's near correspondence in Class 01 masks the possibility that their use of nouns may be vastly different, but since

[85] Addison is selected advisedly because his quantitative outline resembles Swift's in many details. Whether this is due to the contemporaneity of his work with Swift's is not as important as finding means to distinguish between them.

those other differences are not being investigated, we must conclude that in the matter of Class 01 words Swift and Addison are alike. Only quantitative difference is being measured by the means in use here.

Therefore, in order to differentiate between Swift and the controls it will be necessary to devise other ways of using the available information. The simplest that presents itself is that of amalgamating word-classes into groups of perhaps greater stability. The matter, however, ought not to be pursued in the spirit of trying to open a combination lock by guess-work. To be meaningful, a grouping should be theoretically justified. For instance, it would be illicit or dubious to combine Classes 08, 51 and 81 because it looked as if these figures might behave as desired in combination. Because of random variation, this property might hold only for this particular set of numbers and fail to do so for another set of random samples; thus it would not represent the characteristics of the total population. But if the hypothesis adhered to suggests a likely combination without prior reference to the values embodied, the predictive results should be far more satisfactory. A grouping which is inevitable is that into Parts of Speech and Function Words, which both the layout of the Tables and the theoretical exposition which introduces this chapter strongly imply.[86] The figures are developed by summing Classes 01 to 08, the total of which represents the P/S[87] value, and summing Classes 11 to 91 to achieve the FW value. Table 6.10 displays what looks more or less like a 40-60 division for both sets of samples. On closer inspection, however, it may be noticed that all the P/S values of Swift lie below 40 per cent. Swift, that is, always uses more than sixty per cent of Function Words. Macaulay, on the other hand, uses fewer than sixty per cent in both his samples

[86]   See pp. 144-145, above. The question of how real this distinction may be and what the criteria of differentiation are is studied in Ralph Dana Winter's unpublished Ph. D. Dissertation, "English Function Words and Content Words: A Quantitative Investigation" (Cornell, 1953). The loss of information resulting from grouping is discussed by Alvar Ellegård, *A Statistical Method for Determining Authorship* (Göteborg, 1962), pp. 17-18.
[87]   The abbreviations P/S and FW stand for Parts of Speech and Function Words, respectively, as defined in this chapter.

and Gibbon even fewer than Macaulay. Although both of Johnson's values fall below sixty per cent, they are probably too close to Swift's for adequate separation. With Addison, the measurement goes wholly agley, for his two samples fall smack in the midst of Swift's.

Nonetheless we may derive some interesting indications from this grouping. Noticing that the highest P/S values were registered by Gibbon, whose style is obviously "formal",[88] we may be justified in equating high P/S values with "formality", especially since the largest component of Gibbon's bulge in the P/S total comes from his large noun total [89] and since nouns are usually associated with formality (even pomposity). Consequently, low P/S (and high FW) values might be exepcted from writers whose style has "colloquial" quality, such as that sought for by the writers of Queen Anne's time. Addison and Swift are obviously in agreement there, historically and quantitatively. But on this basis Macaulay would appear more formal than Johnson, a ranking that many might question (including Macaulay). To verify the

TABLE 6.10

Grouping of word-classes into Parts of Speech (P/S) and Function Words (FW), for all whole samples, with computed mean

	10	12	13	20	25	26	29	x̄
P/S	39.8	38.0	36.6	38.4	39.3	37.8	39.1	38.4
FW	60.2	62.0	63.4	61.6	60.7	62.2	60.9	61.6

CONTROLS

	61	62	65	66	71	72	75	76	x̄
P/S	41.6	43.3	38.8	39.1	43.7	44.9	40.4	41.2	41.6
FW	58.4	56.7	61.2	60.9	56.3	55.1	59.6	58.8	58.4

[88] Nearly every writer who mentions Gibbon's style makes this point, though the descriptive word varies: "patterned", "balanced", "self-conscious" are examples. "Ironic gravity and formality" is D. W. Jefferson's phrase in *From Dryden to Johnson* (Harmondsworth, 1957), p. 72.
[89] A glance at Table 6.8, above, shows Gibbon's dominance in Class 01.

simple formula just discussed – high P/S equals formality; high FW, colloquiality – would require far more data than are available. Moreover, other factors than part-of-speech density contribute to the impression of a formal style.[90] In rejecting the P/S-FW grouping as a useful discriminator, we must consider the likelihood that for writers less closely bunched in time the results might be quite different.[91] It is probable that the grouping is subject to too many contradictory forces, that it is the resultant of a number of mutually cancelling pressures which are too intertwined to permit rational sorting. A better grouping would be one which proceeded from a more minute approach to the dynamics of word-classes.

A set of groupings answering to this requirement might be expected to develop if the two word-class types, modifiers (Classes 31-34) and connectives (Classes 41-45), were separately grouped. It is probable that such a grouping as connectives (C) would have a higher consistency than its member classes because the process of syntactic connection is a constant necessity though the means of achieving it may vary. Different stylistic effects are achieved by major dependence on coordinating conjunctions, subordinating conjunctions, or relatives, respectively, but the frequency of total need may be constant. A writer who tends to write short, unconnected sentences would probably have a low total value for Group C. Another writer, less loath to qualify his statements, might hesitate between *but, though* and *which* but would finally decide to use one of them. The sum of his decisions would be constant and would be reflected in the value of C. Let us test this hypothesis.

The figures given in Table 6.11 for Classes 44 and 45 are too small to be considered individually though their contribution to the total weight of Group C is not to be ignored. For Swift the percentages of Class 41, 42 and 43 are reasonably well-bunched, though Class 43 has a bulge under Sample 13 and the range for

[90]   The matter is again considered below under the nominal-verbal style, p. 195.
[91]   What would Hemingway or T. S. Eliot score? On the other hand it might be that P/S values between 35 to 45 per cent represent a linguistic constant. But see the Stability Factor below, p. 187.

Class 41 seems rather wide. If the values are summed,[92] it is seen that the Group value C has a range no greater than the greatest range of its component values.[93] If the C values for the controls are examined in pairs (representing individual authors), only one author seems really consistent (Johnson), the other varying over a range of nearly one-third the mean C value. The Macaulay values, though substantially below Swift's are not close together; the Addison values overlap Swift's. Only Gibbon's values fulfill the requirements: they are close together and distinguishable from the Swift values.

The observant reader will already have noticed that Gibbon and Addison have more meaningful roles in this study than Macaulay or Johnson. So far, Gibbon's figures have been found always to be comfortably distant from Swift's and from the other controls. Gibbon's style, quantitatively at least, has a satisfying uniqueness. It is truly peculiar, as probably its author intended.[94] But Addison's figures are nearly always like those of Swift and the main problem is to find licit measurements which can help to distinguish them. It is evident that the grouping of connectives does not successfully perform this, despite its other discriminative abilities.

The grouping of modifiers (M) in Table 6.12 gives a range for Swift about twice that for Group C, but the mean value is also about double. The estimate, therefore, may be considered roughly

[92] The C values may not be precisely equal to the sum of 41 through 45 because these were independently computed from the raw scores (rather than by summing the rounded percentages) for the sake of greater accuracy.
[93] The measurement of range is a simple method of evaluating the mean as a good or bad estimate of the population. It is calculated by subtracting the lowest from the highest value. If the range is equal to or greater than the mean, the mean is a worthless estimate (e.g. Class 44). But if the range is small compared to the mean, the mean is a good estimate of the population.
[94] Gibbon tells us that he worked at his style consciously (*The Autobiography of Edward Gibbon*, ed. John Murray (London, 1896), p. 308), but it is doubtful whether this effort had as much influence as his ability to write and think in French, which he mentions in a letter to Hume (*The Letters of Edward Gibbon*, ed. J. E. Norton (New York, 1956), I, 222). Gibbon's frequency in the use of nouns is closer to French than to English, assuming that the other writers of our group are representative. According to Barth (pp. 96-7), French regularly prefers substantive constructions.

TABLE 6.11

Connectives as individual word-classes and grouped (Group C), in percentages for all whole samples, showing mean and range

Class	10	12	13	20	25	26	29	x̄	w̄
41	5.3	5.0	4.6	4.6	4.9	4.8	4.9	4.9	.7
42	2.7	2.8	2.6	2.6	3.1	2.9	2.5	2.7	.6
43	2.1	2.0	2.7	2.1	2.0	1.9	1.9	2.1	.8
44	.0	.1	.1	.3	.0	.0	.1	.1	.3
45	.3	.3	.5	.3	.4	.2	.5	.4	.3
C	10.4	10.2	10.6	9.9	10.4	9.8	9.9	10.2	.8

CONTROLS

	61	62	65	66	71	72	75	76	x̄	w̄
41	4.5	4.0	4.1	4.6	5.3	6.6	5.0	4.8	4.9	2.6
42	2.3	1.7	2.6	2.7	1.7	1.1	2.3	2.6	2.1	1.6
43	2.1	1.8	2.4	2.8	2.2	1.0	2.3	2.4	2.1	1.8
44	.0	.0	.0	.0	.0	.0	.1	.0	.0	.1
45	.4	.1	.2	.4	.3	.2	.5	.4	.3	.4
C	9.3	7.7	9.4	10.6	9.5	8.9	10.1	10.2	9.5	2.9

of the same quality. Among the controls, the most attractive values for M are Johnson's, which are both close together and significantly distant from Swift's. Gibbon's figures are also close together but overlap those of Swift. Both Macaulay and Addison are indistinguishable from Swift. Curiously enough, if only the values for Class 31 are examined, we find that Gibbon's consistency increases and his overlap disappears. Johnson, however, loses his individuality; Macaulay and Addison remain the same. The difference which exists at one level of the group is wiped out at another. Because Gibbon uses a large number of nouns, which entails a large number of determiners (31), his values for Class 31 are highest. Because Gibbon's verb and verbals figures are low, his adverbial (32-34) modifiers are also low.[95] When the two

[95] Table 6.8, above.

TABLE 6.12

Modifiers as individual word-classes and grouped (Group M), in percentages, for all whole samples, with computed arithmetic mean and range

Class	10	12	13	20	25	26	29	$\bar{x}$	$\bar{w}$
31	15.6	14.7	15.6	14.9	15.9	16.3	14.4	15.3	1.9
32	.5	.6	1.0	.5	.5	.7	.4	.6	.6
33	2.3	2.3	2.6	2.5	2.2	2.0	3.0	2.4	1.0
34	1.8	2.6	2.1	1.7	1.7	2.2	2.1	2.0	.9
M	20.2	20.2	21.3	19.7	20.2	21.1	19.8	20.4	1.6

CONTROLS

	61	62	65	66	71	72	75	76	$\bar{x}$	$\bar{w}$
31	14.9	16.4	16.1	15.5	19.3	19.4	14.7	14.4	16.3	5.0
32	.2	.4	.9	.6	.1	.0	.4	.2	.4	.9
33	2.9	1.5	2.4	2.6	1.4	.7	1.4	2.2	1.9	2.2
34	1.5	2.0	1.4	1.6	.9	1.0	2.0	1.8	1.5	1.1
M	19.5	20.3	20.8	20.3	21.5	21.1	18.5	18.6	20.1	3.0

are added, however, the effect disappears and the Swift samples are hard to distinguish from the control population.[96]

Groupings such as the two foregoing, then, fail to prevent the neutralizing effect which results when something is measured which represents a necessity common to all writers, or, at least, to all writers of essentially the same type of material. Expository composition requires connection of some sort and modification of other nouns or verbs. It appears, therefore, that the best groupings are not those which involve a wide range of choice. Preferable would seem to be those in which the available choices are wholly optional and dispensable but not so free as to be chaotic or circumstantial. It is probable that the verb system will yield some valuable groupings of this kind.

The classes which contain elements of the verb system are

---

[96]   Compare the means: 20.4, 20.1.

five: 02 (finite verbs), 05 (infinitives), 06 (participles), 07 (gerunds), and 21 (auxiliaries). Classes 05, 06 and 07 are obviously related, being generally considered "verbals", or "infinite forms of the verb".[97] As a group these words represent a way of suppressing or limiting the frequency of finite verbs, a peculiarly modern development.[98] Therefore, a writer whose work contained an appreciable quantity of these forms might seem more modern than one who avoided them. If the verbals are placed in one group (VB), the finite verbs and verbal auxiliaries are left to comprise another group (VA). Inasmuch as each component of a compound verb is counted once by this system, a high value for this group might merely reflect a great use of such verbs, though such a value might also result from the use of many finite verbs. This may, of course, be verified by reference to the component classes of the group. At any rate, we would feel justified in considering a high VA score a sign of considerable activity with finite verbs. Let us consider these first.

Table 6.13 shows a curiously even distribution for Swift, the averages for each of the component classes being identical. As to the range, little is gained by the grouping, for the range is static. Except for Samples 25 and 26, the number of auxiliaries is higher than that of finite verbs, a circumstance which reflects the pronoun-verb narrative characteristic of *Gulliver's Travels*.[99] The group value for Sample 25 is the lowest but Sample 26 is the median value.[100] The controls, however, except for Macaulay, have higher 02 than 21 values. Gibbon's figures are at one end of the range and Johnson's (less close together) at the other,

---

[97] Curme, *Syntax,* p. 448.
[98] Lucius A. Sherman, "On certain facts and principles in the development of form in literature", *University of Nebraska Studies,* I, 4 (July 1892), finds that the decrease of predication per sentence increases as English becomes more modern (p. 353). Curme, *loc. cit.,* speaking of infinite forms of the verb, says "No other part of our grammar is at the present time developing as vigorously."
[99] This is supported by the high values for pronouns (11) in Samples 25 and 26: 8.5 and 9.3, respectively, highest of all the samples, Swift and controls. See Tables 6.7 and 6.8 above.
[100] The middle value if the items are arranged in a sequence from lowest to highest.

TABLE 6.13

Finite verbs and auxiliaries as individual word-classes and grouped (Group VA), in percentages, for all whole samples, showing mean and range

Class	10	12	13	20	25	26	29	$\bar{x}$	$\bar{w}$
02	6.7	7.2	7.4	6.9	7.8	8.4	6.0	7.2	2.4
21	7.1	7.5	8.2	8.1	5.7	6.0	7.8	7.2	2.5
VA	13.8	14.7	15.6	15.0	13.4	14.4	13.8	14.4	2.2

CONTROLS

	61	62	65	66	71	72	75	76	$\bar{x}$	$\bar{w}$
02	7.4	7.2	7.7	8.2	7.2	7.0	10.5	8.2	7.9	3.5
21	8.2	7.2	7.1	6.8	5.7	5.1	7.6	7.9	7.0	3.1
VA	15.6	14.4	14.8	15.0	12.8	12.1	18.1	16.1	14.9	6.0

Addison's scores again following those of Swift, though his predominance of finite verbs over auxiliaries resembles *Gulliver's Travels* more than the *Examiner*, with which Addison's samples are really contemporary. Macaulay also overlaps Swift. Thus the VA grouping fails to distinguish both Macaulay and Addison from Swift, a failure which is perhaps attributable to the indistinct character of Class 21, which includes (as was explained above) auxiliaries and all forms of the verb *to be*. It is plain that there might be some advantage in keeping pure auxiliaries separate from copulative verbs in order to be able to relate the number of auxiliaries to the number of finite verbs in a sort of ratio expressing the tendency to use compound verbs. The presence of independent forms of *to be* along with auxiliary forms in Class 21 obscures this relationship. But the issue is whether the additional information supplied by such a distinction would exceed the disadvantages of adding a new class. The issue which is thus raised is: how much additional information is returned for every successive refinement in the procedure? [101]

[101]   It is well known that increases in exactness of measurement require

The division of words in twenty-four classes, though obviously more elaborate than the traditional division, still represents a compromise between the desire for the greatest precision and the need for a practical and usable system. Class 03 words might have been subdivided into participial adjectives ("a sleeping child") and common descriptive adjectives ("a sleepy child"). The unique *not* and the extraordinarily frequent *the* and *and* might have been isolated from their respective classes, which are dominated and all but swamped by their participation. Classes 34 and 61 might have been reorganized, the latter broken down into three classes, each containing one word. But it is problematic whether these and other refinements would have done more than merely increase the difficulty of analyzing the text and require larger samples. The assumption which favors finer and finer sub-division implies that consistency of use will be manifested everywhere. But there is no especial reason to believe so. Some word-classes may be more powerfully influenced by the unifying force of the language, whereas others may be more susceptible to variation. Though guesses may be made about which word-classes belong to which category, the desire to sub-divide should be checked by the self-evident observation that each class is really a sub-sample and that a larger number of such classes decreases the size of each sub-sample with the consequence that it becomes necessary to increase the size of the whole sample if the reliability is to be kept the same. In fact the very process of grouping suggests the increments of stability expected from gross rather than minute classification. Though perhaps grouping of classes has not so far provided any positive stylistic criteria, a consideration of the verbals group (VB) will show a change for the better.

The modernity of constructions with verbals has been noticed by Sherman and Curme, though it is not mentioned by Baugh, who in a review of modern developments in English does cite the

---

disproportionate expenditures of effort. To make a one-foot slide rule more exact by one decimal, one would have to make it ten feet long. Winter, *op. cit.,* found that his 90 word-classes provided no advantage over Fries's 19-class system (pp. 8-9).

progressive tense ("is reading") and verb-adverb combinations ("call up").[102] The more "modern" writer would presumably use many finite-verb suppression devices, whereas the old-fashioned writer would continue to articulate his thought with dependent clauses. In Table 6.14 is clearly shown the extent of Swift's predominance over the controls in this aspect of style. It is interesting that infinitives (05) compose the major part of the VB total, but that in Samples 25, 26 and 29 in which the 05 contribution drops, the number of participles (06) rises to keep the total nearly constant. The most "formal" writer, Gibbon, is of course lowest in the VB figure, but it is surprising that it should be Johnson and not Addison who is treading on Swift's heels. Johnson's value for *Rasselas* slightly exceeds one of Swift's values for

TABLE 6.14

Verbals as individual word-classes and grouped (Group VB), in percentages, for all whole samples, showing mean and range

Class	10	12	13	20	25	26	29	$\bar{x}$	$\bar{w}$
05	2.4	2.6	2.7	2.7	1.9	1.9	1.8	2.3	.9
06	1.0	.6	.8	.8	1.3	1.3	1.5	1.0	.9
07	.5	1.0	.6	.9	.3	.6	1.0	.7	.7
VB	3.9	4.3	4.2	4.4	3.5	3.8	4.3	4.1	.9

CONTROLS

	61	62	65	66	71	72	75	76	$\bar{x}$	$\bar{w}$
05	1.4	1.6	1.7	1.5	1.3	1.0	2.6	1.6	1.6	1.6
06	.7	.8	.4	.4	.4	.3	.8	.7	.6	.5
07	.6	.5	.6	.7	.2	.3	.3	.6	.5	.5
VB	2.7	2.8	2.7	2.6	1.9	1.6	3.7	2.9	2.6	2.1

[102]   Albert C. Baugh, *A History of the English Language*, 2d ed. (New York, 1957), pp. 351 f., 401 f. The word-class system has no provision for identifying the progressive tense, but the verb-adverb frequency is represented by Class 32, which counts prepositional adverbs in that function exclusively. Swift and Addison are highest in the use of that device and Gibbon predictably the lowest by much. Johnson and Macaulay are level.

Gulliver's Travels, perhaps a slight reflection of the influence of the genre.[103] This reliance of Swift on verbs of infinite predication, clearly established by Table 6.14 and Figure 6.A,[104] permits a number of inferences. It would account for the feeling that Swift's prose seems modern (which means colloquial).[105] It might also explain the seeming variety of Swift's prose, since he apparently availed himself freely of possible substitutes for finite verbs.[106] Inferences apart, however, this grouping gives promise of providing a stable discriminator for the purpose of text identification.

It would be interesting to explore the relationship between these verbals, whose stability I have established, and the VA group. The obstacles to clarity in the constitution of the VA group have already been explained. But perhaps a graphic rendition of the relationship might reveal the contents of Tables 6.13 and 6.14 in such a way as to disclose a new pattern. Perhaps not surprisingly, the meaning of Figure 6B supports the hypothesis that the verb system of these writers contains part of the solution of their individual mystery.

[103] That Johnson avoided verb-suppression ordinarily is shown, for example, by the distortions he introduced into sentences he quoted from memory. It is natural that such distortion should follow his normal stylistic bent. For example, quoting a remark by Tonson ("He had thoughts of getting that Lady from his first being recommended into the family"), Johnson renders it: "He formed the design of getting that lady from the time when he was first recommended into the family", *The Lives of the Poets,* ed. G. B. Hill (Oxford, 1905), II, 110. Johnson has converted two verbal clusters (a verb idiom, a passive gerund) into finite verbs.

[104] It is also supported by the figures computed by George W. Gerwig, "On the decrease of predication and of sentence weight in English prose", *University of Nebraska Studies,* II, 1 (July 1894), 17-44. His percentage-of-clauses-saved index (by means of participles and appositives but excluding gerunds and infinitives) shows the following figures: Addison 3.72, Johnson 7.09, Macaulay 5.06, Swift 9.23. Though the criteria are somewhat different, the ranking is almost identical with that of Table 6.14: Swift highest, followed by Johnson, Addison and Macaulay tied.

[105] Rudolph Flesch, *The Art of Readable Writing* (New York, 1949), Chapter XII and passim, argues that written English has more and more closely approached spoken English.

[106] The danger of such speculations is evidenced by the fact that Swift's most "modern" work (*Gulliver's Travels*) is lowest in VB totals and only a little below his least "modern" work, *A Tale of a Tub.*

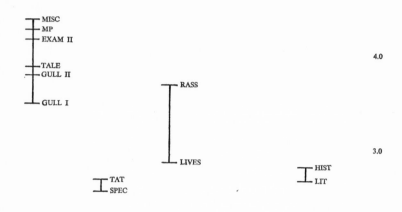

Figure 6a—Values of VB for Swift and controls as a percentage of total words

A number of writers about style have felt that the use of verbs distinguished some writers.[107] Perhaps not much is to be made of this view because verbs are central to competence in using any

[107]   G. Wilson Knight, p. 32, above, refers to Swift's "fine use of the active verb".

Figure 6b—Values of VA plotted against values of VB for Swift and controls

Indo-European language. If one is going to speak about prose one has mostly the choice of verb and noun, though adjectives (lack of) may be mentioned,[108] and Locke and Coleridge cannily noticed connectives.[109] Still, verbs are doubtless of great importance and in Figure 6B may be seen a picture of the verb wardrobe of Swift and his peers.

The little polygon in the center of the graph encloses the heads of Swift's VA-VB vectors. The chances are very good that further samples of Swift would fall within or near it. It is important that the Swift polygon is quite distinct from the lines represented by the other writers. Gibbon's position in the lower left of the graph shows a combination of low VA and VB values. The Addison and Macaulay samples and Johnson's *Rasselas* are clustered in the low center of the graph. It would be difficult to tell them apart. Johnson's *Lives* is alone on the far lower right, somewhat further away from his other sample than that is from the extreme point

---

[108] Perhaps this follows the apocryphal (Voltaire?) tag "The adjective is the enemy of the noun". The adjective-verb quotient (p. 198, below), implies quite a different view of adjectives.
[109] See above, pp. 122-124.

of the center cluster (Macaulay-H). This seems to suggest the influence of fiction on Johnson's style or perhaps reflects a lower order of quantitative consistency in Johnson. It is risky to say more on the basis of two samples.

So much only may be speculated about Johnson, whose work is represented here by just two samples. But about Swift it is possible to be more definite. As attested by Figure 6B, Swift's individual use of the verb system can serve to distinguish his work from that of the other writers.[110] It must not be supposed that the boundaries of the polygon described by the Swift values in Figure 6B will inevitably enclose any value derived from another work by Swift under test. I only claim a high probability that such a value would fall within or very near outside it, but owing to random variation it may perhaps fall elsewhere on the graph. Two ways exist of guarding against this uncertainty. If the work being tested were extensive enough, a number of samples could be drawn from it. Since it is unlikely that this procedure would be practical, the alternative is to find some other discriminators which, in combination, would produce a profile of Swift's style of considerable predictive power. Such additional discriminators will be sought in an examination of the patterns produced by the arrangement of word-classes in the works of our authors. But before proceeding to that stage of the discussion, I must pause to examine whether anything of value remains to be discovered in the word-class frequency distributions.

THE STABLE STYLE STATISTIC (SSS)

It is apparent from a cursory inspection of such arrays as Table 6.7 and 6.8 that an essential order prevails, beyond the modifications produced by random variation and individual difference.

[110] The discriminator obtained by the study of Swift's verb-system and others which will be taken up hereunder, have not been tested, it should be remembered, against anything but a limited range of prose produced by writers of great distinction between 1700 and 1850. It seems highly likely that Swift would be easier to distinguish from a less homogeneous group of writers.

This has already been noticed as the centripetal tendency of a given language. Setting aside the effects of chance which affect any sample, we are left with the modicum of difference which constitutes the individual contribution of the writer, his particular quantitative selection from the common pool. The individual word-classes, being relatively small, least reflect this individual hall-mark, or at least it is swallowed up in the larger fluctuations resulting from the play of other forces. Grouped word-classes, it has been seen, show a valuable cohesiveness in some one part of the syntactical spectrum. It is possible that all four grouped word-classes (VA, VB, M and C), taken together in a particular way might reveal a consistency and an order hidden from the naked eye.

There are elaborate statistical methods for comparing the congruence of sets of numbers with each other.[111] Nothing of the sort will be used here. The four group values for each sample will be simply compared with the group values for every other sample and the sum of their differences will be tabulated under the designation **SSS**. Table 6.15 shows simply how the figures are

TABLE 6.15

Stable Style Statistic (SSS) for Swift's Tale *compared with other Swift samples, showing absolute differences for the four word-groups and total absolute difference*

Word-group	10	12	Diff.	10	13	Diff.	10	20	Diff.
VA	13.8	14.7	.9	13.8	15.6	1.8	13.8	15.0	1.2
VB	3.9	4.3	.4	3.9	4.2	.3	3.9	4.4	.5
M	20.2	20.2	.0	20.2	21.3	1.1	20.2	19.7	.5
C	10.4	10.2	.2	10.4	10.6	.2	10.4	9.9	.5
Total (*SSS*)			1.5			3.4			2.7

	10	25	Diff.	10	26	Diff.	10	29	Diff.
VA	13.8	13.4	.4	13.8	14.4	.6	13.8	13.8	.0
VB	3.9	3.5	.4	3.9	3.8	.1	3.9	4.3	.4
M	20.2	20.2	.0	20.2	21.1	.9	20.2	19.8	.4
C	10.4	10.4	.0	10.4	9.8	.6	10.4	9.9	.5
Total (*SSS*)			.8			2.2			1.3

[111] The Chi-square test, for example.

developed. It may be seen that the columns under "Difference" are merely the absolute differences [112] between Sample 10 and the other samples of the Swift group; their total constitutes the SSS. The range of sums of absolute differences (or SSS) for this sample is between .8 and 3.4. To estimate the value of this characteristic, it will be necessary to perform the same operation for every combination of samples. Table 6.16 shows an array of these figures.

TABLE 6.16

SSS values for all samples

	10	12	13	20	25	26	29	61	62	65	66	71	72	75	76
10		1.5	*3.4*	2.7	.8	2.2	1.3	4.8	4.5	*3.8*	2.8	5.2	6.4	6.5	5.1
12			2.5	1.2	*2.3*	2.1	1.6	*4.1*	4.4	*3.1*	2.5	6.3	7.5	5.8	4.4
13				*3.1*	4.2	2.6	*4.1*	4.6	6.5	*4.0*	3.2	6.4	8.0	5.3	*3.9*
20					3.5	2.7	1.4	*3.1*	5.0	*3.5*	3.1	6.9	8.1	5.2	*4.0*
25						2.8	2.1	4.8	4.5	3.8	2.8	4.4	5.6	6.7	5.1
26							*2.5*	4.4	*3.9*	2.2	3.4	4.2	5.4	6.7	5.5
29								4.3	4.8	*4.1*	4.1	5.5	6.7	6.4	5.2
61									3.7	2.2	2.8	5.8	6.6	5.3	2.5
62										2.7	3.7	5.5	5.5	8.8	6.0
65											2.0	3.6	4.6	7.3	4.5
66												5.2	6.4	6.5	3.5
71													2.0	9.7	7.9
72														9.2	9.2
75															3.0
76															

The values in the upper triangular block constitute the SSS figures *within* the Swift samples. Those in the rectangular block result from comparing the Swift values with those of the controls. Each of the numbers in the individual boxes is the result of a comparison between the two samples of each control. The remaining figures, in the lower triangular block, derive from a comparison *among* the controls. As they are arrayed, the numbers resulting from the comparison within the Swift samples seem to be smaller than those reflecting the comparison between Swift and the controls. This is according to expectation, as low SSS values result when the groups being compared are similar, as

---

[112] Absolute differences ignore plus or minus signs.

they would be in samples from the same author. High values, on the contrary, reflect differences between the samples, such as might arise between different authors. But although the Swift-Swift SSS values seem to be generally lower than the Swift-Controls figures, there is not a perfect boundary between them. Some values in the Swift-Swift block are higher than the lowest single Swift-controls value and naturally some in the Swift-Control block are lower than the highest Swift-Swift figure. There is a considerable overlap,[113] mostly with Addison. Does this invalidate the apparent tendency of the respective blocks? It does not, as will be seen when the components of the table are separately examined. It should be noted, however, that this measurement (SSS) is not proposed as a discriminator, capable of acting with a single sample. It is rather an attempt to demonstrate some of the residual stability of the word-class frequency distributions.

In Table 6.17 may be found a summary of the contents of Table 6.16, accompanied by some statistical measures designed

TABLE 6.17

Detailed summary of SSS values, showing extremes, mean, median, range and number of items for individual authors and groups

1.	2.	3.	4.	5.	6.
Extremes	$\bar{x}$	M	$\bar{w}$	N	
.8/4.2	2.4	2.5	3.4	21	A. *Swift-Swift*
2.0/3.7	2.7	(2.5)	1.7	4	B. *Within Controls*
2.2/8.1	4.9	4.8	5.9	56	C. *Swift-Controls*
2.2/4.1	3.3	(3.3)	1.9	14	Swift-Addison
3.9/6.7	5.4	5.3	2.8	14	Swift-Johnson
4.2/8.1	6.2	6.3	3.9	14	Swift-Gibbon
3.1/6.5	4.6	4.5	3.4	14	Swift-Macaulay
2.2/9.7	5.6	5.5	7.5	24	D. *Among-Controls*
3.5/7.3	5.5	(5.5)	3.8	4	Addison-Johnson
3.6/6.4	5.0	(4.9)	2.8	4	Addison-Gibbon
2.2/3.7	2.9	2.8	1.5	4	Addison-Macaulay
7.9/9.7	9.0	9.2	1.8	4	Johnson-Gibbon
2.5/8.8	5.7	(5.7)	5.3	4	Johnson-Macaulay
5.5/6.6	5.9	(5.7)	1.1	4	Gibbon-Macaulay

Note: parentheses indicate an interpolated median.

[113] This is indicated by italicizing the overlapping values.

to clarify the relationship of the figures.[114] The expectation is that *within* figures (A and B) will be low and *among* figures (C, D) will be high, in means and medians. On Line A, Column 2 shows the value 2.4. This is the average sum of the differences of all the samples *within* the Swift group. The median (Column 3) agrees very well with this mean.[115] Column 2 of Line B shows a very slightly higher figure for the agreement *within* the controls: 2.7. This figure is somewhat less reliable than the one for Swift because the Swift value resulted from an average of twenty-one values, whereas the controls numbered only four (one comparison for each control). If we turn to the values resulting from the comparisons between Swift and the controls and those among the controls, we find the values to be 4.9 and 5.6, respectively. This is about double of the *within* figures and therefore may definitely be considered a meaningful difference.

But what of the several groups of comparisons making up these totals — to what extent are they uniformly in agreement with their average? Of the four Swift-Controls comparisons, only Swift-Addison (3.3) is much lower than the average. That it should be Addison is not surprising. The range of values for this pairing is 2.2 to 4.1, which is fully enclosed by the Swift *within* figures, whose average, however, is nearly 1.0 lower. Although this circumstance seems to militate against the usefulness of the SSS measurement, we shall see that it behaves perfectly reliably under the conditions of an actual test.[116] Similarly Addison is again the culprit, this time paired with Macaulay, in the *among-*

---

[114]   Column 6 explains which figures are being compared. Italicized rubrics (A, B, C, D) represent the four resultant possibilities of comparison. Non-italicized comparisons are expansions of the major rubrics. Column 1 encloses the spread from the highest to the lowest figures in the comparison. Columns 2 and 3 give the arithmetic mean and the median, respectively. Column 4 is the range, result of subtracting the lower figure in Column 1 from the higher. Column 5 indicates the number of figures (as items) involved in each comparison.

[115]   Because the mean is sensitive to extreme values, the median is computed (by taking the midpoint value of the items involved) to furnish a check upon the mean. Medians in parentheses were arrived at by interpolating (halving the difference) between two figures. Since the means and medians agree almost exactly, no further use of the medians need be made.

[116]   See Unknown test, below, Chapter VII.

controls (Line D) in the Table. Whereas the other pairs are all above 5.0, Johnson-Gibbon reaching 9.0, the Addison-Macaulay pair with its value of 2.9 is even nearer to *within-Swift* (2.4) than Addison-Swift is. That Addison-Swift should resemble Swift-Swift in this criterion is understandable, as Addison is similar to Swift in several others. But the Addison-Macaulay figure seems circumstantial (perhaps the result of the low numbers of items involved: 4), unless of course the affinity that Macaulay felt for Addison is in some sense responsible. Without more samples of the writing of the controls, it is not possible to examine more closely the relation between Addison and Swift, at least with reference to this SSS criterion. Since it has been possible to find discriminators which separate Swift from all the controls, including Addison, this SSS is not presented for that purpose but as a convenient short method and as a way of suggesting the underlying stability of the word-class frequency distributions.

THE STABILITY FACTOR

A far more elaborate method for testing the consistency of the averages is available but its computation is laborious and the results indecisive. It is nonetheless presented because it offers some interesting comments on method and materials. The Stability Factor (abbreviated S) requires the initial assumption that the values examined will follow the Binomial model.[117] That is, if the word-class tested is 01, which has an average probability for Swift of .20, the assumption is that when the author is considering the choice of a word, there is a 20 per cent chance of his picking a noun and 80 per cent of everything else, as if he did not

---

[117]   Or it might be said that the Stability Factor represents an attempt to discover whether the Binomial assumption is applicable. The formula is $S = \dfrac{(p \cdot q)100^2}{N \cdot s^2}$, where p is the average probability of occurrence of a word-class or grouping (expressed as a number less than one), q is 1-p, N is the number of words in the sample and s^2 is the variance of the sub-samples. The formula is the creation of Professor Colin Mallows of the Mathematical Statistics Department at Columbia University.

know what word he had written last. Obviously, this model is not congruent with the facts, as a writer who has just written *the* (probability .15) has a zero probability of producing another unit from the same class and around 70 per cent of class 01, with much smaller probabilities for 03, 31 and so on. The same limitation applies in varying degrees to all word-classes. Despite this approximation, however, the factor is worth pursuing because it will measure the stability of a given word-class or grouping in the tenth sub-samples which were regularly produced as part of the yield of the computer. Unlike the standard deviation (which it resembles) the Stability Factor takes account of the size of the sample and even of the probability of the event (in the numerator).

To explain briefly the meaning of the Stability Factor, Table 6.18 is presented. This table contains a selection of the material given in Table 6.9, whose purpose was to show the greater cohesiveness of the Swift samples over the Controls samples taken as a population, by comparing the standard deviations of each word-class. In Table 6.18, three individual word-classes (01, 31, 51) and the four functional groupings (VA, VB, M, C) are compared in terms of standard deviations and Stability Factor. It should be remembered at the outset that the standard deviation *increases* and the Stability Factor *decreases* as the dispersion (lack of uniformity) *increases*. Thus in the Swift columns the class with the highest S.D. has the lowest S value (01), and the lowest S.D.'s are appropriately found next to the highest S values. The discrepancy between the similar S.D.'s (.31 and .32) for Group C and Class 51 (under Swift) is due to the fact that the Stability Factor takes account of the absolute size of the class or group and the standard deviation does not. The S values for Swift are greater than those of the controls by a factor between three and sixteen, and the greater stability of the Swift group is thus again demonstrated. The same conclusion, of course, had followed from the standard deviations given in Table 6.9 but the limitations of that measurement did not permit the comparison of stability between classes of the same author. The S factor shows quite plainly the higher stability of Class 51 and Group C and the

TABLE 6.18

Standard deviations (S.D.) and Stability Factors (S) of three word-classes and four word-groups compared in the Swift and control populations

	SWIFT			CONTROLS		
	Per cent	S.D.	S	Per cent	S.D.	S
01	20.3	.93	.5	23.4	2.60	.1
31	15.3	.69	.7	16.3	1.98	.1
51	12.6	.32	3.2	13.8	1.37	.2
VA	14.4	.77	.6	14.9	1.88	.1
VB	4.1	.33	1.0	2.6	.64	.2
M	20.4	.62	1.2	20.1	1.12	.4
C	10.2	.31	2.6	9.5	.90	.3

relatively lower stability of Classes 01 and 31 and Group VA.

That the Stability Factor should be able to distinguish between the Swift samples and the Controls population is not very surprising, as the differences are quite large (almost an order of magnitude). What it may reveal about the internal stability of a particular sample is less predictable and will furnish both a challenge to the Stability Factor and information about the figures themselves. Examination of Table 6.19 shows that when Sample 20 is divided into ten sub-samples (each of which has its own frequency distribution), the extent of variation along any given line seems to be considerably more than that of Table 6.7. A comparison of the range of variation for several word-classes between the Swift samples and the sub-samples of Sample 20 ought to make explicit the difference. Table 6.20 shows that the range of variation for eight classes and groups is about three times greater among the one-tenth sub-samples of a Swift sample (20) [118] than among all the Swift whole samples. The fact of the variation is due to the difference in the size of the units surveyed, the samples each containing 3500 words and the sub-samples 350, a factor of ten. The relation between the factor of three and that of ten is taken account of in the computation of the Stability Factor, which covers dispersion as well as range.

If the Stability Factor is now computed for all the classes of Sample 20, on the basis of the sub-samples arranged in Table

[118] Each sub-sample is approximately equal to a page of text.

6.19, the results will be those in Column S of Table 6.21. The values range between .4 and 3.6 but with the exception of three (34, 51, C) they are clustered around 1.0 and may therefore be considered equal. Of the three exceptions, only Class 51 has behaved previously in such a way as to make this outcome likely. The Stability Factors for the Parts of Speech seem to be more uniform than those for the Function Words. That is, the Parts of

TABLE 6.19

Frequency distribution of word-classes and word-groups in Swift's Miscellaneous *sample (20), divided into one-tenth sub-samples*

	20_1	20_2	20_3	20_4	20_5	20_6	20_7	20_8	20_9	20_{10}	20
01	16.1	19.3	24.3	19.0	19.7	18.3	21.3	20.5	21.4	22.5	20.2
02	8.3	9.1	6.4	8.4	6.9	6.3	5.8	6.3	4.8	7.3	6.9
03	4.3	5.1	4.8	2.6	7.5	6.9	5.8	5.7	5.9	7.3	5.6
04	2.0	.3	1.1	.6	2.3	.6	—	2.3	1.4	1.2	1.2
05	3.2	2.3	1.7	3.2	1.7	4.6	3.5	1.4	3.1	2.3	2.7
06	—	—	.3	.9	1.2	.3	.6	1.4	1.4	2.0	.8
07	1.7	.9	.8	—	.3	1.4	.6	1.7	.9	.9	.9
08	.6	—	—	.6	—	—	—	—	—	—	.1
P/S	36.1	36.8	39.4	35.2	39.6	38.3	37.5	39.2	38.9	43.4	38.4
11	9.5	7.9	6.4	7.8	4.6	8.3	6.9	6.8	3.7	5.5	6.7
21	9.7	7.7	6.4	10.1	8.1	7.7	8.7	8.5	7.9	5.8	8.1
31	14.3	18.4	14.8	13.5	14.7	14.0	15.0	14.5	16.1	13.4	14.9
32	.3	.6	.8	.6	.9	—	1.2	.3	.6	—	.5
33	2.0	2.6	1.4	3.2	2.9	2.3	1.7	1.4	4.5	3.2	2.5
34	1.4	1.7	1.4	1.7	2.3	2.0	2.0	1.7	1.1	2.0	1.7
41	4.6	2.8	5.6	5.5	2.6	5.1	3.8	5.1	5.1	5.5	4.6
42	2.6	3.1	3.4	3.2	3.2	2.0	1.7	2.8	2.0	2.0	2.6
43	2.6	3.1	1.1	.6	2.9	2.6	2.6	2.0	2.5	1.5	2.1
44	1.2	.3	—	.9	—	—	.3	—	—	—	.3
45	—	—	.8	.6	—	.6	.6	.3	—	—	.3
51	11.2	11.3	14.5	11.5	13.0	12.0	11.5	14.2	13.0	12.5	12.5
61	3.2	3.4	2.2	4.0	4.6	4.6	3.8	2.0	3.9	2.6	3.4
71	—	—	—	—	—	—	—	—	—	—	.0
81	—	—	1.1	.3	.3	—	1.4	.6	.6	2.3	.7
91	1.4	.3	.6	1.4	.3	.6	1.4	.6	.3	—	.7
FW	63.9	63.2	60.6	64.8	60.4	61.7	62.5	60.8	61.1	56.6	61.6
VA	18.1	16.7	12.8	18.5	15.0	14.0	14.4	14.8	12.7	13.1	15.0
VB	4.9	3.1	2.8	4.0	3.2	6.3	4.6	4.5	5.4	5.2	4.4
M	18.1	23.2	18.4	19.0	20.8	18.3	19.9	17.9	22.3	18.7	19.7
C	10.9	9.4	10.9	10.7	8.7	10.3	8.9	10.2	9.6	9.0	9.9

TABLE 6.20

Comparison of range of variation in three word-class and five word-group percentages among Swift whole samples and among sub-samples of Swift Miscellaneous

	SWIFT	20
	$\bar{w}$	$\bar{w}$
01	2.4	8.2
31	1.5	5.0
51	.9	3.3
VA	2.2	5.8
VB	.9	3.5
M	1.6	5.3
C	.8	2.2
P/S	3.2	8.2

Speech have a similar rate of stability, a more or less constant fluctuation. The Function Words, on the contrary, vary between the numerals (81), which have the lowest S and therefore do not appear in the sub-samples with any regularity to the connectives of Group C and the miscellaneous function adverbs of Class 34 which are distributed more evenly among the sub-samples.

If the results given by the Stability Factor were always so easy to reconcile with expectation, it would be of considerable use in these evaluations. Unfortunately, however, it has a tendency to be erratic, as an examination of Table 6.22 will confirm. In this table are given the S values computed for the five word-groups for various-sized sub-samples of Swift Sample 25. These range from one-hundredth sub-samples to ordinary one-tenth sub-samples, employing from ten one-card units to ten ten-card batches. Barring indications to the contrary, it might have been expected that the values in each word-group would have a family likeness. It is seen, however, that they do not. The values under Group M seem close enough to suggest membership in a common family. But the others vary by more than a factor of two (between the highest and the lowest). The least uniform is VA which ranges through a factor of five. The cause of this disagreement must be sought in the lack of congruence of the process under analysis with the binomial model taken as a prototype.

Sample 25 was selected for this comparison because its make-up, through stratified random sampling, was expected to intensify the evenness of distribution of word-classes through the sample. It might, therefore, give less idiosyncratic results than a normal random sample. The peculiar appearance of Column VA, how-ever, makes this expectation questionable. The highest S values (and in fact the highest value in the Table) is found in the con-sistency of finite verbs in a sample taken 35 words (one card) at

TABLE 6.21

Percentage and Stability Factor of all word-classes and word-groups in Swift's Miscellaneous *sample*

	Per cent	S
01	20.2	.9
02	6.9	1.0
03	5.6	.7
04	1.2	.5
05	2.7	.8
06	.8	.5
07	.9	.8
08	*	*
11	6.7	.6
21	8.1	1.2
31	14.9	1.7
32	.5	.9
33	2.5	.7
34	1.7	3.6
41	4.6	1.0
42	2.6	1.9
43	2.1	.9
44	*	*
45	*	*
51	12.5	2.2
61	3.4	1.1
71	*	*
81	.7	.4
91	.7	.7
VA	15.0	.8
VB	4.4	1.0
M	19.7	1.3
C	9.9	3.5

* *Note:* these values have been omitted on account of insufficient size (less than .3).

TABLE 6.22

*Comparison of Stability Factors (S) for sub-samples of different sizes,
all drawn from Swift's* Gulliver I *(Sample 25) by word-groups*

Fraction of sample	VA	VB	M	C	P/S	N	No. of IBM cards
A. 1/100	5.3	1.1	1.4	1.4	2.1	35	1
B. 1/50	1.1	1.1	1.9	.9	2.5	70	2
C. 1/25	1.8	1.6	1.1	2.5	.9	140	4
D. 1/20	2.9	1.3	1.0	1.6	1.2	175	5
E. 1/10	3.5	2.5	.9	1.1	.8	350	10

a time. Measured seventy words at a time, the stability drops almost to the bottom, only to recover gradually as the size of the sample approaches one tenth. It must be that there is an interplay between the size of the sample and the syntactical function under scrutiny such as to render almost unpredictable the direction of the Stability Factor. Inasmuch as there is a built-in allowance for the size of the sample, the Stability Factor should remain constant regardless of the size of the sample. Word-group M, whose largest component is Class 31, which includes articles, has the highest consistency of S values.[119] VA (finite verbs) has least. Whatever may be the cause of this discrepancy, it is clear that the binomial model on which the Stability Factor is based is an inadequate representation of the complex of forces surrounding probability of word-choice.

Despite its lack of minute accuracy, the Stability Factor can lead to suggestive implication and the S values have therefore been computed for the three major word-classes and the five word-groups. Provided only the broadest tendencies are considered meaningful, the results may be of some use. They are displayed in Table 6.23.

Among the Swift samples Column 01 is reasonably uniform, centering around unity. Almost the same is true of group P/S. Column VA offers a remarkable uniformity except for Sample 25, which is disproportionately high. This is of course the sample discussed earlier whose stratified randomness seemed likely to

---

[119] That is, its lack of consistency tends to remain at the same low level, whereas other groups do not have such a uniform lack of consistency.

TABLE 6.23

Stability Factors for all samples, in three word-classes and five word-groups

Sample	01	31	51	VA	VB	M	C	P/S
10	1.6	2.1	1.0	.8	.3	2.1	2.8	.5
12	.8	.8	.7	.7	.7	.8	1.2	1.7
13	.7	.5	.9	.5	1.6	1.8	.8	1.5
20	.9	1.7	2.2	.8	1.0	1.3	3.5	1.3
25	1.3	2.0	1.9	3.5	2.5	.9	1.1	.8
26	1.0	2.9	1.0	.6	.6	1.4	1.4	.9
29	1.4	.6	.8	.8	1.5	2.0	1.2	1.3

CONTROLS

	01	31	51	VA	VB	M	C	P/S
61	.8	1.2	1.8	1.4	1.4	2.8	3.1	1.0
62	.7	1.1	1.7	.6	.4	1.0	.9	.8
65	3.4	1.0	4.3	3.0	1.1	1.8	1.7	2.9
66	.9	1.5	1.2	.6	.9	1.7	1.7	.7
71	2.1	5.2	3.0	1.0	.8	2.0	4.6	2.5
72	1.2	2.8	2.6	1.1	.7	2.9	1.6	1.9
75	1.8	1.2	1.4	5.6	1.0	2.8	2.8	3.4
76	1.8	.9	.8	.9	.6	.8	.9	2.4

produce greater uniformity.[120] If the other values of this sample are compared with the other Swift samples, they seem to show a somewhat higher tendency.[121] By the same ocular inspection, Sample 12 seems to be the least homogeneous, showing only two values above one. The instability may be the result of the nature of the work *(The Examiner)*, a periodical, written on a number of separate occasions in which the unifying tendency would have least opportunity to operate. The writer probably would not consider the previous issues of the periodical part of his context, unlike the writer of a connected work whose daily task might well begin with the re-reading of the previous installment. The other sample drawn from the same work (13) is in the same range of instability. This conjecture may be weakened, however, by the performance of Sample 29, which is the only continuous piece of

[120] This might suggest the adoption of the stratified sampling procedure if it is desired to keep random variation down.
[121] Because of the inaccuracy of the figures, no averages have been computed.

prose among these samples and which is only somewhat more stable than the *Examiner* samples.

Except for Gibbon, the members of each pair of control samples show remarkable divergence from each other. Macaulay in the word-groups, Addison in two word-classes and two word-groups, Johnson in the word-groups. Among those which call for comment are Johnson's S value of 5.6 for Sample 75 in Column VA and .9 for Sample 76. The stable value derives from *Rasselas,* the unstable from the *Lives.* There are three clear variables here: differences in genre, length of time spent on composition, and stage of the writer's life. Which is the significant factor cannot be elicited from the data, but it may be noteworthy that Addison's *Tatler* writing is more stable than his *Spectators.* The difference in time may not be great enough to count: a mere four years. Gibbon's early volumes, however, also are more stable than his late ones, though his over-all stability is higher than anyone else's (except perhaps *Rasselas*).[122] If this factor weighs, it may be that with advancing age, fatigue, carelessness or some other factor increases the likelihood of stylistic instability. A more definite characteristic of Gibbon, however, is his preference for the nominal style, which is reflected in the high values he achieves under the three word-classes comprising prepositional phrases (01, 31, 51).

NOMINAL, VERBAL AND ADJECTIVAL STYLES

The existence of a nominal as opposed to a verbal style has some significance in such a study as this. The almost universal prescription for bad English requires the use of a great many nouns and a consequent decrease in the number of verbs.[123] Yet despite

[122] The Macaulay samples are out of the running, as they are not selected according to time of writing but according to subject matter: literary or historical.

[123] It may be observed in operation in almost any manual of composition. Sheridan Baker, *The Practical Stylist* (New York, 1962), includes in a section titled "The Terrible Essay" the following Rules: "3. Use no adjectives, use nouns instead ... 6. Use only big abstracts nouns ... 7. Use plenty of *of*'s ..." (pp. 107-8). The same view is cited by Rulon Wells, "Nominal

this seeming agreement, there are writers – and very good
ones – whose conscious or unconscious preference is for the
nominal style. In view of Gibbon's pronounced affection for
prepositional phrases and his high Class 01 percentages, one
might reasonably look for him among the nominalists, but what
of the others? Swift's "fine use of the active verb",[124] suggests
that his reputation would land him in the other camp. About the
others, there seems to be no particular rumor, except that Johnson's formality suggests a nominal tendency.

The simplest procedure is just to separate those word classes
which are nominal in character (01, 03, 31, 51) from those that
are verbal in character (VA, VB, 04, 32, 33, 34, 42, 43), add each
group separately, and find their ratio. Table 6.24 gives the ratio
as nominals to verbals.[125] As expected, Gibbon is found at the
summit of the group, although his later work is more nominal
than the earlier. Macaulay's historical essays are more nominal
than his literary ones. Swift's average of 1.9 makes him quite
verbal, though it is impossible to set an arbitrary boundary between the two styles. Addison is a little higher than Swift but so
close that if Swift is verbal so is Addison. The most surprising
finding is that Johnson is more verbal than any one, Swift included, both his samples agreeing in this respect. In this also, he
differs markedly from Gibbon, with whose balanced manner the
Johnsonian style is often mistakenly lumped.

The characteristics of the nominal style, as set forth by one
critic,[126] are monotony of pattern,[127] ease of writing, impersonality,
formality. The formality of Gibbon has already been discussed
and is in any case not likely to provoke controversy. Addison's
"middle style" [128] and Swift's "homely" [129] style accord well
enough with their nominal-verbal ratios. But Johnson's does not.

---

and Verbal Style", in *Style in Language,* ed. Thomas A. Sebeok (New
York, 1960), p. 214 f.
[124] G. W. Knight's phrase. See above, p. 32.
[125] The ratio is the result of dividing N by V.
[126] Rulon Wells, *op. cit.,* pp. 217-8.
[127] Cf. results of pattern study, below, p. 204 ff.
[128] Johnson's phrase.
[129] See p. 26, above.

Johnson's writing is considered formal and formality is associated with the abstractness of nouns. Yet he is the most verbal author of the lot. Where does the difficulty lie? Are the figures of the ratio misleading? It hardly seems probable (though it is of course always possible) by reason of the agreement between the two values of each author and the fact that Johnson provides one pole of the range. The samples are drawn from two representative works, which have in other tests shown results accordant with expectation. The only remaining source of the seeming contradiction is the definition of formality. It is clear that if formality is secured by order in structural arrangement (for example, balance, parallelism, inversion),[130] Johnson (as well as Gibbon) is formal. But if formality can only result from a nominal style, Johnson is not formal. The difficulty, as so often with the terms of the criticism of style, resides in definition and in the relation between objective phenomena and impressionistic labels. In short, Johnson's formality is the consequence of structural design, a characteristic shared by Gibbon, who adds to it a heavy nominal emphasis.

As to the other characteristics of the nominal style, impersonality may be considered an aspect of formality and monotony of pattern is reserved for later discussion: there remains ease of writing. If the nominal style is easier to write than the verbal, one might expect that a writer would become 'nominal' when he was tired or when the task had begun to pall. Such conditions might coincide with the characteristic state of writers in their later periods. Then a writer's later works would be more nominal than his earlier, a speculation supported by the Johnson [131] and (especially) Gibbon figures in Table 6.24 but discountenanced by the Addison figures (though these may be considered contemporary with each other) and by the lack of trend among the Swift ratios. Gibbon himself confesses that he was subject to

---

[130] Wimsatt, *The Prose Style of Samuel Johnson,* passim.
[131] Wimsatt specifically disavows the widespread theory that Johnson's style became lighter (less nominal) with age. Johnson had "different degrees of his own peculiar style" and used them according to the demands of the subject matter without regard to time (*op. cit.,* p. 78).

TABLE 6.24

Ratio of nominals to verbals in the samples of Swift and controls

	N	V	Ratio
10	56.5	27.6	2.0
12	53.0	30.2	1.8
13	52.4	31.4	1.7
20	53.2	30.0	1.8
25	55.8	27.0	2.1
26	53.8	28.6	1.9
29	55.5	29.0	1.9

CONTROLS

	N	V	Ratio
61	58.5	28.5	2.1
62	63.3	25.5	2.5
65	57.9	27.5	2.1
66	56.7	28.3	2.0
71	68.2	21.8	3.1
72	71.6	18.0	4.0
75	52.8	30.5	1.7
76	56.5	28.9	1.9

some such influences,[132] but other factors are also involved: his Gallicism and the vastness and unity of the work he was engaged on. However apposite such an explanation may be, it leaves untouched the more profound question of how reality is construed by means of the functional-semantic process of noun and verb. Such a question does not readily yield to analysis but the examination of the evidence from different sides may help to give us a better idea of the process. Another side from which to view it is provided by a German psychiatrist's [133] hypothesis about the relation between verbs and adjectives. The adjective-verb quotient (AVQ) that he worked out assigned psychological values to these two parts of speech. The quotient is easily compiled from

[132]   His own testimony: "The style of the first volume is, in my opinion, somewhat crude and elaborate; in the second and third it is ripened into ease, correctness and numbers; but in the three last I may have been seduced by the facility of my pen, and the constant habit of speaking one language and writing another may have infused some mixture of Gallic idioms" (*Memoirs,* ed. G. B. Hill, p. 224). This reflection accounts for the fact that the author felt there was a difference between the early and the late volumes. But the reasons he gives do not have the same weight.
[133]   F. Busemann; see Boder's account (next footnote) for references to his original work.

the word-class frequency distributions and is worth pausing to examine because it purports to comment on the emotional stability of the subjects, a trait of considerable interest for the group of writers under consideration.

Busemann in an experiment with some children, whose oral storytelling he recorded, noticed that the relationship between active constructions (verbs) and qualifying constructions (adjectives) varied from child to child. Moreover, over a period of time, an increase in the number of verbs paralleled an increased emotional instability (as independently observed by the children's teacher), while an increase in the number of adjectives reflected greater emotional adjustment. The underlying difference was assumed to be translatable into two types of adult personality: the subjective (active) and objective (qualitative). A later researcher, Boder,[134] using Busemann's work as a basis, tackled the problem from a more literary angle, using a great variety of adult American writing for his material. In a number of samples of 300-350 words from each source, Boder found a wide range of values, varying greatly from one type of material to another. Table 6.25 [135] reproduces some of his findings for the spectrum of sources. The scores for highest and lowest AVQ fluctuate so greatly that the figure for a single sample can hardly be trusted.[136] But since the quotient for each type of source material has been

[134] D. P. Boder, "The Adjective-Verb Quotient", *Psychological Record*, III (March 1940), 309-343.

[135] The AVQ is computed by the following formula: $100 \cdot \frac{03}{02 + 05 + 06}$, which will give a number usually of two digits, expressing the number of adjectives for each hundred words. Though Boder uses adjectives only in attributive position, there is no way to exclude those in predicate adjective position; but these are doubtless very few. Verbs do not include copulas or auxiliaries. The numbers 03, 02, 05 and 06 represent Parts of Speech: adjective, finite verb, infinitive and participle.

[136] The difficulty seems to lie in the size of sample Boder worked with (300-350 words). The monthly samplings which Boder took from Emerson's *Journals* for the year 1825 give the figures 32, 72, 138, 34, 58, 63, 37, 61, 54, 41, 71, 33 (average 58), which have a standard deviation of 29.0. The same computation carried out for the one-tenth sub-samples of Swift Sample 10 (*A Tale of a Tub*) gives a standard deviation of 35.0. But the standard deviation of the seven Swift whole samples is 9.8, which shows a much greater cohesion.

TABLE 6.25

Boder's Adjective-Verb Quotient (AVQ) for various types of writing

Source	Mean	AVQ Low	High	No. of Samples
Plays	11	0	69	226
Legal	16	0	31	13
Business	19	0	33	7
Fiction	35	10	80	20
Poetry	36	0	75	18
A. Brisbane ("Today")	42	28	72	15
Letters	43	13	100	39
Emerson ("Journals")	47	11	138	132
Scientific	64	37	90	20
M. A. Essays	64	10	130	30
H. L. Mencken (*Mercury*)	72	31	160	36
Advertisements	78	33	167	18
Ph. D. Theses	88	50	200	30

Note: entire table is adapted from Boder, Table I, p. 318.

drawn from a sufficiently great number of samples, the averages may be considered representative. On the whole, these figures accord with expectation: the dialogue of plays is expected to be active, the prose of doctoral dissertations circumspect. One is not prepared for so much objectivity in advertisements, but that may be due to the practice of an earlier era.[137] Unfortunately, none of the categories of material seems precisely congruent with the texts under consideration here. However the line from Fiction to Mencken, including values 35 of 72, may be considered roughly parallel to the work of Swift and the controls.

The figures for our authors are set out in Table 6.26.[138] The highest and the lowest of Swift are exactly 30 units apart and the mean of 57 and the median of 58 agree. Gibbon is clearly the highest scorer, followed by Macaulay. Johnson seems to be low and Addison level with Swift. How do these results square with Boder's values? An easier to visualize representation of the same

[137] Boder's research dates from 1927, though his paper was published in 1940.
[138] Vv is the sum of 02, 05 and 06. AVQ results when 03 is divided by Vv and the result multiplied by 100. AVQ figures are rounded to the nearest whole number.

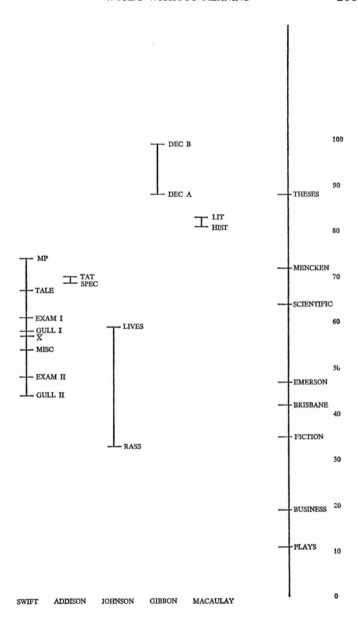

Figure 6c—Adjective-verb Quotient (AVQ) for Swift and controls compared with Boder's scale

TABLE 6.26

The Adjective-Verb Quotient for Swift and controls

	03	Vv*	Sum**	AVQ***
10	6.8	10.1	16.9	67
12	6.3	10.4	16.7	61
13	5.2	10.9	16.1	48
20	5.6	10.4	16.0	54
25	6.4	11.0	17.4	58
26	5.1	11.6	16.7	44
29	6.9	9.3	16.2	74
Mean ($\bar{x}$)	6.0	10.5	16.5	57

CONTROLS

	03	Vv*	Sum**	AVQ***
61	7.9	9.5	17.4	83
62	7.8	9.6	17.4	81
65	6.9	9.8	16.7	70
66	7.0	10.1	17.1	69
71	8.8	8.9	17.7	99
72	7.3	8.3	15.6	88
75	4.5	13.9	18.4	33
76	6.2	10.5	16.7	59
Range ($\bar{w}$)	4.3	5.6	2.8	

* $Vv = 02 + 05 + 06$
** Sum of $03 + Vv$
*** $AVQ = 100 \times \dfrac{03}{Vv}$

information is given in Figure 6C, with Boder's continuous scale for purposes of comparison. When we look at this graph, we see a slightly clearer picture. Gibbon's erudite work is properly located with the works of scholarship which it resembles. Johnson's lower value is *Rasselas,* quite appropriately at the level of Fiction on Boder's scale. The other Johnson value falls almost level with the average of Swift, another witness to the affinity between these two writers. *Gulliver's Travels* (26) is only a little above *Rasselas* and Fiction but *Gulliver's Travels* (25), which is higher, may be reflecting the difference in sampling method. Addison's two values fall close together very near the line of another good middle-brow essayist, Mencken. Macaulay, whose matter has a kinship with Addison's, however, is a good dozen points higher.

It is evident that this criterion (AVQ) is very dependent on the type of material tested, as this variable seems in some sense to govern the frequency of the adjective.

The adjective had been earlier noticed as unusually unstable,[139] even in the works of the same author, and it is perhaps the only part of speech which has given rise to an irrational folklore of recommendation and prohibition.[140] Boder calls attention to the greater linguistic sophistication required of the user of attributive adjectives. The verb's function is straightforward, almost inevitable: the adjective names a quality we believe inheres in an object and so makes a modicum of analysis and evaluation prerequisite to its use.[141] The inter-relation of these two parts of speech may be noticed if the third column of Table 6.26 is examined, in which the sum of 03 and Vv is given. To two elements tend to damp each other out, as is implied by the range,[142] which is considerably less for the sum than for either of the elements alone. This circumstance suggests the possibility that the writer must choose the active or the qualifying construcion and gives a certain latitude for the interpretation of these data according to the psychological constitutions of their authors.

[139] See above, p. 159 and Tables 6.4, 6.5, 6.6.
[140] The classic aphorism is the apocryphal Voltairism "The adjective is the enemy of the noun". A comment with a better claim to be Voltaire's is "Though the adjective may agree with the noun in gender, number and case, nevertheless the adjective and the noun may not agree." Both are cited by Henry L. Mencken, ed. *A New Dictionary of Quotations* (New York, 1946), p. 13. F. L. Lucas, *Style* (London, 1955), in a passage which espouses the view that epithets are somehow a source of danger to the writer, combines the two comments into one which he attributes to Voltaire (pp. 110-1). On the other side – the side of greater rationality – may be found Margaret M. Bryant and Janet Rankin Aiken, *Psychology of English* (New York, 1940), who note that "the adjective appears today to be under a cloud, while the verb is praised by teachers of composition..." (p. 177). They question the value of "discrimination between the parts of speech", citing an ironic passage from Mark Twain: "When you catch an adjective, kill it ... An adjective habit, or a wordy, diffuse, flowery habit, once fastened upon a person, is as hard to get rid of as any other vice" (*ibid.*). This is the suffrage of the professional, to whom the deliberate sacrifice of any part of his word-hoard is simply naive.
[141] Boder, p. 314.
[142] The difference between the extreme values in any column, given on line w̄.

If Boder's psychological views are adopted, at least temporarily, and the variable provided by the type of material is disregarded, the following ranking emerges, in an increasing order of emotional stability: Swift (lowest), Johnson, Addison, Macaulay, Gibbon (highest). The significance of the ranking is found in the division of personalities into two types: the kinaesthetic or active (subjective) and the reflective or qualitative (objective). The former is characterized by energy, emotionality, lower objectivity, less concreteness and less intellectuality and avails itself of an abundance of verbs. The latter has the opposite traits and favors adjectives.[143] Whatever may be the accuracy of such a simple dichotomy in dealing with such a complex quantity as a writer whose abilities operate at the level of genius, it is striking that Swift has been called energetic and subjective and he himself refers to his emotional excess,[144] whereas Gibbon's writing is something like the antithesis of Swift's in these qualities. Irony, of course, they have in common.

THREE-WORD PATTERNS

Although this last speculation verges on the tenuous, the quotient which prompted it does not exhaust the possible uses which may be made of the word-class frequency distributions. The analysis into word-classes contains almost more information than can ever be extracted from it. As it stands, it remains available for the testing of new relationships and ready to answer certain kinds of questions about the grammatical structure of Swift's (and the controls') style. However, frequency distribution is not the only way in which the words of the texts, analyzed into their individual word-classes, can be deployed. There is another perhaps not so obvious way in which to study them: by examining the *arrangement* of the word-classes, not just their quantitative distribution. This method is not as obvious as the other because it requires the solution of several difficulties in theory and practice, of which

[143]   Boder, pp. 312-3.
[144]   E.g., the "saeva indignatio" of his epitaph.

the greatest is the problem of technique – how to do it. But preliminary of this is the question of the type and size of arrangement to be studied.

If words are not taken in isolation, they must be taken in groups. These groups must be small enough to occur often and so form a pattern of preference springing from individual difference among authors. For example, the words of the text may be taken two at a time, three at a time, ten at a time and soon. However, the number of different possible arrangements of word-classes increases very steeply as the number of units in the group is increased. For instance, since there are 24 word-classes, the number of possible combinations of two words each of which may be a member of any of 24 word-classes is 24 x 24 or 24^2, that is, 576. If the size of the group studied is three, we have 24^3 or 13,824 possibilities. Patterns of four may occur 331,776 different ways (24^4). These are of course only the theoretical totals for items which can be arranged any which way (like marbles). Words are not so obliging. If the first word is *a* or *the*, it is very likely that the next word will belong to Class 01. After *very* or *to,* the choice is also quite restricted. Scarcely any opportunity occurs for unrestricted choice, even in the first word. Practically speaking, this limitation works to hold down the number of combinations that arise freely. Naturally, there is no very good way to estimate the relationship between theoretical and practical possibilities except to try them all. But let us say that for groups of three the practical total is between one-tenth and one-twentieth of the theoretical.[145] For any given author, this practical total is expected to be further reduced because of individual preference.

The decision as to the size of the pattern to be obtained (whether two, three, four-words) was based on two requirements; it must be extensive enough to make visible some of the syntactical structure of the writing; it must be small enough to permit in a sample of 3500 words a reasonable distribution of the most and least frequent with a gradation between. If the number of practical possibilities exceeds the number of words in the sample, it is unlikely that any kind of distribution will

[145] Some confirmation of this estimate will be provided later, p. 208.

result. This would be true for all combinations of four or more. There are 331,776 different ways of combining four items of this type. If only five per cent are practical possibilities, that is still more than fifteen thousand or more than the total number of words in the sample. Therefore only two or three-word combinations are available. Two-word patterns can be inferred from three-word patterns and are scarcely any advance over single words; and so three-word patterns have been chosen. Since the practical total probably lies between 600 and 1200 possibilities,[146] there seems to be room in the sample for a sufficient distribution. Three-word patterns are just large enough to include prepositional phrases and most compound verbs, so they seem justified from the theoretical viewpoint as well.

The procedure consists of taking the same reduction of the texts to numerical word-class designators (the data decks) and processing them via the computer with a different set of instructions. Beginning with the first word of a sentence [147] the computer takes successive groups of three words (each word in turn, thus making an overlapping sequence) and compares each with the previous ones, keeping a record of each different pattern and the frequency of its occurrence. When it reaches the end of a sentence, it stops and skips to the beginning of the next. Thus no groups are recorded which begin with the last or next-to-last words of a sentence.[148] As a consequence, the total number of patterns in a sentence is two less than the total number of words, since a new pattern begins with each word of the sentence save the last two. Thus the number of total patterns in a sample [149] is equal to the number of words less twice the number of sentences.[150] It is not surprising that the processing of samples with a program devised to produce a list of the different patterns to-

[146]   This is five to ten per cent of 24^3 or 13,824.
[147]   The first word-designator coming after a record-mark (‡ ‡).
[148]   E.g., in the sentence "The boy came to our house" (‡ ‡ 31 01 02 51 31 01 ‡ ‡), the patterns extracted would be 310102, 010251, 025131, 513101, a total of four patterns against the six words in the sentence.
[149]   "P" distinguished from "D", the number of *different* patterns.
[150]   Swift's Sample 29 has a total number of words (N) equal to 3324, a total number of 62 sentences. Thus, $3324 - (62 \cdot 2) = 3200$, which is the total number of patterns (P).

gether with the frequency of occurrence of each should take even a computer [151] a relatively long time to do.[152] A person working with pencil and paper might manage it eventually but it is to be feared that by then he would have lost interest in the results and that the monotony of the work would have led to error.

In short, this second processing of the same material might be called a study of word-order in the small. As has been explained, the study of long patterns would have required much larger samples, almost astronomical in fact.[153] Of course, other methods might have been devised to study sentence structure but only by jettisoning the word-class analysis which is considered the basis of this research. It was anticipated that certain preferences in the arrangement of words by various authors would be reflected in different "favorite" patterns, which might serve as identifying fingerprints. This expectation turned out to be naive,[154] but by a kind of serendipity a result materialized which has proved useful, even valuable. This result consists of the remarkable variation in different number of patterns for each author.

Table 6.27 shows under Column D the number of different three-word patterns used by each author in each sample. Column P shows the total number of patterns and Column N the total number of words. The D values show that Swift's numbers of different patterns are almost uniformly higher than those of the other writers. Swift is remarkably consistent, except in Samples 25 and 26 *(Gulliver's Travels),* which drop by nearly one hundred, though the stratified sample has the higher value. Three of the controls, Addison, Johnson and Macaulay, each average around 700, though they all have the peculiarity that one of the samples is about 90 units lower than the other. Johnson's *Rasselas* is lower

[151]   The IBM 1620, with 60K memory and indirect addressing.
[152]   Between 30 and 75 minutes of machine time for each sample.
[153]   If it is required that the sample be three times the size of the number of practical possibilities (which is taken as one-twentieth the number of theoretical possibilities), then Swift's entire canon (estimated as a million words) would be just insufficient for five-word patterns, whose 7.5 million theoretical possibilities would yield 375,000 practical possibilities.
[154]   At least this is so for the works under examination in the given sample sizes. Different-sized samples of authors writing in other traditions at other times might have justified the expectation.

TABLE 6.27

Three-word patterns in Swift and controls, showing number of different patterns (D), total patterns (P) and total words (N)

	D	P	N
10	868	3323	3499
12	864	3338	3500
13	844	3315	3489
20	857	3334	3501
25	789	3343	3509
26	768	3333	3501
29	844	3200	3324

CONTROLS

61	755	3122	3438
62	669	3108	3424
65	657	3298	3490
66	752	3299	3487
71	497	3342	3522
72	440	3290	3482
75	680	3189	3453
76	769	3220	3462

than his *Lives,* a trend which parallels Swift's. But there seems to be no obvious trend in the fluctuation of Macaulay or Addison. Striking as have been Gibbon's departures from the performance of the other writers, I was not quite prepared for the extent to which his variety seems circumscribed. His repertory of patterns is a little more than half of Swift's. And, characteristically enough, his results agree better together than those of the other three controls. But what might be the significance of these results? [155]

The D value represents the number of different arrangements of the twenty-four word-classes in the samples of each author's work. If the value is high, the author would seem to arrange his word-classes in relatively more ways than if it is low. He has, we may assume, a varied repertory of possible syntactical construc-

[155] It may be noticed that the practical possibilities range between 440 and 868 (as against the anticipated 600 to 1200), which is between 3 and 6 per cent of the theoretical possibilities for this sample size. It is evident that the larger the sample the more possibilities are likely to occur, though at a diminishing rate.

tions. A writer whose D value is high would seem to have a style with more syntactical variety than one whose D value is low, like Gibbon's. Of course, variety may be achieved by more means than arrangements of grammatical functions, that is, with word-order. A large vocabulary, for example, or one which reflects choices from several levels of usage, or a wide range of sentence-length may be used to achieve or simulate variety. But probably syntactical variety is more basic and gives a richer texture than other means. It is evident that Swift's style bears not only the outward marks but also the underlying stamp of variety.[156]

Whatever the meaning of this syntactical variety (high D value) may be, it is likely that it will help to identify Swift. Figure 6D gives a picture of the variety (D) levels for our writers. It is true that there is the merest overlap between Swift's 26 and Johnson's 76 and that Macaulay's 61 and Addison's 66 are not very far below, but in combination with other discriminators the D value will doubtless be found reliable. Further, additional samples of each of the others may well cluster around their common midpoint, and Swift's average is well above theirs. Not the specific unit value but the general tendency tells us the meaning of this measurement. Its testimony to Swift's greater variety than three other considerable stylists is irrefutable.[157]

A list of the most frequent three-word patterns of an author, I had hoped, would furnish a guide to his favorite small constructions. Therefore a matter of the first interest in the study of the results of the pattern processing is the identity of these favorite patterns. Table 6.28 tells the surprising tale of the three most frequent patterns in each sample. In every case the single most frequent pattern is the same (513101), and the two that follow

[156] Variety has always been considered a desirable quality in writers (as in women, if Enobarbus's "infinite variety" tribute to Cleopatra is representative) and therefore the temptation is great to credit it to one's own man and deny it to others. Both Swift and Gibbon, of course, have been awarded it (Jefferson, *From Dryden to Johnson,* p. 231 and Bond, p. 136).
[157] It is naturally possible to regard Swift's variety as instability and Gibbon's monotony as steadiness. Such is the risk of subjective response. Lucas, *Style,* endorses variety achieved by consciously manipulating sentence length as well as variety in "mood, feeling, and tone" (p. 109).

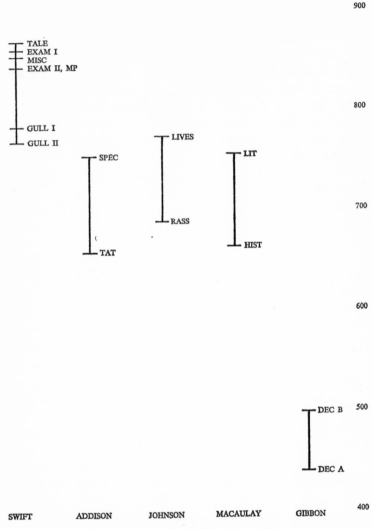

Figure 6d—Actual values of D for Swift and controls

are only slightly less uniform. In the entire table there are five exceptions to the standard order, which is 513101, 310151, and 015131. This find is not quite as surprising as it might be, for 513101 is the pattern of the prepositional phrase (preposition, article, noun). On the basis of this result it can be unhesitatingly declared the most frequent three-word structure in the language.[158]

The most frequent pattern (Column 1) is the prepositional phrase in regular order. The second most frequent is of the form article, noun, preposition ("the man of") and the third most frequent, noun, preposition, article ("man of the"). It will be noticed that all three of these are in whole or in part prepositional phrases. And as for the exceptions, there are only two, the others merely being displaced from the standard ranking. The exceptions are 310301 (article, adjective, noun: "the good man"), which might be part of an expanded prepositional phrase, and 015101 (noun, preposition, noun: "man of courage"), which includes a minimal prepositional phrase. All this suggests the commanding

TABLE 6.28

The three most frequent three-word patterns in Swift and controls

	1	2	3
10	513101	*310301*	015131
12	513101	310151	015131
13	513101	310151	015131
20	513101	310151	015131
25	513101	*015131*	*310151**
26	513101	310151	015131
29	513101	310151	015131

CONTROLS

	1	2	3
61	513101	310151	015131
62	513101	310151	*310301*
65	513101	310151	015131
66	513101	310151	015131
71	513101	310151	015131
72	513101	310151	015131
75	513101	310151	015131
76	513101	310151	*015101*

* The difference between Rank 2 and 3 for Sample 25 is minute: 111 to 109 occurrences.

[158] It might in fact be named the most common construction of any size in English. A study by E. L. Thorndike et al., "An Inventory of Grammatical Constructions, with Measures of their Importance", *Teachers College Record,* March 1927, pp. 580-610, supports this finding, although his categories are not commensurable with those used here.

position of the prepositional phrase in the inventory of English syntactical structures.[159]

However, it is not specifically the prepositional phrase which we are considering here but pattern 513101, which is only one possible form of the prepositional phrase. Inasmuch as this pattern is everyone's favorite, it is fruitless to look for individual variation in the identity of the favorite pattern. Perhaps it resides in the quantitative distribution. Table 6.29 shows the relative frequencies of the most frequent pattern. Except for Gibbon, whose nominal style makes him the heaviest user of prepositions, the figures are indistinguishably bunched. The pattern 513101 seems to have an overall frequency of around five per cent. It is again remarked that the three samples drawn from fiction (25, 26 and 75) are out of line with their fellows.

TABLE 6.29

Frequency distribution of the most frequent single three-word pattern (513101), in actual occurrences and as a percentage of total patterns (P)

	Count	Percentage
10	143	4.3
12	180	5.4
13	163	4.9
20	163	4.9
25	184	5.5
26	210	6.3
29	163	5.1

CONTROLS

	Count	Percentage
61	150	4.8
62	150	4.8
65	163	4.9
66	163	4.9
71	222	6.6
72	249	7.6
75	177	5.5
76	160	5.0

[159] No exact estimate is made of the number of prepositional phrases per sentence because sentences vary so much in size from work to work, author to author, period to period. However, there seems to be a prepositional phrase every eight or nine words (more in Gibbon): two in a Macaulay sentence, four in a Swift-sized one.

If we turn from the most frequent pattern to the least frequent, we have a considerable choice, for the number of patterns which occurs only once is very large. Table 6.30 shows the relation between the total number of words (N), the total number of Patterns (P), the different number of Patterns (D), and the number of patterns appearing only once (I). The main item of interest is the last column, which shows how great a percentage of the total number of patterns those patterns which occurred with a frequency of one represent. Oddly enough, they appear to be fifty per cent of each value of D, regardless of the relative size of that number. Gibbon's unique patterns occur slightly less than half of the time and Swift's slightly more. But essentially all the samples show a uniform relation of these two characteristics.

That the one-time patterns should total half (more or less) of the number of different patterns is very curious but it is also misleading. It may suggest that this proportion would hold for samples of any size. A moment's thought will suggest that this is

TABLE 6.30

Number of patterns appearing only once (I) as a percentage of the number of different patterns (D), showing also number of words in sample (N) and number of total patterns (P), for whole samples of Swift and controls

	N	P	D	I	I/D
10	3499	3323	868	458	52.8
12	3500	3338	864	458	53.0
13	3489	3315	844	457	54.1
20	3501	3334	857	442	51.6
25	3509	3343	789	397	50.3
26	3501	3333	768	401	52.2
29	3324	3200	844	432	51.2

CONTROLS

	N	P	D	I	I/D
61	3438	3122	755	377	49.9
62	3424	3108	669	330	49.3
65	3490	3298	657	329	50.1
66	3487	3299	752	402	53.5
71	3522	3342	497	239	48.1
72	3482	3290	440	212	48.2
75	3453	3189	680	355	52.2
76	3462	3220	769	408	53.1

unlikely. For instance in a sentence (sample of 25 words) it is possible that all the patterns will have a frequency of one. As the sample is increased, individual preferences and the organizing tendency of the language compel the re-use of more patterns until the number of available possibilities is almost exhausted.[160] So, as the sample becomes larger, the number of different patterns and the number of unique patterns increase at a decreasing rate. No particular linguistic reason requires that the curves diverge. A comparison of the rather complex values involved in these relationships is shown in Table 6.31.[161] The first column shows (first for Gibbon, then for Swift) the fraction or multiple of the standard sample used for the calculation. The actual number of words (N) is given in Column 2. Columns 3 and 4 show the total number of three-word patterns (P) and the number of different patterns (D), a distinction exactly parallel to the total number of words in a piece of writing and its vocabulary (different words).[162] Column 5 shows the number of different patterns each of which occurs only once (I). Columns 2-5 give the actual numerical values of the quantities. Columns 6, 7 and 8 are percentages representing ratios between various pairs. Column 6 shows the varying relationship between I and D, that is, the decreasing percentages of D represented by I as P increases. In other words, as the size of the sample increases (by doubling) from 55 words to 7000 and beyond, the number of different patterns and the number of unique patterns increase, *at different decreasing rates*. Their respective relationship to P is expressed in Columns 7 and 8 and their relationship to each other is given in Column 6. To make the abstract relations easier to visualize, however, five graphs have been included, Figures 6E, 6F, 6G, 6H, and 6I. Figures 6E, 6F and 6G represent the relationships $\frac{I}{D}$, $\frac{D}{P}$ and $\frac{I}{P}$ respectively, the same as Columns 6, 7 and 8 of Table 6.31, taken vertically, one

---

[160]   It follows the same general trend as vocabulary items, as described in the Zipf curve. See Miller, *Language and Communication,* pp. 90-93.

[161]   Values for Gibbon were taken from his two samples (71 and 72); those used for Swift include 10, 12, 13 and 20.

[162]   This is the type-token ratio. See Miller, pp. 122-124.

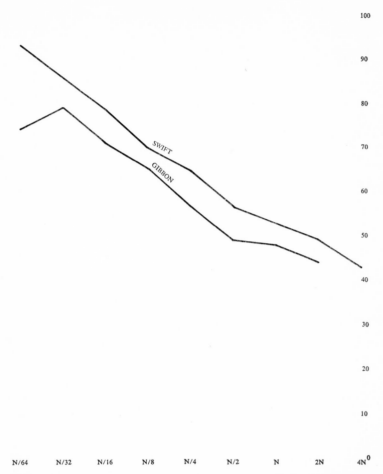

Figure 6e—Unique patterns (I) as a percentage of different patterns in doubling sizes of sample (N) for Swift & Gibbon: $\dfrac{I}{D}$

at a time. Figures 6H and 6I represent the performances of Gibbon and Swift, respectively, in all three relationships.

To examine Figure 6F first $\dfrac{D}{P}$, we find that the smallest fractional samples (55 words) included some patterns that are re-

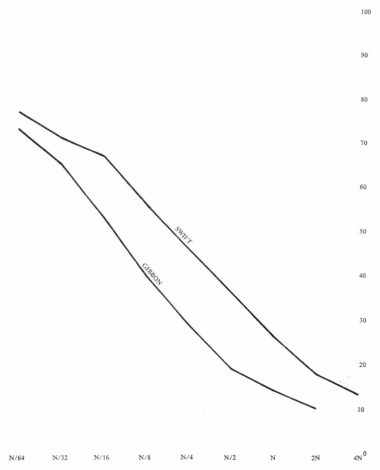

Figure 6f—Different patterns (D) as a percentage of total patterns (P) in doubling sizes of sample (N) for Swift & Gibbon: $\dfrac{D}{P}$

peated, though the largest proportion occur only once. As samples become larger, the patterns begin to repeat more and more at a steady rate (indicated by the more or less straight line) until another change occurs (at 1750 words for Gibbon and 7000 for Swift) and the number of different patterns ceases to diminish as

TABLE 6.31

Comparison of the relative changes in D and I for two samples of Gibbon and four of Swift as the size of the sample increases, showing N, P, D and I as number of actual occurrences and I/D, D/P and I/P as percentages

1.	2.	3.	4.	5.	6.	7.	8.
Sample	N	P	D	I	I/D	D/P	I/P
			GIBBON				
N/64	55	52	38	28	74.0	73.0	54.0
N/32	110	104	68	53	78.0	65.0	51.0
N/16	220	207	110	78	71.0	53.0	38.0
N/8	440	414	167	108	65.0	40.0	26.0
N/4	875	828	238	135	57.0	29.0	16.0
N/2	1750	1658	324	160	49.0	19.0	9.0
N	3500	3316	468	225	48.0	14.0	7.0
2N	7000	6632	652	289	44.0	10.0	4.0
			SWIFT				
N/64	55	52	40	37	93.0	77.0	71.0
N/32	110	104	74	64	86.0	71.0	62.0
N/16	220	208	139	109	78.0	67.0	52.0
N/8	440	416	235	165	70.0	56.0	40.0
N/4	875	832	379	246	65.0	46.0	30.0
N/2	1750	1664	592	335	57.0	36.0	20.0
N	3500	3328	858	454	53.0	26.0	14.0
2N	7000	6611	1251	608	49.0	18.0	9.0
4N	14000	13311	1699	727	43.0	13.0	5.0

regularly as it has. That the two lines are parallel for much of the distances tells us that the process is common to both Gibbon and Swift and may be a constant of linguistic statistics.

Similarly Figure 6G reveals that the percentage of unique patterns diminishes steadily until the half-sample size is reached (1750 words), when it takes a turn upward. If it had continued at the same rate, a point would have been quickly reached when the number of unique patterns would have been zero. Theoretically, (and perhaps practically too), if an author writes enough, he will sooner or later have used every pattern he is capable of (as also every item of his vocabulary). In actual fact, this probably does not happen, but curve $\frac{I}{P}$ must intersect zero at some no very distant point: eventually every combination must have been

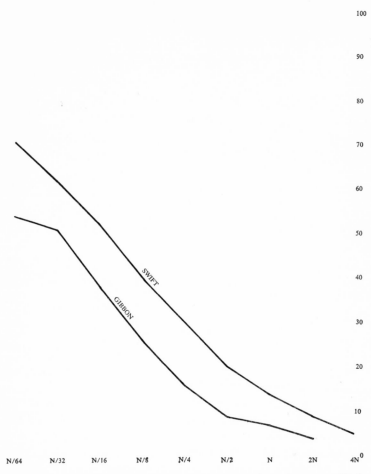

Figure 6g—Unique patterns (I) as a percentage of total patterns (P) in doubling sizes of sample (N) for Swift & Gibbon: $\dfrac{I}{P}$

used more than once. The same is not true of $\dfrac{D}{P}$, the relation of different to total patterns. The number of different patterns is finite. No matter how big the sample becomes, the number of different patterns cannot go beyond a certain point. Therefore, if D

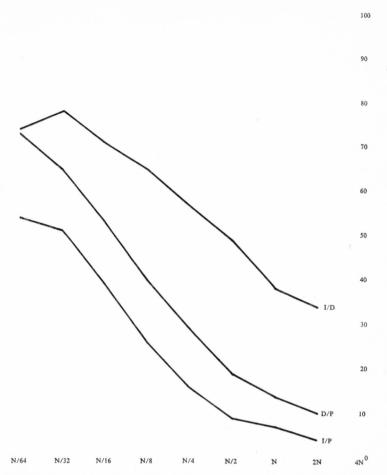

Figure 6h—Relationship of total, different and unique patterns for Gibbon, in doubling sizes of sample, expressed as percentage ratios

and $\frac{D}{P}$ remain steady while P increases, the numerical equivalent of the expression $\frac{D}{P}$ will become a smaller and smaller percentage but it can never become zero. The superficial resemblance between the curves in Figures 6F and 6G is due to the fact that the

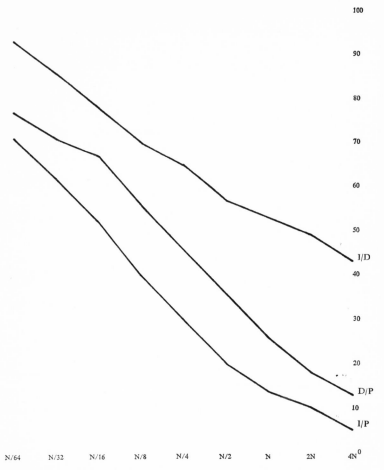

Figure 6i—Relationship of total, different and unique patterns for Swift, in doubling sizes of sample, expressed as percentage ratios

sample size never reaches those values where the distinction would be operative.

Figure 6E, which represents the inter-relation of I and D seems to occupy a higher-valued area of the graph. We have seen that unique patterns (I) and different patterns (D) increase at different falling rates, but that their eventual fates differ. Eventually

I vanishes (when every pattern has been used at least once), but D must continue to grow till it reaches its limit, practical or theoretical – until all available different patterns are in use. D's progress is plain but I is deceptive because its domination might not become apparent until a sample of several million had been taken, a whole population. From Figure 6E, it looks as if the value I will remain at or near 30-40 per cent of D for values of N up to 16 or 32 (50,000-100,000 words). As the foregoing discussion suggests, the relations $\frac{I}{P}$ and $\frac{D}{P}$ are more likely to resemble each other, in the work of one author for samples of 14000 words or less than $\frac{I}{D}$, as is clearly shown in Figures 6H and 6I, where the three curves are compared for each author separately. In both of these Figures, the two lower curves are very closely approximative, whereas the upper one is divergent. What these relationships seem to point to, more than anything, is the uniform behavior of languages in the gross. Gibbon and Swift are very different writers but certain uncontrollable forces compel them to use the language at something like the same rate, in a manner almost determined. It would be difficult for a writer deliberately to alter his performances on these curves. But too much must not be made of this uniformity, which proceeds after all in part from

TABLE 6.32

The ten most frequent three-word patterns in all the samples combined, ranked in descending order and showing equivalents in English

1. Rank	2. Pattern			3. English Equivalent
1.	51	31	01	of the man
2.	31	01	51	the man of
3.	01	51	31	man of the
4.	31	03	01	the good man
5.	01	51	01	man of goodness
6.	01	41	01	man and boy
7.	03	01	51	good man of
8.	51	31	03	of the good
9.	31	01	41	the man and
10.	02	51	31	went to the

the simple fact that they are speaking the same language, whose mutual comprehensibility depends on internal uniformity. Moreover, since our interest is in individual differences, it would be well to turn to the question whether any individuality is detectable in the choice and preference of three-word patterns.

Some emphasis was placed on the interesting discovery that all the writers agree in their most favorite patterns. The three most frequent nearly coincide. Let us see how this agreement holds for places other than the first three. If all the samples are combined, the ten most common patterns are those given in Column 2 of Table 6.32.[163] Table 6.33 [164] shows the relative rank

TABLE 6.33

Relative rank of the ten most frequent patterns, by individual whole sample

	1.	2.	3.	4.	5.	6.	7.	8.	9.	10.
	513101	310151	015131	310301	015101	014101	030151	513103	310141	025131
10	1	4	3	2	5	6	7	8	9	10
12	1	2	3	4	6	9		8	5	7
13	1	2	3	4	5		8	10	7	
20	1	2	3	4	5		6	7		8
25	1	3	2	4	6		9	8	5	10
26	1	2	3	4	9			10	5	8
29	1	2	3	4	5	7	6	10	8	

CONTROLS

	1.	2.	3.	4.	5.	6.	7.	8.	9.	10.
61	1	2	3	5	4		9	8		10
62	1	2	4	3	5		7	6		8
65	1	2	3	4	5		7	6	10	
66	1	2	3	4	5	10	7	6	9	
71	1	2	3	4	6		7	5	10	8
72	1	2	3	4	5	6	10	7	8	9
75	1	2	3	7	6				5	9
76	1	2	4	5	3		9		8	

Note: blanks show that pattern ranked lower than tenth.

[163] Column 3 gives equivalents in English.
[164] The number in each vertical space designates the rank held by each pattern among the most frequent for a given sample. If the space is empty the rank of the pattern is lower than tenth.

TABLE 6.34a

*Distribution of the 18 Most Frequent Patterns in the combined samples
(MFP), ranked in numerical order, as a percentage of total patterns (P),
for Swift samples*

Pattern	10	12	13	20	25	26	29	x̄
012102	.7	.7	.7	.5	.5	.4	.5	.6
014101	1.7	1.1	.8	1.0	1.1	.6	1.2	1.1
015101	2.0	1.5	2.0	2.0	1.4	1.2	2.0	1.7
015131	2.8	3.3	3.2	3.3	3.3	3.2	3.2	3.2
023101	1.1	.9	1.3	1.1	1.3	1.7	.9	1.2
025131	1.2	1.3	1.1	1.1	1.2	1.2	1.0	1.2
030141	.6	.4	.3	.6	.5	.5	.6	.5
030151	1.6	.9	1.3	1.5	1.2	1.0	1.6	1.3
112102	.7	.6	1.1	.7	.8	.8	.4	.7
210251	.6	.7	.7	.8	.5	.7	.7	.7
310121	1.0	1.1	1.1	1.1	.7	1.3	1.2	1.1
310141	1.5	1.9	1.4	1.0	1.5	2.0	1.2	1.5
310151	2.7	4.0	3.7	3.8	3.3	3.5	3.5	3.5
310301	3.0	2.0	2.2	2.4	2.5	2.1	2.2	2.3
313101	1.2	.7	1.7	1.0	1.0	1.0	.7	1.0
510151	.5	.5	.6	.7	.5	.5	1.0	.6
513101	4.3	5.4	4.9	4.9	5.5	6.3	5.1	5.2
513103	1.5	1.2	1.2	1.2	1.2	1.2	1.0	1.2

TABLE 6.34b

Control samples

Pattern	61	62	65	66	71	72	75	76
012102	.8	.7	.3	.6	1.3	1.7	1.3	1.0
014101	1.1	1.0	1.0	1.2	1.3	2.6	1.0	.7
015101	2.8	3.1	2.3	1.9	2.8	3.9	1.8	2.9
015131	2.9	3.6	3.9	3.9	5.8	6.2	2.9	2.4
023101	1.6	.9	1.5	1.6	1.4	1.9	2.3	1.7
025131	1.1	1.6	1.4	1.0	2.2	2.2	1.5	.8
030141	.9	.7	.8	.7	.8	.7	.4	.8
030151	1.4	1.8	1.8	1.5	2.5	2.0	.6	1.2
112102	.5	.5	1.7	.8	.5	.4	1.2	.8
210251	.6	1.2	1.2	.8	1.7	1.8	1.1	1.0
310121	1.6	1.2	.7	.6	1.3	1.2	1.5	1.6
310141	1.0	1.0	1.4	1.5	1.5	1.4	1.9	1.2
310151	4.8	4.6	4.1	4.4	6.2	7.0	3.7	4.1
310301	2.8	3.9	3.1	3.2	5.3	4.7	1.6	1.9
313101	.6	.9	1.2	1.0	.3	.3	.7	.5
510151	.5	.8	.7	.6	.2	.8	.8	.6
513101	4.8	4.8	4.9	4.9	6.6	7.6	5.5	5.0
513103	1.4	1.9	1.8	1.7	3.3	2.5	1.0	.9

of each of these ten most popular patterns in each sample. The rankings show the perfect agreement in the first place and the substantial though decreasing agreement in the next three.[165] On the whole, there is no more agreement on the Swift side than on the controls' side. Obviously, individual preference cannot assert itself by means of this instrument either. Sample size, type of composition, inadequate pattern size, may be the variables that interfere with the expression of individual preference. It seems odd that three-word units should be less able to illustrate individual choice than words taken singly as parts of speech. Perhaps, however, the items are not sufficiently grouped. After all, the most common pattern appears only 7.6 per cent of the time. A new grouping may be constructed from the most frequent patterns.

If the ten most frequent patterns in each sample are selected (instead of the ten applicable to all samples) and combined, all together, we find that there are eighteen in all. In other words, there is so much overlap that eighteen patterns include the ten most frequent patterns for every sample. If these are arranged in numerical order and the percentage of the total (P) is computed for each one, the result looks like that in Tables 6.34a and 6.34b. The sum of the 18 Most Frequent Patterns varies between 28.0 per cent (Swift) and 49.9 per cent (Gibbon). The values are well-bunched but the information they give us is not entirely new. The totals, as given in Column 3 of Table 6.35 are clearly related to the D values of the various samples.[166] The more different patterns there are (the higher the D) the lesser percentage of the total will be included in any number of most frequent patterns: Swift's patterns are most numerous and his total is lowest; Gibbon has the fewest and his total is the highest. Nonetheless, the information supplied by this order is important when it is finally elicited.

It may be noticed that among the patterns listed in Tables

---

[165] Only two samples (Swift 10 and *Decline B*) contain all ten patterns and are therefore most typical of the whole group in the matter of most frequent patterns. None of the samples reproduces the preferred order of the whole group.

[166] Cf. Table 6.27 and Figure 6D.

TABLE 6.35

Verb and non-verb component of 18 Most Frequent Patterns (MFP),
as a percentage of total three-word patterns (P)

	1. Verb	2. Non-Verb	3. Total
10	5.3	23.4	28.7
12	5.3	22.9	28.2
13	6.0	23.3	29.3
20	5.3	23.4	28.7
25	5.0	23.0	28.0
26	6.1	23.1	29.2
29	4.7	23.3	28.0

CONTROLS

61	6.2	25.0	31.2
62	6.1	28.1	34.2
65	6.8	27.0	33.8
66	5.4	26.5	31.9
71	8.4	36.5	44.9
72	8.2	41.7	49.9
75	8.9	21.9	30.8
76	6.9	22.2	29.1

6.34 are some that include the finite verb designators 02 and 21. There are six of these: 012102, 023101, 025131, 112102, 210251, 310121. The other twelve include the designators 01, 03, 11, 31, 41 and 51, which may be called nominal or non-verb. If these two components are totalled separately and the results are compared, they fall into a certain order, as shown by Table 6.35. The non-verb component, plotted on Figure 6J, clusters very satisfactorily for each author. This information of course resembles the nominal-verbal ratio [167] computed earlier, but these results are more distinct. Apart from supporting the evidence of the earlier test, they provide an additional feature in Swift's stylistic profile.

INTRODUCTORY CONNECTIVES

Before proceeding to the concluding stage of this discussion, one more feature may be considered, though it was taken up earlier. In Chapter III, Swift's propensity for opening his sentences with

[167] See Table 6.24.

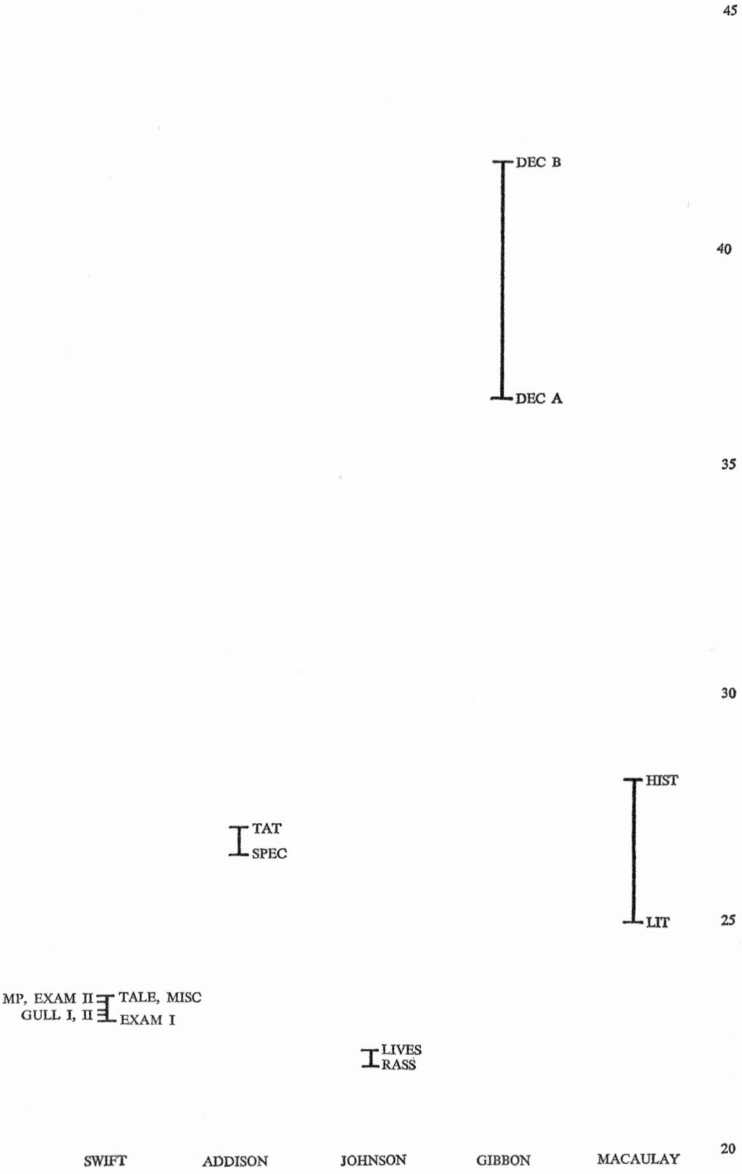

Figure 6j—Values of non-verb component of 18 Most-frequent-patterns (MFP), as the sum of percentages of different patterns

connectives was documented. Using the different texts now under scrutiny, the same feature may again be inspected. The relevant connectives are coordinating (41) and subordinating conjunctions (42) and conjunctive adverbs (91).

The first element of each sentence is tabulated and the occurrence of each word-class as first sentence-element is expressed as a percentage of the total number of sentences in each sample. Since sentence-lengths vary, there are more sentences in some samples than in others, a factor which might introduce a question about the strict comparability of the data. The reliability, however, is not at all doubtful: the figures are closely verified by earlier tests; the differences are so clear-cut as to be unmistakable. Tabel 6.36 shows the over-all pattern of first sentence-element preference.

Certain general preferences can be seen to assert themselves: some word-classes are never called on (05, 07, 32), some are very infrequent (02, 04, 06, 33 . . .), some are very popular (11, 31). Individual preferences emerge very easily. Swift is not partial to initial nouns, which are usually names. It is obvious why Macaulay-Historical (62), Gibbon (71) and Johnson *Lives* (76) should be highest in this row. Pronouns are naturally very popular among writers of personal essays and of fiction: therefore Addison is highest, *Rasselas* and *Gulliver* next, Gibbon and the *Lives of the Poets*, lowest. Swift, Addison and Johnson are lowest in opening articles, Gibbon and Macaulay highest. Of the remainder, only Classes 41 and 91 show a pronounced tendency. But if they are grouped with Class 42 and the results totalled, the tendency is striking. Table 6.37 gives this interesting layout. The "Total" Column demonstrates Swift's overwhelmingly greater use of initial connectives than the controls: over-all it is on the order of three to one. Though there is a certain dispersion in Swift's samples (24.0 to 41.8), it can be accounted for easily. The two lowest are the *Gulliver* samples, which being fiction probably require less intense connection. *Rasselas*, similarly, is the lowest of the controls. The remainder fluctuate within a range centering around 11.5.[168]

[168] Compare the results of the manual count, shown in Column "Manual"

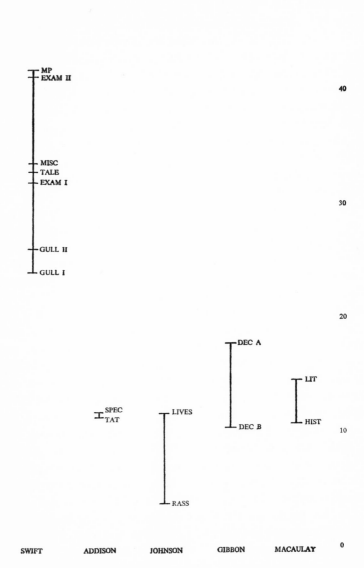

Figure 6k—Introductory connectives (IC) as a percentage of total sentences for Swift & controls

TABLE 6.36a

First sentence-elements by word-class, as a percentage of total sentences

Class	10	12	13	20	25	26	29
01	2.3	2.5	1.1		1.2	2.4	3.2
02	1.1			1.2		1.2	
03		2.5				2.4	
04							
05							
06				1.2			1.6
07							
08			1.1				
11	12.5	25.9	19.5	20.4	37.3	27.3	32.2
21	3.4	1.2	4.6	3.6			
31	20.4	18.5	16.1	18.1	20.4	23.8	9.7
32							
33		1.2	1.1				
34	3.4		1.1	1.2	2.4	1.2	
41	12.5	14.8	26.4	19.2	16.8	13.1	19.3
42	2.3	9.7	10.3	7.2	3.6	7.1	1.6
43	2.3	2.5	1.1			4.8	1.6
44				3.6			
45			1.1				
51	11.3	7.4	6.8	4.8	8.2	7.1	3.2
61	8.0	4.9	4.6	7.2	6.0	2.4	6.5
71	2.3						
81						1.2	
91	18.1	7.4	4.6	7.2	3.6	5.9	20.9
Total Sentences	88	81	87	83	83	84	62

As for the components of the "Total" figure, it is curious that there is considerable fluctuation there. Apparently, when a connective is wanted, it is not a matter of consistent preference which type is chosen. Thus Swift Samples *Examiner II* (13) and *Modest Proposal* (29), which have nearly identical totals, vary considerably in the way they reach them: 13 has many *but*s and *if*s and few *however*s, whereas 29 has almost no *if*s but a plethora of *however*s. Less extreme fluctuations of the same kind may be seen in the other writers. At any rate this demonstration confirms

in Table 6.37. Results are averaged for each author. Gibbon was not included among the controls in the manual count.

TABLE 6.36b

Control samples

	Macaulay		Addison		Gibbon		Johnson	
Class	61	62	65	66	71	72	75	76
01	6.3	10.8	1.0	5.3	7.8	3.1	8.3	14.9
02							1.5	
03	1.3	2.5		1.1	1.1	1.0	1.5	.8
04	.6				1.1		.8	
05								
06	.6						1.5	
07								
08						1.0		
11	24.7	19.0	43.8	40.4	7.8	3.1	35.6	14.0
21		.6	3.1	3.2		1.0	1.5	.8
31	32.9	33.5	25.0	23.4	43.3	49.0	23.5	27.3
32								
33		1.9				1.0	.8	.8
34	.6	5.7	1.0		2.2	2.1	1.5	3.3
41	10.1	7.0	3.1	3.2	11.1	8.3	3.8	5.8
42	3.8	3.2	4.2	8.5	6.7	2.1		3.3
43							.8	1.7
44				1.1			3.0	
45	1.3		1.0		1.1			
51	11.4	9.5	5.1	7.4	14.4	25.0	7.6	18.2
61	5.1	4.4	8.3	6.4	3.3	2.1	2.3	9.9
71							3.0	
81	.6	1.3				1.0		
91	.6	.6	4.1					2.5
Total Sentences	158	158	96	94	90	96	132	121

Swift's position as a writer with high connective emphasis,[169] a characteristic which may reasonably be used to help identify his work.

THE SWIFT PROFILE

A great deal of information is produced by such analysis as has just been described. Some of the ways of organizing the resulting data have been detailed. Naturally, from the viewpoint of the

[169] The same test was applied to closing sentence-elements, but the results only revealed that nouns (01) are everyone's favorite way of ending a sen-

identification of styles not all are successes. Both successes and failures have been encountered and discussed. Failures, of course, are such only if the elicitation of individual differences is a requirement. Otherwise, they are aspects of the language itself, linguistic constants. A knowledge of these is not without value, but they are not dwelt on here because the concern is with the particulars.

The details of individual difference for the groupings and rapprochements discussed in the foregoing may be found summarized in Table 6.38.[170] This list of the eleven most meaningful tests

TABLE 6.37

Total introductory connectives, for Swift and controls, as a percentage of all introductory elements, showing individual values for the three connective word-classes

	41	42	91	Total	Manual
10	12.5	2.3	18.1	32.9	
12	14.8	9.7	7.4	31.9	
13	26.4	10.3	4.6	41.3	
20	19.2	7.2	7.2	33.6	
25	16.8	3.6	3.6	24.0	
26	13.1	7.1	5.9	26.1	
29	19.3	1.6	20.9	41.8	
$\bar{x}$	17.4	6.0	9.8	33.1	33.9
CONTROLS					
61	10.1	3.8	.6	14.5	13.0*
62	7.0	3.2	.6	10.8	
65	3.1	4.2	4.1	11.4	15.9*
66	3.2	8.5	—	11.7	
71	11.1	6.7	—	17.8	
72	8.3	2.1	—	10.4	
75	3.8	—	—	3.8	13.4*
76	5.8	3.3	2.5	11.6	
$\bar{x}$	6.6	4.0	1.0	11.6	
Total $\bar{x}$	11.6	4.9	5.0	21.6	

* Average for each author.

tence, from a minimum of 55.9 per cent (Swift's 26) and reaching a maximum of 92.8 per cent (Gibbon's 72). No other word-class showed enough distinctiveness to offer competition. See Appendix F.

[170] All values are averages for each author. Rank 1 means highest.

shows how each author ranked in each test and the respective values achieved. The noteworthy aspect of this Table is not the absolute rank but the relative ranks of Swift and various controls. Thus Swift and Gibbon are found at the extremes on three occasions and nearly so on four more. Only twice are they in contiguous places. Gibbon and Swift, however, we expect to be different. What of Addison and Swift? They are in contiguous places on six occasions and obviously quite difficult to keep apart. However they are very well separated on three occasions (6.14, 6.27 and 6.37) and these three are obviously crucial to the success of this demonstration because they are not only very clear-cut but theoretically meaningful criteria. They will be used to construct the style profile of Swift.

Not only Addison, but Johnson has been found similar to Swift in the course of the study. The Table shows eight occasions when Swift and Johnson were in contiguous places, which argues a remarkable affinity between these two Tories. Johnson's dislike

TABLE 6.38

Summary table of identification criteria for all authors showing relative rank and value for each criterion

Table No.	Swift Rk	Val.	Addison Rk	Val.	Johnson Rk	Val.	Gibbon Rk	Val.	Macaulay Rk	Val.	Description
6.10	1	61.6	2	61.0	3	59.2	5	55.7	4	57.5	FW
6.11	1	10.2	3	10.0	2	10.1	4	9.2	5	8.5	C
6.12	2	20.4	3	20.5	5	18.5	1	21.3	4	19.9	M
6.13	4	14.4	3	14.9	1	17.1	5	12.4	2	15.0	VA
*6.14	1	4.1	4	2.6	2	3.3	5	1.7	3	2.7	VB
6.24	4	1.9	3	2.0	5	1.8	1	3.5	2	2.3	Nominal-Verbal Ratio
6.26	4	57	3	69	5	46	1	93	2	82	AVQ
*6.27	1	833	4	704	2	724	5	468	3	712	D
6.29	3	5.2	4	4.9	2	5.3	1	7.1	5	4.8	513101
6.35	4	23.2	2	26.7	5	22.0	1	39.1	3	26.5	Non-Verb MFP
*6.37	1	33.1	5	11.5	2	15.4	3	14.1	4	12.6	Introductory Connectives

* Constituent of the Profile.

of Swift is probably a symptom of that kinship.[171] That it should
be reflected quantitatively is extremely interesting, but it does
not threaten the usefulness of the discriminators, partly because
of the distance between them in at least two (6.27 and 6.37) and
partly because refinements are available to supplement the present
set of discriminators, if necessary.[172] The success of this approach
lies in its ability to discriminate between the related pairs: Swift
and Addison, Johnson and Gibbon.[173]

If Table 6.39 is examined, it will be found to contain, under
Columns 1, 2 and 3, the discriminators derived from the author's
use of verbals (VB), from pattern quantity (D), and from devotion to introductory connectives (IC). The values given in each
column are the result of considering the average for Swift as 100
per cent and calculating the departures from it. Thus, Gibbon's
1.9 VB value is less than half as big as Swift's average, 4.1, 46
per cent of it, in fact. Gibbon's value in Column 1 is therefore 46.
The same obtains for all the other values. Swift's samples are
shown individually and are therefore naturally to be found
grouped around their own average. Figure 6L[174] attempts to
display the consanguinity of the Swift samples and their lack of
kinship to the others. The family likeness [175] is attested to by the
relative exiguity of the cross-hatched area, within which is enclosed all the dispersion of the Swift samples around their own
mean. The lack of kinship to the others is demonstrated by the

---

[171]   It has been explicitly noticed by literary men, e.g., W. B. C. Watkins,
Perilous Balance (Princeton, 1939), pp. 25-48, and implicitly by those who,
like G. M. Trevelyan, make a point of comparing the two men's styles: *An
Autobiography and Other Essays* (London, 1949), p. 210.

[172]   E.g. Class 31 in Table 6.12; Tables 6.7 and 6.8, passim.

[173]   According to Leo Rockas's unpublished Ph.D. Dissertation, "The Description of Style: Dr. Johnson and His Critics" (Michigan, 1960), Johnson's critics have not been able to differentiate his style "from a style more
closely similar to Johnson's, for example Gibbon's" (*Dissertation Abstracts,*
XXI, 339). Table 6.38 shows with what success I have been able to accomplish this differentiation.

[174]   Rankings of individual authors for each discriminator, as well as for
the other criteria, may be consulted in Table 6.38.

[175]   No attempt is made to demonstrate the likeness of the control pairs,
partly because of their insufficient number, though some kinship is clearly
evident.

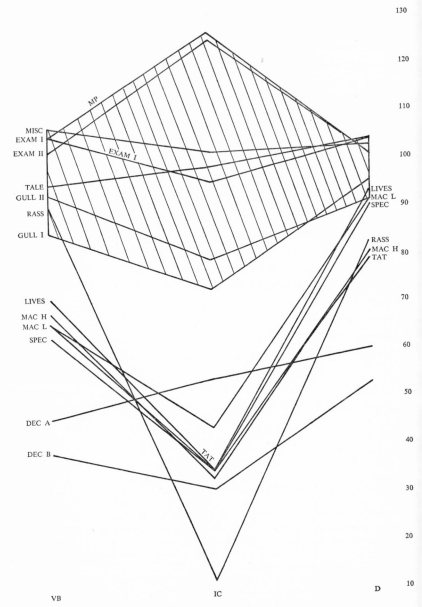

Figure 6l—Three-discriminator profile of the style of Swift and controls, all values being expressed as percentages of Swift's average

TABLE 6.39

Three-discriminator style profile (normalized)

	1 VB	2 I.C.	3 D
10	95	99	104
12	105	96	104
13	102	125	101
20	107	102	103
25	85	73	95
26	93	79	92
29	105	126	101
$\bar{x}$	100	100	100

CONTROLS

61	66	44	91
62	68	33	80
65	66	34	79
66	63	35	90
71	46	54	60
72	39	31	53
75	90	12	82
76	71	35	92

minimal impingement of the controls' lines on the cross-hatched area. One such line timidly crosses a corner under the first criterion and another line just touches the lowest edge under the third criterion.

The three criteria in the profile are not random choices: they are meaningful features of style. The emphasis on verbals that reflects a modernizing element in Swift; the variety of patterns; the use of introductory connectives – all these point to important aspects of the man's thought and personality. But in presenting this profile, I do not intend to suggest that it is a real epitome of the analysis described. It is both a symbol and a shortcut. If it should be desired to test the attribution of a work to Swift,[176] the

[176] It should be kept in mind that the preceding analysis (especially the profile) is Swift-oriented. If it is desired to test attribution to some other author, that author's work would require an analysis of this sort in which *his* salient features were brought out. In fact, if Macaulay were central to an investigation, some discriminators would be sought which would place

matter may be quickly verified by reference to the three points of the profile. But to produce the confidence required by responsible investigation, the entire analysis should be gone through and each detail of the physiognomy scrutinized. However convenient it might be to be able to identify a work on the basis of a single criterion of style, writers are too complex for that. Within the limited context of word-class and pattern analysis, the total picture should be allowed to develop, if we are to say with any certainty that such and such a composition is the work of this or that hand.

him in the foreground. If, in the present set of figures, he does not seem to have a clear-cut position, that is because he is not a protagonist but a control.

VII. A CASE IN POINT: *A LETTER TO A YOUNG POET*

The previous chapters of this study have attempted to bring together a number of peculiarities in Swift's style partly in the hope of developing a reliable method of attribution by internal evidence. In Chapter VI, particularly, a systematic approach to a quantitative method was undertaken. The goal of such an approach, of course, is a wholly objective method, one that does not depend on a special interpretation of the data in order to yield uniform results. Although it is true that subjective attribution can be quite accurate,[1] it is not really a method in that everyone's subjective attribution will not yield the same results.[2] No discounts for the subjective interpretation of evidence are required

---

[1] For instance, Jacob E. Cooke's attribution of the disputed papers in *The Federalist* (Cleveland and New York, 1961) to Madison is made on the basis of circumstantial evidence (pp. xxix-xxx). This procedure, despite its dependence on external evidence, is plainly subjective: the assessment of how plausible the evidence is must be a personally variable matter. Cooke rejects the usefulness of internal evidence in this dispute because of the "remarkably similar prose styles of Madison and Hamilton" (p. xxviii). If the conclusions of the Harvard Federalist Project are accepted, Cooke's subjective attribution is validated by the objective methods he considered uncertain (See Appendix D).

[2] C. W. Everett, in his edition of the *Letters of Junius* (London, 1927), ascribed them to the Earl of Shelburne on what appeared at the time to be sound circumstantial grounds, though the reviewer in the *Times Literary Supplement* (March 8, 1928), did not take the attribution seriously (p. 161) and though no one else in modern times has done so. Alvar Ellegård, however, surveying the same evidence, dismisses the attribution and establishes the authorship of Sir Philip Francis by internal evidence in *Who Was Junius?* (Stockholm, 1962), pp. 89-90 and *A Statistical Method for Determining Authorship* (Göteborg, 1962), passim. See Appendix G.

in the method I propose. This claim can be both illustrated and tested by reference to a work of disputed authorship in the canon of Swift.

The fortunes of Swift's critical reputation have at times deprived him of what was plainly his due: Johnson thought *A Tale of a Tub* to be above Swift's usual manner; Gray thought the *History of the Four Last Years of the Queen* too much below Swift's manner to be his. Of late, however, only one work of any consequence has excited editorial disagreement: *A Letter to a Young Poet* (1721).[3] Herbert Davis, the most recent editor of Swift's prose work, has relegated this pamphlet to an appendix of dubious attributions despite the fact that it has been considered part of the Swift canon since 1768. Davis's objections to Swift's authorship are essentially subjective, consisting primarily of an intuitive detection of stylistic peculiarities supported by reference to circumstantial particulars of apparent incontestability.[4]

Davis finds three main circumstantial obstacles to the acceptance of the *Letter* as a genuine Swift work: 1) that no reference to it by Swift or his friends, during Swift's lifetime, has been found and that neither Swift nor Faulkner included it in the collected works; 2) that the date offers difficulties because Swift was then at work on *The Bubble*, a long poem of fifty-five stanzas which he sent to Ford on December 15, 1720, around which time "he had an attack of his recurring illness"; 3) that the same publisher (J. Hyde) had in the previous year (1720) brought out a pamphlet entitled *The Right of Precedence between Physicians and Civilians Enquir'd Into*, which, when it was reprinted by Curll in London, had been fathered on Swift but which, in a letter to Ford, he had specifically disavowed and in which Davis sees some un-Swiftian stylistic affinity with the *Letter*.[5] Despite his own doubts, Davis admits that "many will say [the *Letter*] bears marks of his work and recalls his point of view in other writings, and therefore is unlikely to have come from any other

[3]   *Works,* IX, 325-345.
[4]   The matter has been contested by Paul Fussell, Jr., who ignores the external evidence and evades the stylistic particulars (p. 36, above).
[5]   "Introduction", *Works,* IX, pp. xxv-xxvi.

hand".[6] In other words, many readers have by just as intuitive a process concluded that it was like Swift's work. To this intuitive consensus, Davis opposes what he may believe to be objective rebuttals but which are without exception subjective readings of the available data and with one exception erroneous or inconclusive findings.

The force of these circumstantial objections is not great enough to compel belief. To take 2) first: who can pretend, at this distance, to account for time that Swift spent during nearly the most obscure part of his life? This is surely the weakest possible kind of objection: even to include it casts doubt on the strength of the case. The first of his objections, however, makes the clearest appeal to common sense. But the same charge – that the *Letter* was never acknowledged by Swift – can be made against works that Davis accepts as genuine, as for example, *The Story of an Injured Lady*.[7] In any event, many explanations can be given to account for an author's leaving a given short paper out of his collected works: lapse of memory, loss of the copy, lack of interest in the issues, dissatisfaction with the performance. That Swift and Faulkner should have failed to include the *Letter* in Swift's works may occasion suspicion, but it is not a sufficient ground for disbelief. As for the third objection, Swift, after all, did not disavow the *Letter* but the *Right of Precedence,* a work which is connected with the *Letter* by three tenuous threads: the same publisher, the ascription of both to Swift, and "certain trivial resemblances" of style.[8]

It is not clear from Davis's account whether the resemblances that he is citing are those which are present in both pamphlets and

[6]   *Ibid.,* p. xxv. Davis notes that the *Letter,* though never printed by Faulkner, even after Hawkesworth had included it in his 1768 edition, has been accepted without comment by succeeding editors and critics. But, he makes nothing of the fact that J. Hyde of Dublin was the publisher of a later unquestioned work of Swift's, *Some Arguments against Enlarging the Power of Bishops* (1723).
[7]   This is the first item in the same volume, *Works,* IX, 3-9. It may be recalled that *A Tale of a Tub* did not achieve inclusion in Faulkner's 1735 edition either.
[8]   *Ibid.,* p. xxvi. The question of Swift's credibility when talking about the authorship of his own works may also be raised in this connection.

agree in being unlike Swift or whether he is merely listing his stylistic objections to the *Letter*, whether these be present in the other pamphlet or not. Regardless, after admitting that the *Letter* is a better piece of work than *The Right of Precedence,* Davis cites the following stylistic practices in the *Letter* which he considers to be unlike Swift: 1) phrases like "But to proceed" to start a new paragraph, and other transitional devices; 2) many parentheses like "I will take upon me to say", "As I was saying", "And truly"; 3) "a heavy use of adjectives"; 4) a tendency to indulge in punning and word-play; 5) the unfinished condition of "the latter part" of the *Letter*, whose last dozen pages contain the phrases "Another point", "Once more", "To conclude", and five *lastly*'s.[9]

The easiest of these points to verify is the third. If a *heavy* use of adjectives means merely more adjectives than usual (rather than a particular way of using them), the matter can be settled by referring to the word-class frequency distributions. Swift's average use of Class 03 words (descriptive adjectives) is 6.0 per cent of the total number of words.[10] The average for the *Letter* is 7.25 per cent.[11] This is a substantial difference, which would not often arise by chance, though this does not mean that it could not happen.[12] At first glance, it certainly seems as if Davis's intuition had been sound. Although he says nothing about how the density of adjectives was estimated – counting, inspection, or introspection – his claim is substantiated by the evidence. Though the decision was reached subjectively, it can be validated by objective means.

But if we turn now to a consideration of Davis's first point, his claims do not seem so well-grounded. First of all, Davis's objection is not itself of the greatest clarity: "the use of the phrase

[9]   *Ibid.,* pp. xxvi-xxvii.
[10]   See Table 6.7, above. The range in individual samples is between 5.1 and 6.9 per cent.
[11]   Specifically, the values are 7.1 for the first half of the *Letter* and 7.4 for the second. See Table 7.2, below.
[12]   On the basis of the Student t-test, the probability that the two values come from the same population is .01 (1/100). In other words, if a hundred random samples of Swift's work were drawn, one sample would probably have 7.25 per cent adjectives.

'But to proceed' to start a new paragraph, only one example of a number of various devices to hook his arguments together." [13] Although we may probably assume that it is the crudeness of the "hooking" mechanisms – and not the mechanisms themselves – that is here being aimed at, the matter is a trifle uncertain. At any rate, some of Swift's authenticated paragraph openings are not much less crude: "I must repeat . . ." (*Works*, IX, 50), "To return, then . . ." (74); "I will add one Thing . . ." (94); "But to return . . ." (XII, 99); "To return from digressing . . ." (124); "I now return . . ." (226). It would not be difficult to find, in Swift's tracts and pamphlets, additional examples to support the view that the transitional practice of Swift and the author of the *Letter* had much in common, and that it certainly would not serve to distinguish their work.

There are also many parentheses of the type that Davis in his second point objects to: "Therefore I say" (*Works*, XII, 70); "if those (I say) openly profess . . ." (IX, 157); "I say, that in such a Nation . . ." (209). Though this feature is less characteristic of Swift in rapid argument than the "hooking" procedure in the work of this period,[14] one might argue, without perversity, that such second-order comments – self-conscious remarks about the fact that he is speaking – are a hallmark of Swift's writing.[15]

Davis's fourth point is again rather difficult to paraphrase with any accuracy. It reads: "a tendency to overwork a figure or even to indulge in such play as this – 'To these devote your spare hours, or rather spare all your hours to them.' " [16] There is no denying that the illustration reaches a rather mechanical level of wit, but it does not seem to follow that Davis was stigmatizing the author of the *Letter* for the poor quality of his wit. Over-

---

[13] "Introduction", *Works*, IX, xxvi.

[14] The examples chosen for illustration have been drawn, as much as possible, from work of the same or contiguous periods in Swift's writing life.

[15] These comments are very similar to the "autoclitics" that B. F. Skinner describes as a special group of verbal responses which "have a function in starting, stopping, or deflecting" the reader's reactions. See *Verbal Behavior* (New York, 1957), p. 321.

[16] *Works*, IX, xxvi.

working a figure and indulging in play both imply an interest on
Swift's part in the mere use of words, the existence of which the
editor of Swift's work ought to be the last to deny. Swift's persist-
ent punning, his Castilian language, the "bites", the *Polite Conversation*, the Anglo-Latin correspondence, the little language,
even the *Proposal for Correcting the English Tongue* – all testify
to Swift's enduring fascination with the tools of his trade, the
English language and language itself.

It is unlikely that Swift's tendency to pun is seriously being
questioned. The man who is capable of "You may call them a
triumvirate; for, if you please to try-um, they will vie with the
best",[17] is not likely to draw a line at "in some measure vers'd
in Poetry".[18] Though paronomasia is perhaps not the only figure
Davis is thinking of, it is probably fruitless to pursue a search
for every example of chiasmus, zeugma, synecdoche, that might
be found in the *Letter* or in Swift's works. Conscious rhetorical
artifice may be too easily put on or avoided to serve as any conclusive measure of identification.

The final point – that the *Letter* is badly finished because of
the plethora of concluding machinery, including five *Lastly*'s
(not unlike a Rossini overture) – is, first of all, in disagreement
with our objective findings, which detect more agreement between
Swift and the second half of *Letter* than with the first half.[19] It
is really not strange that a polemical or satiric work, which
pursues a series of argumentative heads, should contain a number
of concluding mechanisms. In less than a dozen pages, *The
Publick Spirit of the Whigs* displays two *Lastly*'s, with "And to
sum up all", and "His last demand".[20] Elsewhere, in the space
of four pages, Swift uses "Further", "And whereas", "And

---

[17]   *The Correspondence of Jonathan Swift*, ed. F. E. Ball (London, 1910),
I, 177.
[18]   *Works*, IX, 327.
[19]   Details of these findings are set out hereafter, passim. Davis refers to
the unfinished character of the "last dozen pages" but the whole work occupies only nineteen pages in his edition. His halves are therefore one-
third and two-thirds, whereas my comparison was made between two nearly equal halves.
[20]   *Works*, VIII, 62-8.

again", "To conclude", and "Therefore, upon the whole".[21] In sum, this work seems no more unfinished than some others which are accepted without question.

The single matter of adjective density aside, it may be seen that the weight of Davis's objections to Swift's authorship is not overwhelming. How are we to account for a seasoned editor's rejection of an author's work on such grounds? It seems likely that the formulated objections represent merely the formulable portion of his response to the material. That is, if we may speculate about thought processes, the feeling may have grown upon the editor that the *Letter* was not quite the Swift he had become used to. Eventually, he concluded that it was not his work, all this taking place to some extent on an unconscious or intuitive level. When it came time to document the basis for his rejection of the work, however, a truly sound basis was not available because the process of decision was hidden from consciousness, and it was necessary to fall back on apparently plausible features of dissimilarity. But because the evidence proffered and the decision reached are not in an organic relationship, they will not withstand close examination. An editor's intuitive decision is not to be lightly dismissed, with or without evidence, but it is after all only an opinion, though an expert one.[22] It can be countered with the opinion of other experts. Consider the unrestrained lack of qualification with which Ricardo Quintana seems to vouch for the *Letter:*

Not only has it a peculiar importance by virtue of the fact that Swift nowhere discoursed of poetry at such length, but it is also distinguished by the texture of its satire and irony, for it is a grave discourse, evenly modulated, but with crushing irony lurking in every phrase.[23]

---

[21] "Reasons Humbly Offered to the Parliament of Ireland", *Works,* VII, pp. 292-5.
[22] It is, as Lewis P. Curtis says in "Forged Letters of Laurence Sterne", *PMLA,* L (1935), 1077, "so much a matter of my ear versus thy ear".
[23] *The Mind and Art of Jonathan Swift* (New York, 1936), p. 274. Two other writers, coming after Davis's expressions of doubt about the *Letter* but apparently eager to analyze its satiric technique as part of Swift's entire system, have recourse to an unconvincing compromise involving a skillful imitator: William B. Ewald, Jr., *The Masks of Jonathan Swift*

Obviously, when the game of witnesses is invoked, some way of comparing the credibility of the witnesses is required. This is not a graceful nor ultimately a possible undertaking. If any greater certainty than that resulting from the mere opposition of opinions, perhaps based on casual evidence, is to be achieved, more objective methods must be used.

It should be self-evident that absolute certainty in the attribution of works to authors is not possible. The existence of a corrected draft in an author's handwriting is perhaps the strongest kind of presumptive evidence, but it does not constitute absolute certainty. In most cases, the matter does not arise. The best proof we ordinarily have of any authorship is that no one has questioned it. All historical data are subject to the same necessity of trust. It would be impossible to prove the existence of Alexander the Great or of Tacitus, but there is no necessity to do so. The authorship of Shakespeare's plays has been questioned for many years, and the loser in the argument will almost certainly be the one on whom the burden of proof rests. It is no easier to prove that Shakespeare wrote *Macbeth* than to prove that some other person did not write it. Fortunately, it is not necessary to prove what every one is willing to acknowledge.

To say about the *Letter* that it does not sound like Swift is to achieve the negative extreme of objectivity. How much better can we hope to do with more rigorous methods? By careful definition, by consistent adherence to sound and standard procedures of objective demonstration, we can reach a conclusion in the form of a probability statement about which we can feel such certainty as is consistent with the soundness of the original assumptions and the reliability of the data. In other words, the conclusions based on objective procedure have all the reliability of statistical demonstration, which is almost always more than that of mere speculation and conjecture.

Let us therefore examine the *Letter* according to the procedure developed earlier. For the analysis, the *Letter* is divided into two

(Oxford, 1954), p. 92; J. Holloway, "The Well-Filled Dish: An Analysis of Swift's Satire", *Hudson Review*, IX (Spring 1956), 22.

halves [24] and, along with a sample from Swift's *History of the Four Last Years of the Queen*, is subjected to a variety of stylistic tests. In essence, the analysis should lead to a choice among the following conclusions: 1) the works were written by Swift; 2) the works were written by one or more of the controls; 3) the works were written by totally different hands. This will be accomplished by comparing the figures yielded by various tests of the "Unknown" samples with the figures characteristic of Swift and the controls. If the resemblance to Swift is sufficient, we may infer that nothing in this evidence – in the particular features tested – is inconsistent with the theory of Swift's authorship. If, on the other hand, the resemblance favors one or more of the controls, it will be necessary to reject the theory of Swift's authorship. Of course, there is also the possibility that there will be no resemblance to either Swift or the controls. In that case, it will be necessary to postulate an anonymous author of the *Letter*.

The inclusion of a sample from Swift's *History* is designed to test the assumption made earlier that Swift's anonymous writings constitute his typical work, whereas his signed and posthumously published writings are atypical and do not share a common style with the former.[25] The sample from the *History* will be considered an unknown together with the two halves of the *Letter*. The purpose of this procedure is of course not to cast doubt on its genuineness but to judge whether the atypical work could be identified as Swift's if all other evidence were lacking.

To illustrate the method to be followed, let us examine the results given by a criterion that is not part of the series discussed

[24] The two halves are slightly uneven: the first half (to be called *Letter* I) contains 3591 words, runs from p. 327 to the end of the sentence in line 12 on p. 336 and requires 102 IBM cards; the second half (*Letter* II) contains 3777 words, runs from the point just mentioned to the end of p. 345, excluding the last paragraph, and requires 107 IBM cards. The reason for dividing the work into halves is the necessity of maintaining the standard sample size so that the results might be comparable. The reason for dividing the work into first and second halves, rather than for example randomly chosen halves, is that this might help to isolate the location of extraneous influence, if any. A further test has been made, of the central section of the work – the second and third quarters – the results of which may be found in Appendix H, below.

[25] The point is discussed on p. 80, above.

in the previous chapter, average number of words in a sentence. Because sentence-length is an easy number to calculate, the use of this criterion developed early in the quantitative phase of the history of style analysis, and a body of literature has grown up about it, which furnishes some interesting comparisons.[26] Its reliability as a test of authorship, however, is seriously open to question because of a variety of factors: the possibility (even likelihood, at some periods) that an editor or printer might have tampered with punctuation; the variability of sentence-length according to the mood and the type of composition; the necessity for a very large sample to achieve a meaningful average, which nonetheless might have a large scatter around it. Merely as an illustrative preliminary, then, let us look at some sentence-length figures.

In Table 7.1 are displayed the sentence-length averages for each author and for each unknown, with comparative values derived from the work of other students.[27] The Swift samples, it may be seen, bunch together at around 40.0, except for *Modest Proposal*, which is ten words higher than the Swift average, but not inconsistent with it. The four controls are all self-consistent and, perhaps Gibbon excepted, reasonably distinct from Swift. The comparative figures are, if we recall the difference in size of sample and in method, remarkably in agreement with our values. On the basis of these figures, which are set out chronologically (except for the unknowns) in Figure 7A, it is possible to see a relationship between the three unknowns and the upper end of the Swift distribution. If we had no other criterion, we should feel reasonably secure in attributing all three unknowns to Swift on sentence-length.[28]

[26]   The work of Sherman, Moritz, and Aurner is discussed on pp. 59 ff., above.
[27]   Lucius P. Sherman, "Some Observations ...", p. 130, considered 300 sentences necessary for reliability. As my samples all contain fewer than 200 sentences, they are probably unreliable by his standard. In addition, the figures are distorted by the fact that I counted some phrases as single words, though this effect is well under one per cent.
[28]   Incidentally, Figure 7A also corroborates Sherman's observations that the size of sentences has gradually diminished since the beginning of printing, "On Certain Facts ...", p. 353.

TABLE 7.1

*Average length of sentences (in words), for samples of Swift, controls
and unknowns, compared with results of earlier researchers*

	Length	Other Results
10	39.8	
12	43.2	
13	40.1	
20	42.3	
25	42.3	
26	41.7	
29	53.6	
$\bar{x}$	43.3	

CONTROLS

61	21.8	} 24.[a]
62	21.7	
65	36.4	37-40[b]
66	37.1	
71	39.1	
72	36.3	
75	26.2	(44)[c]
76	28.6	34.[d]

UNKNOWNS

History	50.7	55.[e]
Letter I	49.9	
Letter II	53.2	

[a] Sherman (1888, 1892) gives this figure for all of Macaulay's prose.
[b] Sherman (1888, 1892) gives 37 and 38: Aurner (1923) gives 40.
[c] Aurner (1923) gives this figure for the *Rambler*.
[d] Aurner (1923).
[e] Moritz (1903).

Eleven criteria of varying reliability have emerged from the discussion in the previous chapter. In order not to depend on inadequate measuring tools, it will be advisable to sort out the testing criteria according to their reliability. The three most reliable indicators are the three points of the Discriminator Profile: Verbals (VB), Different Patterns (D), and Introductory Connectives (IC).[29] The eight remaining tests have been classified as either Not-certain or Not-reliable. If they do not show adequate

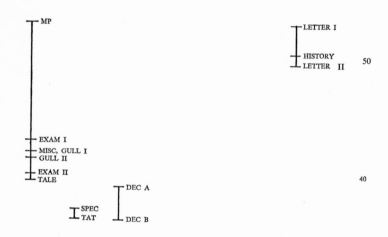

Figure 7a—Average sentence-length in words for Swift, controls and unknowns

consistency, if they are unduly sensitive to the type of writing tested, or if they fail to discriminate between greatly different authors, they are considered Not-reliable.[30] If their performance is not as indiscriminate as these but fails to meet the criteria for reliable tests, they are considered Not-certain.

To begin with the reliable tests, let us first examine the word-class frequency distribution of the three unknowns, as it is given in Table 7.2.[31] Looking only for substantial differences, we find that *History* is different from *Letter* I and *Letter* II in five classes (01, 03, 11, 31, 51). In the remaining classes, the differences seem to be of an order probably due to random variation. It may be noticed that all five of these classes – noun, adjective, pronoun, determiner, preposition – are nominal in character, that is, inter-related. Thus, because *History* is higher in nouns (lower in pronouns), it is also higher in determiners and in prepositions than *Letters* I and II. Its number of adjectives, however, is lower.

Casual inspection of the arrays of figures in Table 7.2 with the comparable arrays for Swift and the controls in Tables 6.7 and 6.8 shows a better agreement of *Letters* I and II with Swift than with any of the controls. The five nominal classes apart, *History* also seems to conform to the Swift figures. Because of the essentially fixed nature of the basic distribution of words into word-classes in English, however, no significant conclusions can be drawn from comparing the whole tables of any samples or authors.[32] A closer examination is required to uncover the relationships of the unknowns.

The first of the reliable criteria is the percentage of Verbals (VB). Table 7.3 gives these figures in the form of averages and individual values for Swift, the controls and the unknowns. *His-*

---

[29]   These may be found detailed in Tables 6.14, 6.27 and 6.37.

[30]   Their being considered not reliable does not imply that the results are false: it means only that they are useless for discrimination.

[31]   This table should be compared with the similar tables for Swift (6.7) and for the controls (6.8).

[32]   The Chi-square test fails to distinguish the word-class distributions of even the most extreme authors tested. On the basis of ten classes, the value of Chi-square for Gibbon against Swift is only 8.4, which for nine degrees of freedom represents a .50 probability.

TABLE 7.2

Word-class frequency distribution for unknowns, as percentages

Class	History	Letter I	Letter II
01	24.0	19.8	21.4
02	6.5	5.7	6.1
03	4.0	7.1	7.4
04	.6	1.0	.5
05	2.1	2.2	2.4
06	.9	.5	.6
07	1.1	.6	.8
08	.1	.2	.1
11	2.5	7.4	6.6
21	6.6	8.2	7.2
31	19.0	14.6	15.3
32	.6	.5	.7
33	2.0	2.7	1.9
34	1.9	2.5	2.4
41	4.1	5.3	5.7
42	2.5	3.5	2.7
43	2.0	2.0	1.8
44	.0	.0	.2
45	.5	.4	.4
51	15.3	12.3	12.7
61	2.6	2.8	2.7
71	.0	.1	.0
81	.8	.1	.2
91	.3	.5	.5

tory coincides exactly with the Swift average of 4.1, but *Letter* I coincides with the Johnson average. *Letter* II has the value of 3.8, which is 0.5 greater than Johnson and 0.3 lower than Swift. Should it be credited to Swift or considered too aberrant to fit under any available writer and therefore the work of our anonymous author? Reference to Table 6.14 shows that the Swift distribution symbolized by the average of 4.1 represents a range between 3.5 and 4.4. The 3.8 value of *Letter* II coincides exactly with that of *Gulliver* II. It seems unnecessary therefore to postulate any other author than Swift for this unknown.[33] In sum, according to the

[33] If we estimate the statistical probability that the value of 3.8 for *Letter* II belongs with the Swift figures, we discover, using the *t*-test that the chance is one in twenty. *Letter* I (3.3) has one chance in a thousand, according to the same test. That is, one Swift sample in twenty would have the value

TABLE 7.3

*Individual sample and average VB values for Swift controls
and unknowns, as percentages*

SWIFT

10	3.9
12	4.3
13	4.2
20	4.4
25	3.5
26	3.8
29	4.3
x̄	4.1

ADDISON

65	2.7
66	2.6
x̄	2.7

JOHNSON

75	3.7
76	2.9
x̄	3.3

GIBBON

71	1.9
72	1.6
x̄	1.8

MACAULAY

61	2.7
62	2.8
x̄	2.8

UNKNOWNS

History	4.1
Letter I	3.3
Letter II	3.8

3.8 and one in a thousand would have the value 3.3. These probabilities
cannot be taken wholly to the letter because of the possible divergence of
the word-class distribution from a normal distribution. Cf. Herdan, *Language as Choice and Chance:* "Although applicable in general, significance
tests are not always to the point in the particular sphere of linguistics ..."
(p. 8), in which he includes stylistics.

first criterion of the Discriminator Profile, *History* and *Letter* II
are by Swift and *Letter* I like Johnson, or unlike Swift.

The second point of the Discriminator Profile is the number of
different three-word patterns that occur in a 3500-word sample
(D). Table 7.4 gives the averages and individual values of all
the samples and Figure 7B displays them graphically. *History*
(value 744) falls closest to Johnson's average of 724, which is
highest among the controls. *Letter* I is much higher than any
average, even Swift's. In fact, as may be seen from the values for
individual Swift samples shown in Table 6.27, it is even higher
than the highest single Swift value of 868. We are therefore led
to conclude that this sample is unlike any of our authors and
perhaps the work of our hypothetical anonymous author. *Letter*
II, however, though above the Swift average, fits into the group
of his individual sample values, falling closest to the 857 of
Swift *Misc.*[34] The verdict, then, of this second criterion is that
History is most like Johnson, that *Letter* II is very much like
Swift and that *Letter* I is the work of an anonymous author.

The third and final Discriminator is the percentage of sentences introduced by a connective of Classes 41, 42 and 91 (IC).
The values given in Tables 7.5 show a clear separation between
all the unknowns and Swift, on the one hand, and all the controls,
on the other. *Letter* II is almost exactly equal to the Swift mean
and *History* is a little below it, though well within the range of individual Swift values shown in Table 6.37. *Letter* I, though close
to the highest individual Swift value (41.8 for *Mod. Prop.*), yet
falls outside the range.[35] Unquestionably, this criterion shows
Letter II to be indistinguishable from Swift and *History* also
Swiftian, but it compels the attribution of *Letter* I to the unknown
author.

So much, then, is told us by the most reliable criteria I have

---

[34]   According to the *t*-test, the probability that Swift and *History* came
from the same population is one in one thousand, on the basis of the
D criterion. The relevant probabilities for *Letters* I and II are one in two
hundred and one in five.
[35]   According to the *t*-test again, the probabilities for *History*, *Letter* I and
Letter II are one in six (.15), one in one hundred (.01) and eight in ten (.80),
respectively.

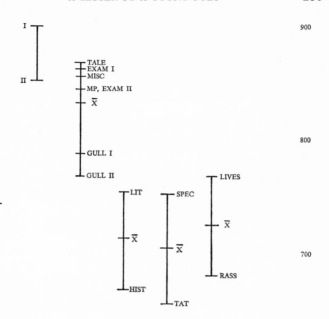

HISTORY   LETTER   SWIFT   MACAULAY ADDISON   JOHNSON   GIBBON   400

Figure 7b—Values of **D** for Swift, controls and unknowns, with means indicated

TABLE 7.4

Individual sample and average D values for Swift, controls and unkowns

	D
SWIFT	
10	868
12	864
13	844
20	857
25	789
26	768
29	844
$\bar{x}$	833
ADDISON	
65	657
66	752
$\bar{x}$	704
JOHNSON	
75	680
76	769
$\bar{x}$	724
GIBBON	
71	497
72	440
$\bar{x}$	468
MACAULAY	
61	755
62	669
$\bar{x}$	712
UNKNOWNS	
History	744
Letter I	901
Letter II	855

been able to devise. They seem to be saying that *Letter* II is by Swift on all three counts, *History* on two out of three and that *Letter* I is by an anonymous writer, who is like Johnson in one criterion. In other words, it looks as if the atypical Swift sample (*History*) is typical enough to be attributed to him. But, oddly enough, only the second half of the *Letter* seems to be Swift's work. This very curious finding needs some explanation. Before

TABLE 7.5

*Individual sample and average Introductory Connective values for
Swift, controls and unknowns, as percentage of total sentences*

	IC
SWIFT	
10	32.9
12	31.9
13	41.3
20	33.6
25	24.0
26	26.1
29	41.8
$\bar{x}$	33.1
ADDISON	
65	11.4
66	11.7
$\bar{x}$	11.5
JOHNSON	
75	3.8
76	11.6
$\bar{x}$	7.7
GIBBON	
71	17.8
72	10.4
$\bar{x}$	14.1
MACAULAY	
61	14.5
62	10.8
$\bar{x}$	12.6
UNKNOWNS	
History	28.9
Letter I	43.1
Letter II	32.4

that is given, however, a look at some more evidence may give us more assurance.

For convenience, the Not-certain and Not-reliable criteria have been grouped in Reference Table 7.6 and interpreted in Summary Table 7.7. In this latter, the three groups of criteria are set out in decreasing order of reliability and the three unknowns are attributed to the author whose average is closest to their values. If

TABLE 7.6

Reference table of Not-certain and Not-reliable criteria

	Not-certain				Not-reliable			
	6.10	6.13	6.35	6.11	6.12	6.24	6.26	6.29
History	60.8	13.2	29.3	9.0	23.6	2.3	42	6.5
Letter I	62.9	13.8	23.6	11.1	20.3	1.8	85	4.4
Letter II	60.7	13.3	25.9	10.6	20.2	2.1	81	4.9
Swift $\bar{x}$	61.6	14.4	23.2	10.2	20.4	1.9	57	5.2
Addison $\bar{x}$	61.0	14.9	26.7	10.0	20.5	2.0	69	4.9
Johnson $\bar{x}$	59.2	17.1	22.0	10.1	18.5	1.8	46	5.3
Gibbon $\bar{x}$	55.7	12.4	39.1	9.2	21.3	3.5	93	7.1
Macaulay $\bar{x}$	57.5	15.0	26.5	8.5	19.9	2.3	82	4.8

TABLE 7.7

Summary of attributions of three unknowns on the basis of three groups of criteria of varying reliability

Criteria	*History*	*Letter* I	*Letter* II
Reliable			
VB	S	J	S
D	J	X	S
IC	S	X	S
Not-certain			
FW	A	X	A
VA	X	S	X
18MFP	X	S	M
Not-reliable			
C	X	S/A	S/A
M	G	X	S
N-V	M	S/J	A/S/M
AVQ	J	M	M
513101	X	X	A/M

Note: Initials stand for authors S = Swift   G = Gibbon
                                   A = Addison   M = Macaulay
                                   J = Johnson   X = Anonymous

an unknown's value is not in the range of any author, it is considered the work of the anonymous author. Thus, as has just been shown, by the reliable criteria, *Letter* II is like Swift in three out of three. The Not-certain criteria give quite a different version.

The unknown (*Letter* II) which the reliable criteria had adjudged most like Swift is variously attributed by these criteria to Addison, Macaulay and Anonymous. Contrariwise, the presumably non-Swiftian unknown (*Letter* I) is indicated to be Swift's by two out of three of these Not-certain criteria. *History* is attributed to Anonymous in two out of three. Among these Not-certain criteria there is some pattern of consistency for two of the unknowns, but they do not coincide with the patterns afforded by the reliable criteria. There is, therefore, no reason to place confidence in them. The Not-reliable criteria go even further away from certainty. There is no distinct pattern to oppose the evidence of the reliable criteria – merely a disorderly jumble. The Not-reliable criteria, taken as a group, do not show the dominance over the unknowns of any putative author.

As a graphic summary of all the values encompassed by the three reliable criteria, let us now construct the Discriminator Profile, relying entirely on the evidence they provide. The first step is the normalization of all the values yielded by testing for each of the criteria. This is accomplished by considering the Swift average to represent one hundred per cent and calculating what comparative percentage each value represents.[36] The resultant values are given in Table 7.8. These values are now superimposed on the content of Figure 6L and the points for each unknown are connected. The resulting graph may be seen in Figure 7C.

At first glance, this graph seems to allow the inference that all three unknowns are the work of Swift. Closer examination, however, reveals that only one of the unknowns' lines (*Letter* II) falls wholly within the Swift boundaries. In interpreting the graph to reach conclusions about the authorship of *History*, we must pay attention to the precise locations of the three points that determine each line, not to the line itself. The fact that *History's* line falls almost entirely within the Swift polygon must not obscure the fact that its point D falls outside, just below a cluster of control values. *Letter* I, of course, has all three points outside the Swift polygon. What the Profile shows us, however, which the in-

---

[36]   The working out of this calculation may be followed on p. 233, above.

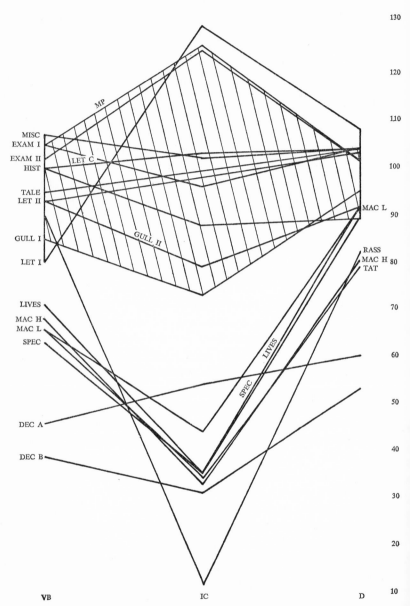

Figure 7c—Three-discriminator profile of the style of Swift, controls and unknowns, including *Letter C,* all values expressed as percentages of Swift's average

TABLE 7.8

Three-discriminator style profile (normalized) for unknowns

	1 VB	2 I.C.	3 D
History	100	88	89
Letter I	80	130	108
Letter II	93	98	103

dividual estimates do not, is that the anonymous author of *Letter* I is the possessor of a style (in these respects) which is not un-Swiftian.

Aside from the criteria so far adduced, is any other information available which might help to clarify the conclusions tentatively reached about the authorship of the three unknowns? One calculation which has been neglected until now is the SSS, the sum of the absolute differences between the four grouped word-classes of any two works (VA, VB, M, C).[37] In other words, this test is based on verbs, modifiers, and connectives and ignores most noun-connected word-classes. It is probably not a wholly reliable test, inasmuch as only one of its four components is numbered among the reliable criteria, the remainder being Not-certain (VA) and Not-reliable (M, C). It has the disadvantage, in addition, of being the sort of test that operates best with a number of samples great enough that a trend may be elicited and that reliance does not have to be placed on a few individual figures. Despite these limitations, the test performs well enough if not overextended.

Detailed values of SSS for the unknowns against Swift and against the other controls and against each other are given in Table 7.9. Summary Table 7.10 provides, as a basis for comparison, a condensed version of Table 6.16. In Lines 1-4 may be read the general tendency of comparisons *within* an author to produce SSS values around 2.5 and comparisons *between* authors to produce values around 5.0. Lines 5-7 show that *Letters* I and II have values of 2.8 and 2.3 and *History* a value of 5.9 against Swift. These figures seem to imply that *Letter* I and *Letter* II are closely related to each other and, since both fall near the 2.5 value

[37] See Table 6.16, above.

TABLE 7.9

SSS values for unknowns

	History	*Letter* I	*Letter* II	
10	5.6	1.4	.8	
12	6.3	2.9	2.3	
13	6.4	4.2	3.8	
20	6.9	4.1	3.5	Unknowns vs. Swift samples
25	5.6	1.4	.6	
26	4.8	3.2	2.8	
29	5.5	2.7	2.1	
61	8.2	5.0	5.4	Macaulay
62	7.1	4.5	5.1	
65	6.2	3.8	4.4	Addison
66	8.2	2.4	3.0	Unknowns vs. Control samples
71	5.2	5.2	4.8	Gibbon
72	6.2	6.4	6.0	
75	11.5	7.5	7.1	Johnson
76	10.3	5.3	5.7	
History 58		6.8	5.4	
Letter I 97			1.6	Unknowns vs. Unknowns
Letter II 98				

characteristic of *within* comparisons, that they are both Swiftian. It also suggests that *History* is less Swiftian because it is closer to the value for *between* comparisons. These results seem to disagree with those of the Profile, which find *History* and *Letter* II to be more Swiftian than *Letter* I. This disagreement is not quite so considerable as appears at first.

Letter I (Line 5) has a higher SSS than *Letter* II (2.8 vs. 2.3), which means it is more distant from Swift. Further, the Swift-*Letter* II value is almost identical with the *within*-Swift average of 2.4. But the Swift-*Letter* I value (2.8) is closer to the Addison-*Letter* I value (3.1) than to Swift-*Letter* II (2.3). Apparently, then, when the tendency of this test to emphasize the similarity between Swift and Addison is taken into account, the relative results do not contradict the findings of the Profile: that *Letter* II is very much like Swift but that *Letter* I is more like someone else.

It is with reference to *History* that the disagreement between

TABLE 7.10

Summary of SSS values for all samples, showing average SSS and items involved in computation

		$\bar{x}$	N Items
*1.	SWIFT-SWIFT	2.4	21
*2.	WITHIN CONTROLS	2.7	4
*3.	SWIFT-CONTROLS	4.9	56
*4.	AMONG CONTROLS	5.6	24
5.	SWIFT-97	2.8	7
6.	SWIFT-98	2.3	7
7.	SWIFT-58	5.9	7
8.	CONTROLS-97	5.0	8
	MACAULAY-97	4.8	2
	ADDISON-97	3.1	2
	GIBBON-97	5.8	2
	JOHNSON-97	6.4	2
9.	CONTROLS-98	5.2	8
	MACAULAY-98	5.3	2
	ADDISON-98	3.7	2
	GIBBON-98	5.4	2
	JOHNSON-98	6.4	2
10.	CONTROLS-58	7.9	8
	MACAULAY-58	7.7	2
	ADDISON-58	7.2	2
	GIBBON-58	5.7	2
	JOHNSON-58	10.9	2
11.	97-58	6.8	1
12.	98-58	5.4	1
13.	97-98	1.6	1

this test and the Profile may be found. It centers around the SSS of 5.9, which is the typical value for a comparison between authors. For instance, the average SSS for controls against *Letter* I is 5.0 and against *Letter* II, 5.2. The value of 5.9 for *History* against Swift exceeds these. Hence, if we assume the reliability of this test, we must conclude that *History* is not by Swift if *Letter*s I and II are. Although we are bound to accept this conclusion, we can adduce two related kinds of evidence to account for the seeming paradox.

The whole problem arises because *History* is an atypical sample,

* For details, see Table 6.16.

whose word-class frequency distribution [38] shows less verb-orientation and more noun emphasis than the typical Swift samples. Consequently, its departure from typical Swift values is to be expected. This expectation is more intense if the samples are subjected to a test which is especially sensitive to verb-orientation (as SSS is and the Profile is not). Thus, on the basis of SSS, *History* is closest to Gibbon (5.7) and farthest from Johnson (10.9), who are the most and least nominal authors among the controls.

The relationships of the unknowns to each other and to the controls are made quite plain if instead of comparing the SSS value of each of them against Swift we compare the SSS values of each author and *Letters* I and II against *History*. The SSS values for these two unknowns and average SSS values for each author against *History* are ranked in Table 7.11 in increasing order of kinship. Thus, Johnson is first on the list because his highly verbal style sets him farthest apart from *History*. Gibbon, it can be seen, is more like *History* than Swift is, though the difference is too minute to be important. And *History* is considerably more like *Letter* II than like *Letter* I, to judge by both the values and the rankings. Thus, this test confirms the results of the Reliable tests in showing greater kinship between *History* and *Letter* II than between *History* and *Letter* I, though the relationship is not unambiguous because of the limitations in range and accuracy of this test.

However, this test also tells us, in Line 13 of Table 7.10, that *Letters* I and II are more like each other than either is like Swift. The value of 1.6 is of the same order as some of the lowest among the *within*-Swift comparisons displayed in Table 6.16. If this permits the conclusion that they seem to be by the same author, and their values against Swift (2.8 and 2.3), in Lines 5-6 of Table 7.10, seem to suggest that this author is Swift, then we do find that the conclusions of this test disagree with the conclusions to be drawn from the Profile. The disagreement resides in the closer kinship between *Letters* I and II implied by the SSS test

---

[38] The frequency distribution for the unknowns is given in Table 7.2, above.

TABLE 7.11

SSS values of History *against Swift, controls and other unknowns, ranked in descending order*

	History
Johnson $\bar{x}$	10.9
Macaulay $\bar{x}$	7.7
Addison $\bar{x}$	7.2
Letter I	6.8
Swift $\bar{x}$	5.9
Gibbon $\bar{x}$	5.7
Letter II	5.4

than by the Profile. This disagreement may be attributed to the incomplete reliability of the SSS test. As such, it may be rejected if only the most stringently objective data are to be considered. If the enquiry is broadened, however, by the introduction of less rigorous evidence, the two sets of results may be brought into closer agreement.

If the text of the *Letter* is now considered in the light of the conclusions about Swift's use of connectives and of seriation that were reached in the early part of this study,[39] some support may be found for the position that *Letter* I and *Letter* II are indeed closely related and perhaps indistinguishable. These earlier calculations established that Swift began one sentence in three with a connective, one in five with a coordinating conjunction and one in six with *and, but,* or *for*.[40] The comparable values for the two parts of the *Letter* are shown in Table 7.12. Although *Letter* I predominates in all three classes,[41] the two parts are not greatly divergent and their average agrees with the expected value to a remarkable degree.

Swift's use of connectives has the additional peculiarity that he tends to accumulate them both at the beginnings of sentences and in medial positions.[42] Without being more precise, we can

[39] Chapters IV and V, above. Part of the information about connectives has of course already been included in the IC component of the Profile.
[40] See pp. 125 ff., above.
[41] If it predominates in the first, all three are likely to be affected.
[42] See pp. 132 ff., above.

TABLE 7.12

*Frequency of introductory connective word-classes, for all
unknowns, as percentage of total sentences*

	Expected	97	98	Letter $\bar{x}$
Introductory Connectives (IC)	33	42	30	36
Coordinating Conjunctions	20	25	15	20
and, but, for	17	22	14	18
N Sentences		72	71	

see that both parts of the *Letter* follow this tendency. Of the
dozen and a half such accumulations which have been noticed
(slightly more than half of which occur in *Letter* I), combinations with *and, but* and *for* predominate: *and since, and if, and
further, and surely, but yet, but altho, but as, for tho, for altho*
(2), *for indeed*. The remainder are miscellaneous and include
sets of three: *or if, whereas therefore, once more if, furthermore
when, however that, and whereas on the other hand, for though
indeed*.[43] These have all the earmarks of Swift's practice, though
the possible work of an able imitator ought perhaps not to be
totally dismissed.

The same uniformity with Swift's practice is true of the *Letter's*
use of seriation (making of lists). There are sixteen series in the
two parts of the *Letter*, eight in each one. According to the earlier
research, one might expect to find one list on every page, on the
average, with substantial variation.[44] In the nineteen pages of the
current edition of *A Letter of Advice to a Young Poet* there are
sixteen lists or slightly less than one to a page. Table 7.13 attempts to summarize these sixteen according to their most prominent features.[45] The most common is the noun series, of which
there are ten, between four and ten items long. They range from
the perfectly regular sequence of four nouns

Love, Wit, Dress and Gallantry (343)

to the "chaotic" order of this series of six items, which contains

---

[43] *Works,* IX, 327-345, passim.
[44] See p. 89, above.
[45] Regularity of order, type of connection, presence and type of continuator, word-class and size of unit, number of items.

TABLE 7.13

*Distribution and classification of seriation items according to
prominent features, listed by page on which they appear*

Page	Order Irreg. Ch.		Connection Poly. Asynd.		Continuator Neut. Sat.		Unit type Word Group		Size
Letter I									
327	x		x				01		5
328			x				01		4
329	x		x		x		01		4
330						x	04		5
330							01		5
330	x							Dep. Cl.	4
333			x				01		4
336	x		x				05		4
Letter II									
338			x				02		4
339	x							Sent.	4
340	x		x				07		4
341		x	x			x	01		6
342	x		x			x	01		8
343							01		4
344						x	01		10
345						x	01		5

Note: As may be seen, no provision is made in the table for the commonest regularity. If, for a given item no mark shows in any of the first
three columns, it may be assumed that order is regular, connection normal or continuator absent.

a "nested" triplet and ends with what I have called a "satiric
continuator": [46]

a *Court*, a *College*, a *Play-House*, and beautiful *Ladies*, and fine
Gentlemen, and good *Claret*, and abundance of *Pens*, *Ink* and *Paper*
(clear of Taxes) and every other Circumstance to provoke WIT.
(341)

There are two series of verbals, both short and irregular:

by Cutting and Slashing, and laying about Him, and banging Mankind. (340)

[He shou'd have them] siz'd, and rang'd, and hung up in order in his
Shop, ready for all Customers, and shap'd to the Feet of all sorts of
Verse (336)

and a regular one of finite verbs:

[46]   See p. 97, above.

wisely Molds, and Polishes, and Drys, and Washes this piece of
Earthen-Ware . . . (338)

The longest series (of ten nouns)

*Gaming-Ordinaries,   Groom-Porter's,   Lotteries,   Bowling-Greens,
Nine-pin-Allies, Bear-Gardens, Cock-pits, Prizes, Puppet* and *Raree-
Shews,* and whatever else concerns the elegant Divertisements of
this Town (344)

is quite tame and regular for its size. In fact, there is only one
"chaotic" series in the lot.[47] But the polysyndetic connection
(which predominates) is generally irregular, affecting ususually
only half the members of the series, and the continuators are
rather unimaginative. Though the quality of the series, subjectively, seems less rich than Swift's usual output, it has considerably the same flavor as Swift's seriate efforts.

We have, it can be seen, moved from objective criteria of internal evidence (the profile, SSS) to significant but less precise
data. The interpretation of the cumulated connective and seriation
data may cause an objection to be raised. A skeptic may very well
admit that these features are present in Swift and in the *Letter*
in appropriately similar numbers, but he may question whether
the spirit in which the writer of the *Letter* uses these features
resembles Swift's spirit. To me it seems that the spirit is the same,
but there is no convincing method of demonstration available.
The impractical nature of such a question is obvious and emphasizes once more the uncertainty of criteria of internal evidence
which require any evaluation. The statistical criteria provided
here, however limited their range, are free of this defect and
therefore more reliable.

What finally is the verdict of the statistical evidence? The
answer is simply stated: *Letter* II is not distinguishable from the
work of Swift; *Letter* I, though generally quite close to the work
of Swift, is statistically distinguishable from it. But *Letter* C, which
overlaps both halves, is almost identical with the Swift average.[48]

[47] *Works,* IX, 341, given above.
[48] *Letter* C is fully treated in Appendix H.

Parenthetically, *History* is very much like Swift, even though it is an atypical work. That is, the test is sensitive enough to perceive through the un-Swiftian outward rind the Swiftian heart that beats inside. The ancillary evidence is all in favor of the kinship of both parts of the *Letter* with Swift. It is therefore impossible to expel the *Letter of Advice to a Young Poet* from the canon of Swift's work. But neither is it possible to accept it without some sort of reservation.

The chances that the same unaided hand could have produced the entire *Letter* are much less than even. But since in literary composition, hybrids are rare, we feel compelled to search for an explanation. In fact, our real task has already been accomplished: we have found as definite an answer as the data will yield under the scrutiny of the present method. This investigation is on solid ground as long as it stays with the evidence and arrives at an answer based on it. So much is objective and rigorous. When we respond to the need to account for what we have found, we step into the limitless and uncertain territory of conjecture and we take the risk of violating the evidence. If we have any trust in our findings, no supporting hypothesis is required. But if a plausible circumstantial clothing is required for our conclusions before they can find a welcome, then the emphasis is placed on ingenuity and plausibility. I do not pretend to any ingenuity greater than that required to produce the findings. Only with reluctance will I be induced to account for them now.

The only theory capable of explaining the findings, without upsetting them, is the presence of an alien hand. Perhaps a draft of the *Letter* was revised by a well- (or ill-) wisher to the Dean; perhaps the printer himself or some associate modified the wording; perhaps the Dean collaborated on the project with one of his Irish friends; perhaps he gave the hints to a friend and impatient with the result finished it himself; perhaps it was hauled out of a wastebasket (after being disowned by the Dean for being un-Swiftian) and sold by a footman to an eager printer; perhaps. Doubtless other theories are possible, but since there is no external evidence of any kind (despite Professor Davis) none of them can have much claim on our attention.

Since the evidence permits the conclusion that Swift was the author of the *Letter,* though it was probably subject to the influence of another hand – a view that would take care of the unusual number of adjectives discovered by Professor Davis – we have no alternative to accepting it. That someone else might have written so much like Swift is beyond belief. The sentiments of the piece are perfectly consistent with what we know Swift's to have been, though the bedevilling of Sir Philip Sidney [49] and the free use of proper names is perhaps unusual. There is at least one concealed reference to another work of Swift [50] and the views about religion, literary hackwork, games, Ireland and the like are such as he would have acknowledged. The skilled imitator or careful student of Swift's satire postulated by Herbert Davis would have had to be as familiar with Swift's mind and work as the

[49] The connection between Swift and Sidney deserves some comment. Their names are associated in several contexts. Henry Sidney (1641-1704), later Earl of Romney, grand-nephew of the poet, was a political associate of Sir William Temple's and a frequent visitor at Moor Park during Swift's residence there. Stella's name is generally assumed to be drawn from Sidney's "Astrophel and Stella". The first paragraph of Sidney's *Defence of Poesie* contains the following curious statement (which had been noticed, however, as early as the middle of the nineteenth century): "then would he adde certaine praises by telling what a peerlesse beast the horse was, the onely serviceable Courtier without flattery, the beast of most bewtie, faithfulnesse, courage, and such more, that if I had not bene a peece of a *Logician* before I came to him, I thinke he would have perswaded me to have wished my selfe a horse." *The Complete Works of Sir Philip Sidney,* ed. A. Feuillerat (Cambridge, 1923), III, 3. As far as is known, the name "Stella" was not used by Swift before he began the series of annual birthday poems in 1719. The close connection between that date and the date of the *Letter* is inescapable. In fact, Herbert Davis noticed it himself and argues persuasively in favor of the conscious literary allusion in Swift's use of the name, *Stella* (New York, 1942), pp. 12 ff. This rapprochement does not turn up in Davis's discussion of the *Letter* (in his edition), even to be dismissed. None of this, of course, is really evidence in favor of Swift's authorship. It merely emphasizes the link between Sidney and Swift and thus ratifies a predisposing condition for Swift's authorship – that he was more than casually familiar with Sidney and his work. He probably admired the man who could inspire in Fulke Greville the desire to lie under a stone that said "Friend to Sir Philip Sidney", a circumstance that Swift mentioned in a letter to Pope (*Correspondence,* IV, 78).

[50] *A Proposal for the Universal Use of Irish Manufacture (1720), Works,* IX, 337.

Dean himself to be capable of this pamphlet. Until definite evidence comes to light about the circumstances under which *A Letter of Advice to a Young Poet* was written, it must therefore be accepted as Swift's work.

CONCLUSION

I have not claimed, in the work just concluded, to provide a complete description of Swift's style and a foolproof method of attribution. I do not know that either is possible. Rather I have tried to steer the study of style away from vagueness and impressionism and toward the maximum of objectivity and precision consistent with the nature of the problem. I have therefore begun with a detailed survey of the traditional commentary designed to reveal the shortcomings of the usual metaphoric descriptions, particularly the prevalent cliché that Swift's style is simple and clear. The greater honesty and value of a description based on observable fact I take to be self-evident.

The style of Swift, it has been argued, reflects the qualities of his mind and personality. The consistency with which the man reveals himself in the work is a tangible verification of the method employed and the assumptions on which it rests. To appreciate the basis of Swift's literary personality, one need only recall his addiction to catalogues, the range and ingenuity of his connectives, and the variety of his structures, particularly as shown in his three-word patterns.

The extent of his contributions to the English word-stock, the tendency to draw his vocabulary from all levels of usage, his especial fondness for colloquialisms and idiomatic phrases might together form the subject of a separate study. The sum of these elements reflects his radicalism in linguistic matters, a position remote from his reputation and influence as a linguistic conservative.[1]

[1] His neologisms are documented in Lois M. Scott-Thomas, "The Vocabulary of Jonathan Swift", *Dalhousie Review,* XXV (1940), 442-447.

If verbal innovation and structural variety may be said to constitute one order of originality, so then may his reluctance to
adhere to any formal pattern, as his irregularly-formed series well
illustrate. And so may his rejection of the usual canons of propriety – heavy use of connectives, especially in initial position,
pleonasm, ellipsis and all the defects of composition for which
men like Blair and Campbell blamed him. And if originality also
means being ahead of one's time, Swift was more modern in his
practice than in either his own preaching or in both the practice
and preaching of his contemporaries and successors. For these
same characteristics – the colloquial tendency of his vocabulary
and the dependence on connectives – as well as the predilection
for verbals are all predictions of the future which make his prose
more modern to the reader of the twentieth century than that of
Addison or Gibbon or Johnson.

Evidence has been adduced that shows him to be original in
another sense too. In guiding his reader with copious signposts,
he demonstrates that his first concern is to convey and safeguard
meaning rather than to write with propriety. This Swift, with a
microscopic sense for the details affecting his reader's response,
is one who keeps his reader alert by denying him the luxury of
predictable endings in sentences and other structures: "Last week
I saw a Woman flay'd, and you will hardly believe, how much it
altered her Person for the worse"; " . . . they are every Day
dying, and rotting, by Cold and Famine, and Filth, and Vermin,
as fast as can be reasonably expected." This Swift is not the fussy
pedant who writes clearly, simply and directly and urges others to,
who dislikes monosyllables, clipped forms, slang and a number
of other irrelevancies. The consciously-expressed dislikes are the
sources of his influence on language, but his practice is the basis
of his fame. If he could have written in accordance with his own
advice, we are justified in thinking, he would have written like
his secretary, whose revision of a letter of Swift's furnishes a

---

Swift's attitude toward words and his influence on linguistic attitudes are
discussed in J. H. Neumann, "Jonathan Swift and the Vocabulary of
English", *Modern Language Quarterly*, IV (1943), 191-204.

useful demonstration of the difference between the value of his precept and his practice:

> I desire that my Prescriptions for Health, which you intend to follow, may be made publick for the benefit of Mankind, although I very much dislike the Animal as it hath acted for severall years past, nor ever valued myself as a Philanthropus.[2]

When this is compared with the original, the stylistic features I have found stand out plainly, even in this short passage:

> I desire that my Prescription of living may be published, which you design to follow, for the benefit of mankind; which, however, I do not value a rush, nor the animal itself, as it now acts, neither will I ever value myself as a Philanthropus, because it is now a creature, taking a vast majority, that I hate more than a toad, a viper, a wasp, a stork, fox, or any other that you will please to add.

The plethora of connectives, the complexity of the structure, the presence even of two verbals excised in the secretary's version and of a short series, complete with continuator – these are the flesh and blood Swift.

As this study objectified the traits of Swift's style, it revealed equally verifiable characteristics in the prose of his contemporaries. In fact, the continual discovery of Gibbon's divergence from his peers at times made it seem as if an independent study of his style were in progress. It is strikingly different from the others examined, most prominently in its limited variety of patterns and highly nominal character. These peculiarities make it easy for me to distinguish his work from Johnson's, with whose style Gibbon's has regularly been linked. Johnson himself has a hidden resemblance to his aversion, Swift, in his inclination to the verbal style. And though Addison and Swift are very much alike, they are distinguishable by my method.

The hope I held of discovering the invisible qualities of Augustan and Georgian English has had to yield before the limitations imposed by the extreme idiosyncrasy of the writers selected and

[2] Both the revision and the original are cited by Herbert Davis in his "Remarks on Some Swift Manuscripts in the United States", in *Jonathan Swift: A List of Critical Studies . . .*, ed. Louis A. Landa and James E. Tobin (New York, 1945), pp. 15-16.

their limited number. A larger collection of controls, unfortunately beyond the limits of practicality, might have permitted some valid generalizations about the English of the eighteenth century. That quite subsidiary aim has been abandoned. For another reason, so has the hope of finding the pattern of change in Swift's style with time: if such an effect occurred, it was too minute to survive the vagaries of random variation. Perhaps, in a version of Quintana's phrase, Swift reached stylistic maturity at a single bound.

Thus although it has not been possible to say much about the particular qualities of eighteenth-century English, a number of inferences about the literary language may be made. The statistical tables contain much precise information about the frequency of word-classes and the distribution of certain patterns. Prepositions and prepositional phrases, for instance, seem to be constant, if not invariable, but pronouns and auxiliary verbs range widely. The simple prepositional phrase is probably the most frequent three-word pattern in the language. A number of other linguistic constants are contained in the tables.

The specific nature of these details furnishes a silent rebuke to those who, without evidence, talk about adjectives and verbs or discuss style in the vague terms of impressionistic criticism. If the exact details of style may be elicited from the texts, what can be the purpose of remaining at the general and imprecise level of description which borrows its terminology from physiology (*nervous, flabby, sinewy, muscular*), from chemistry (*limpid, crystalline*) or even from cookery (*spiced, flavored, bland*).

This study has I hope shown in an attractive light the order of conclusiveness which may emerge from the close examination of texts for the purpose of achieving an objective description of style. To be sure, the categories which here define what is to be measured may need to be modified to pluck out from Swift more of his mystery. And for the study of other authors, the method employed here may be adopted with such modifications as their varying idiosyncrasies suggest. I trust it is fair to claim that the principal effects of this study have been the definition of such a method of stylistic criticism and the reader's new and quite palpable sense for Swift's style.

APPENDICES

APPENDIX I

Make-up of Samples in Chapters IV and V

Table 4.1

Dryden, *Essays,* ed. Ker: I, 29-35; II, 21-26; I, 267-273; II, 197-202; I, 212-217.

Defoe, *Novels,* Shakespeare Head ed.: *Plan,* 19-25; *Roxana,* I, 160-165; *Crusoe,* I, 17-22; *Plague,* 176-181; *Moll Flanders,* I, 157-163.

Steele, *Spectator,* Aitken ed.: III, 181-194; III, 275-288; *Periodical Journalism,* ed. Blanchard: 76-80; *Englishman,* ed. Blanchard: 99-104; 31-35.

Addison, *Spectator,* ed. Aitken: I, 29-41; III, 61-74; V, 267-303; *Works* (1761): II, 106-111; II, 341-348.

Goldsmith, *Selected Works* (1950): 44-49; 301-307; 493-500; 211-216; 246-252.

Johnson, *Prose and Poetry* (1950): 475-480; 701-705; 868-873; 497-501; 179-184.

Swift, *Gulliver's Travels and Selected Writings* (1934): 31-36; 303-308; 267-272; 478-484; 182-187.

Table 4.2

Defoe, *Novels,* Shak. Head ed.: *Plague,* 154-159; *Plan,* 228-233; *Crusoe,* I, 120-125; *Roxana,* I, 141-146; *Englishman,* 23-29.

Addison, *Works* (1761): IV, 8-16; III, 304-310; III, 84-92; IV, 203-210; III, 133-140.

Goldsmith, (1950): 250-256; 24-30; 564-570; 530-537; 448-455.

Johnson, (1950): 673-677; 353-359; 60-64; 584-591; 212-217.

Gibbon, *Decline,* ed. Bury: VII, 136-142; III, 154-159; III, 418-423; VII, 243-249; VI, 420-425.

Swift, *Works*, ed. Davis: I, 155-160; III, 150-155; VIII, 170-174; X, 107-111; XII, 161-165.

Table 5.1 (100 periods beginning at page indicated)
Addison, *Spectator*, ed. Aitken: I, 97; II, 67; III, 157; IV, 107; V, 137. *Works* (1761): I, 427; II, 7, 67, 117; IV, 287.
Johnson, *Lives,* ed. Hill: I, 157, 357; II, 97, 327; III, 157. (1950): 177, 307, 357, 397, 497.
Macaulay, *Essays*, Oxford ed.: I, 297, 597; II, 157, 447, 707. *History,* ed. Firth: 147, 647, 1147, 1647, 2147.
Swift, *Works,* ed. Davis: I, 37, 57, 77, 97, 117; II, 147; III, 17, 57, 107; IV, 7; XI, 37, 87, 137, 187, 237; IX, 67, 177; X, 7, 57, 87.

Table 5.2
Addison, *Works* (1761): IV, 222-4; II, 305-7.
Johnson, (1950): 587-590; 41-43.
Gibbon, *Decline*, ed. Bury: I, 312-314; III, 338-340.
Swift, *Works*, ed. Davis: I, 55-58; X, 112-114.

APPENDIX II

Some Factors of Experimental Design

In any experiment with pretensions to objective validity, some elementary precautions must be taken to avoid disabling error. Three relevant concerns in this research are the choice of the controls, the choice of the samples and the size of the samples.

It was necessary to select, as controls, writers whose practice might be compared with Swift's. These writers represent the contemporary background against which Swift was standing out. To choose contemporaries whose prose is related in subject matter and who were themselves distinguished users of the language is to insure that such differences as are found do not represent merely crude matters of chance or of historical change in fashions of language. It would be easy to show that Swift and the editorial writer of the *Daily News* differ from each other, but it would be pointless to do so because it is expected that they should differ. If it can be shown that Swift differs from Addison, the difference is important and can lead to useful conclusions. Therefore, the main controls are bound to be such authors as Addison, Johnson and Gibbon, but there is room for moderns too, if not for the journalist just adduced, at least for writers like Macaulay or Hemingway, to insure that some permanent characteristic of the language itself is not under test.

The selection of writers of distinction as controls represents my attempt to secure at once the literary backdrop for Swift's writing and writers with idiosyncrasies of writing comparable to Swift's. Failing this latter, I might have found that the writing of each control was not consistent within itself or differentiated from the other controls. Similarly, to limit the natural divergence among any group of writers, I decided to restrict the tested materials (wherever possible) to a homogeneous kind of prose, such as periodical essays, political pamphlets, didactic or historical works, and satire. Dramas, novels, scientific writing were usually avoided.

Once I had decided on the materials to be tested, the choice of the particular samples represented a problem. It might be thought that opening a book at random would provide an adequate amount of arbitrariness for a literary test. But the pitfalls in such a method are dangerous and might easily invalidate all the results obtained. In fact, the factor of bias is the essential one to fence against in sample selection, whether it be the bias of the investigator anxious to prove his hypothesis or the unconscious bias of the materials. A random choice, in statistical procedure, is defined as a method of selection in which every unit has an equal chance to be selected. Obviously, the mere taking of a likely-looking passage is redolent with bias. Opening a book by chance to the first page that comes up involves a similar, though subtler, bias. Books have a tendency to open more readily to places where they have been frequently consulted. Moreover, the thumb tends to seek out the central portion of the book and thus to avoid the introductory and concluding passages of a work, which may have a difference in texture from the body. These and less obvious impediments to truly random selection can only be checked by the use of a random number list.[1] Such a list has been regularly used for the tests in this study.[2]

Determining the size of the sample necessarily preceded the selection of the samples themselves. The size is equally sensitive to the application of statistical principles but in a less uniform way. In addition there are non-statistical factors to take account of. For instance, the sample had to be large enough to include a fair number of instances of the stylistic feature, let us say one

---

[1] Such a list is produced by a random number generator, a set of freely-rotating wheels containing the numerals from zero to nine which are set in motion and allowed to come to a stop, at which time the resulting configuration of digits is recorded.

[2] "A Page of Random Numbers", printed as an Appendix in William Edwards Deming, *Some Theory of Sampling* (New York, 1950), p. 593.

hundred. If the item counted was word-sized (i.e., all the words in a passage), the sample could be anything in excess of one hundred words. But if the item was sentence-sized, the sample needed to be in excess of one hundred periods long. So much is elementary. But a limitation operated as well on the maximum size of the sample. It had to be short enough to fall under the length of any representative work of the author's, or it would become impossible to test the characteristics of work against work and period against period in a writer's canon. Nor could it be so large that it approximated to any substantial portion (say one per cent) of the writer's canon, or it would have left the realm of sampling for that of the census or concordance, both of which are more accurate than the sample but vastly less economical.

A. *Definition of Word-Classes*

01 Nouns: "The *captain* was very well satisfied."
02 Main finite verbs: "My master *alighted* at an inn . . ."
03 Descriptive adjectives: "No wise man ever wished to be *younger*."
04 Descriptive adverbs: "I would *humbly* offer an amendment."
05 Infinitives: ". . . it will be a double charity to *admit* them."
06 Participles: ". . . *offering* to demonstrate . . ."
07 Gerunds: "Tools for *cutting* and *opening* . . ."
08 Quotations, Foreign Words: "*per annum.*"

11 Pronouns (*I, them, himself, this, each, some, both, none*): "I have observed the wit . . ."

21 Auxiliaries (*may, does, be, have, must, can, will, let, ought*): "I am assured . . ."

31 Determiners (*a, an, the, some, every, his, many, all*): Let me place *this* offer in a clear light."

32 Prepositional adverbs (*up, in, around, on, away, off*): "Jealousy like fire may shrivel *up* horns."

33   Intensifiers (*very, much, so, rather, too, more, quite, not*): "Young divines are *more* conversant."

34   Function adverbs (*almost, already, soon, perhaps, then, often*): "As I have *already* observed . . ."

41   Coordinating conjuctions (*and, but, for, nor, or, so, yet*): "*But* to return to madness."

42   Subordinating conjunctions (*because, when, if, as, although, since*): "*As* a war should be undertaken . . ."

43   Relatives (*who, that, which*): "The same spirits *which* would conquer a kingdom . . ."

44   Interrogatives (*who, when, where, how*): "*What* can be more defective or unsatisfactory . . ."

45   Correlative conjunctions (*either . . . or, not only . . . but also*): "They could *either* doubt it *or* forget it."

51   Prepositions (*with, of, on, by, in, up, behind, in relation to, as for*): "And *upon* this account it is . . ."

61   Pattern-markers (*there, it, to*): ". . . *there* are more children born in Roman Catholick countries . . ." "*It* is usual for clergymen," ". . . Cartesius reckoned *to* see before he died."

71   Interjections (*Pray, No, Lord*): "*O faith*, I should be glad . . ."

81   Numerals (*one, eighth, eighteen, million*): "I again subtract *fifty thousand* . . ."

91   Sentence-connectors (*however, moreover, on the contrary, nevertheless*): "*Further*, they have liberty to garrison . . ."

Note: All illustrative examples are from the works of Swift.

B. *Comparison of Two Separate Analyses of "Modest Proposal"*

Class	Manual	EDP	Difference
01	20.7	20.9	.2
02	6.0	6.0	
03	7.2	6.9	−.3
04	1.2	1.0	−.2
05	1.8	1.8	
06	1.5	1.5	
07	1.0	1.0	
08	—	—	
P/S	39.5	39.1	−.4
11	5.3	5.1	−.2
21	7.7	7.8	.1
31	13.9	14.4	.5
32	.4	.4	
33	2.7	3.0	.3
34	1.8	2.1	.3
41	5.0	4.9	−.1
42	2.5	2.5	
43	1.6	1.9	.3
44	.1	.1	
45	.6	.5	−.1
51	12.9	13.3	.4
61	2.3	2.3	
71	—	—	
81	3.0	1.8	−1.2
91	.8	.9	.1
FW	60.5	60.9	
VA	13.7	13.8	
VB	4.4	4.3	
M	18.8	19.8	
C	9.8	9.9	

The "Manual" sample was analyzed by writing each word on a slip of paper (with identifying location and class designation) and filing this slip alphabetically by hand in a box. As a word came up for other than the first time, the appropriate slip was located, an additional notation made on it and it was returned to the file. The Electronic-Data-Processing (EDP) procedure has been described in Chapter VI. The differences between the two sets of results may be traced to these factors:

1. Changes in analytic method
   A. Definition of word
   B. Word-class system
2. Difference in interpretation
3. Error.

The many numerals in *Modest Proposal* were originally broken down into their components, thus "an hundred and seventy thousand" was treated as five words, three of them numbers. But during the EDP reanalysis, numbers counted as one word if they were not separated by another part of speech. Therefore, "an hundred and seventy thousand" varied thus:

Manual - 31 81 41 81 81
EDP   - 31 81 41 81.

As a result, the quantity of numerals in the second analysis has greatly diminished. Some (e.g. *one*) have, when it was appropriate, been moved to class 31.

Some of the difference is traceable to the refinement of analytical skill with practice and to a new policy toward some words. The trend seemed to be slightly in favor of interpreting more words as Function words.

The factor of error results when a procedure like the Manual is used, in which the same piece of paper is often handled and much written on. The chances of omission, duplication and wrong entry are far greater than with EDP procedure.

When these factors are weighed, it is clear that the actual differences are not very important. Apart from Classes 31 and 81, the sum of differences is 2.6 per cent, a low figure considering the lack of uniformity between the two procedures. Swift himself considered a two per cent error trivial.[1] It is probable that the EDP procedure is subject to less than one per cent error.

[1] "An Examination of Certain Abuses...", *Works,* XII, 221.

C. *Make-up of Samples and Sub-Samples in Chapters VI and VII*

Sample					Sub-sample					
	1	2	3	4	5	6	7	8	9	10
	Volume* and page number									
Swift										
10	I* 20	7	154	30	48	26	57	104	88	100
12	III 110	93	29	30	99	159	64	36	145	79
13	III 49	60	165	124	115	39	24	151	149	139
20	II 80	IV 59	VI 14	VIII 17	II 17	IX 74	X 61	X 119	XII 162	XII 45
25	XI**									
26	XI 100	80	192	59	14	17	200	74	194	232
29	XII***									
58	VII 64	35	112	149	136	96	105	78	60	165
Macaulay										
61	I 562	72	321	411	64	36	536	593	303	631
62	II 176	450	737	583	49	456	666	775	671	564
Addison										
65	II 267	179	246	275	199	297	323	265	261	318
66	III 176	450	49	456	527	448	354	60	212	363
Gibbon										
71	II 408	II 349	III 353	I 242	III 132	III 95	III 460	II 43	II 399	II 32
72	V 272	IV 487	VII 136	VI 420	IV 256	IV 200	VII 216	V 369	VI 316	VII 142
Johnson										
75	200	74	194	61	183	119	72	162	27	67
76	IV 118	III 39	I 366	I 59	II 121	III 418	IV 256	IV 200	I 150	IV 152
Unknown										
97	IX***									
98	IX***									

* When no volume number is shown, all sub-samples are drawn from the same volume.

** Stratified sample.

*** Continuous sample.

Note: The Swift and Unknown samples are drawn from *Works*. The control texts are identified in Ch. VI, nn. 57-60, and are starred in the Bibliography.

Names and short titles of samples

Sample	Author	Work	Short title
10	Swift	*A Tale of a Tub*	*Tale*
12	„	*The Examiner*	*Exam.* I
13	„	„	*Exam.* II
20	„	Miscellaneous Works	*Misc.*
25	„	*Gulliver's Travels*	*Gull.* I
26	„	„ „	*Gull.* II
29	„	*A Modest Proposal*	*MP*
58	„	*History of the Four Last Years of the Queen*	*History*
61	Macaulay	*Literary Essays*	*Macaulay*-L
62	„	*Historical Essays*	*Macaulay*-H
65	Addison	*The Tatler*	*Tatler*
66	„	*The Spectator*	*Spect.*
71	Gibbon	*History of the Decline and Fall of the Roman Empire*	*Decline* A
72	„	„	*Decline* B
75	Johnson	*Rasselas*	*Rass.*
76	„	*The Lives of the Poets*	*Lives*
97	Unknown	*A Letter of Advice to a Young Poet*	*Letter* I
98	„	„	*Letter* II

D. *The "Federalist" Experiment*

Shortly before this study was completed, information became available that two important attribution problems had been solved by objective methods. A Swedish scholar, Alvar Ellegård, published two books setting forth his solution to the *Junius* problem (see Appendix G); and the directors of a large group of research workers at Harvard and elsewhere presented results claiming to establish the authorship of the disputed *Federalist Papers* (New York *Times,* September 10, 1962).

According to a fuller account in a press release entitled "Inference in an Authorship Problem" (dated September 9, 1962), Professors Frederick Mosteller of Harvard University and David L. Wallace of the University of Chicago, the co-leaders of the project, claimed to have settled the problem by attributing all the disputed papers to Madison.

The study was based on the individual frequency of two kinds of words in the known writings of Hamilton and Madison, compared with the disputed writings:
1. Function words, such as *any, by, of, but, upon.*
2. Other words, whose discriminative powers had been revealed by preliminary investigation: *fortune, rapid, vigor.*

Altogether, a total of 165 words was used. From the apparent consistent preference of an author for certain words, especially the high-frequency short function words, the researchers were able to estimate the odds in favor of Madison to be very high (at least 80 to 1).

The study was carried out over a period of three years by a group of more than fifty researchers, with the help of the Ford, Rockefeller and National Science Foundations, the Office of Naval Research, the Harvard Laboratory of Social Relations, the Center for Advanced Study in the Behavioral Sciences at Palo Alto, and the IBM 7090 computer at the Massachusetts Institute of Technology.

It is difficult to assess the results achieved in view of the intricacy of the statistics, a full understanding of which is well beyond my reach. However, a number of assumptions made by the researchers require comment. For example, the odds in favor of Madison's authorship of a given paper (80 to 1) are the product of a likelihood ratio developed from the data and a subjective initial estimate about the author's identity. Though the project directors are aware of the dangers of this procedure, which tends to magnify the figures offered to the public, they do not explain why the assumption of ignorance is not simply made.

Moreover, they do not seem to be wholly aware of the possibility that editorial revision might have taken place – that Madison might have changed all Hamilton's *on*'s to *upon*'s, as Swift in 1735 changed all his earlier *has*'s to *hath*'s. After all, if Madison edited Hamilton's text, would he not take care to adjust the function words according to his own preference? Since the change of even a few words has enormous statistical repercussions in the technique used by the project, such editing would probably affect and might even invalidate the results. The project directors discuss the possibility of joint authorship but not of editing.

The "contextual" nature of words has not escaped their notice. And they try to avoid words the frequency of whose use seems to be affected by the context. But to the extent that a writer is consciously aware of the identity of individual words, all words are contextual and their individual importance must be viewed skeptically.

Finally, one has the feeling that some of the literary aspects of the problem has escaped the researchers, whose simple faith in a common-sense approach to language and literature tends to create doubt in the observer. It is disturbing to read in the press release the point duly reported in the newspaper account: "both authors were masters of the popular *Spectator* style of writing – complicated and oratorical" (p. 1).

E. *Parts of Speech Distribution in Three Modern British Writers* compared with one Sample of Swift and the Swift Average*

Class	Woolf %	Huxley %	Greene %	Swift 12	Swift x̄
01	21.9	27.1	24.0	19.3	20.3
11	13.3	7.6	12.9	7.5	7.1
04 + 32 + 33 + 34 + 91 }	9.3	10.1	9.4	6.9	6.3
02 + 05 + 06 + 07 }	19.4	16.8	19.6	11.4	11.2
31** + 03	14.5	18.8	13.3	21.9	21.3
41 + 42 + 51 }	22.6	22.9	21.3	20.5	20.3

*   After Barth, Tables I-VI.
**   Barth excludes articles.
Note: Each writer is represented by a sample of 5000 words (excluding articles).

F. *Closing Sentence-Elements by Word-Class, as a Percentage of Total Sentence* *

Swift samples

Class	10	12	13	20	25	26	29
01	60.	65.	64.	70.	69.	56.	73.
02	8.	9.	9.	4.	6.	4.	5.
03	5.	1.	3.	5.	7.	7.	7.
04				1.		1.	
05				4.	1.	7.	2.
06							2.
07	1.	3.	1.	1.		1.	
08	7.	1.	5.	2.			
11	9.	14.	9.	6.	6.	17.	7.
21							
31	3.	1.		2.	4.		
32		1.	2.		4.		2.
33					1.		
34	5.	4.	3.	4.	2.	2.	2.
41							
42							
43							
44				1.	1.		
45							
51		1.				2.	
61							
71							
81	2.		1.				3.
91							

* Rounded to whole numbers.

290   APPENDIX II

Control samples

Class	61	62	65	66	71	72	75	76
01	66.	73.	75.	71.	90.	93.	64.	63.
02	10.	10.	5.	6.	4.	3.	13.	9.
03	12.	4.	4.	7.		3.	2.	9.
04	1.	1.					1.	1.
05	3.	3.	1.		4.		5.	3.
06		1.						1.
07				1.			1.	1.
08	3.	1.				1.		3.
11	6.	4.	9.	12.	1.	1.	11.	9.
21	1.		1.	1.			1.	
31	1.	1.						
32		3.	2.					
33								
34	1.	1.	1.	1.			3.	2.
41								
42								
43								
44								
45								
51								
61								
71								
81				1.				
91								

G. The "Junius" Problem

In trying to settle the authorship of the *Letters of Junius,* Alvar Ellegård made a number of assumptions parallel to those I have set out in Chapter III. Our procedures, however, diverge considerably. He began by reading the text of *Junius* in search of anything that might strike him as peculiar to Junius, almost exclusively vocabulary items, in a procedure reminiscent of Spitzer's. These he calls "Junius plus-words." From the work of a group of control authors, including all the leading candidates for authorship of the *Letters*, he elicited another series of peculiarities which he felt were not characteristic of Junius. These are "Junius minus-words".

Having tentatively established these two sets of discriminators, he examined the total mass of material (aggregating more than 1.6 million words) with the help of an electronic computer and worked out the relative frequencies of 458 words, expressions and constructions in *Junius*, on the one hand, and in the total mass, on the other. For a given word, for example *decorum*, if the frequency in *Junius* is 9.5 per 100,000 and in the total 1.0 per 100,000, the resulting distinctiveness ratio for such a Junius plus-word would be 9.5. The list of Junius ratios is then compared with those of each of the leading candidates. When the lists match, the author is found. Ellegård believes that Sir Philip Francis was the author of the *Letters of Junius*.

Because his technique, like that of the *Federalist* Project, uses particular words, the quantities he is dealing in are extremely minute and a very sophisticated statistical technique, based on the Poisson distribution (also used by the *Federalist* Project), is required. To diminish the uncertainty of dealing with such minute quantities, Ellegård finds it convenient to group his data. Nonetheless, his results, which he admits are not wholly reliable, are affected by the smallness of the individual samples and the limitations of his word-and-expression technique. As a reviewer of his two books lamented, it is unfortunate "that having laboured so hard he could not have done just a little more, by extending his investigation beyond the examination of mainly vocabulary items . . . to include more syntactical and morphological data . . ." (*Times Literary Supplement*, January 25, 1963, p. 67). There is no doubt, however, that aside from the solution of the attribution problems the *Federalist* workers and Ellegård have uncovered a large amount of new data about late eighteenth-century political English.

H. *"Letter"* C

As I have explained in Chapter VII, the need to maintain the standard sample size of about 3500 words (especially with respect to the "D" criterion) forced the division of *A Letter to a Young Poet* into two parts, each of which approximates 3500 words. The decision to divide into two halves, first and second – rather than even- and odd-numbered pages, for example – is based on the suspicion that the influence of another hand might be more probable at the beginning or the end of the work. In any case, there was no particular reason not to divide the work in that way. Ideally, of course, the non-Swiftian parts of the text might be best brought out if it could be divided into very small parts, each one of which could be tested for genuineness. Unfortunately, such a procedure was out of the question because of the sample size requirement, itself based on the necessity of avoiding the delterious effects of random variation.

The results of the division into linear halves have supported the candidacy of Swift for the authorship of the *Letter*. But, inasmuch as the conclusion might still leave room for doubt, I have decided to present one more examination of the text. In this division (*Letter* C), the second and third quarters of the work are treated as a unit. The new sample runs from the second sentence of the third paragraph on p. 331 (*Works,* IX) to the end of the third paragraph on p.340, skipping two lines on p. 336 (from "Name" in 1.10 to the end of the sentence). The whole sample (numbered 99) takes up 104 IBM cards.

The figures in the accompanying table show the over-all word-class frequency to be not very different from those of *Letters* I and II, as might have been expected. But as the values, both percentage and normalized, of the three Profile criteria disclose, this central section of the *Letter* is more like Swift than even the closer half, *Letter* II. In fact, the resemblance is so close that the Profile values almost exactly duplicate the Swift average, as Figure 7C shows. Thus *Letter* C seems to be more like Swift than any genuine work of Swift's. Its congruence is almost suspicious.

Does this evidence alter in any way the conclusion reached earlier? Fundamentally, little is changed: Swift is still responsible for much of the work, and the possibility of an alien hand is still there. But more accuracy is now possible and somewhat more confidence in voicing this conclusion. Because *Letter* C is more Swiftian than either I or II, we may feel more certain that Swift's nearly unadulterated style is present in the middle section and that something went wrong at the two ends, especially at the beginning. Although it is not essential, the new evidence is welcome because it ratifies, in splendid fashion, what had already been found.

APPENDIX II

TABLE

Letter C (99): Word-class frequency distribution and other statistical details

Class	Percentage	Sentence Openings
01	19.9	4.0
02	5.9	2.6
03	7.4	
04	.7	
05	2.6	
06	.5	
07	1.1	
08	.2	
P/S	38.3	
11	6.8	18.4
21	7.9	5.3
31	14.9	17.1
32	.6	
33	2.6	
34	2.1	4.0
41	5.2	20.1
42	3.0	2.6
43	2.2	
44		
45	0.5	
51	12.3	13.1
61	3.0	1.3
71	.1	
81	.1	
91	.4	10.5
FW	61.7	
VA	13.8	
VB	4.1	
M	20.3	
C	10.9	

Total Words:	3647
Total Sentences:	76
Average Sentence-length	47.99
Different Patterns (D):	869
Initial Connectives (IC):	34.2

Three-Discriminator Profile (Normalized)
VB — 100   IC — 103   D — 104

BIBLIOGRAPHY *

Abrams, M. H., *The Mirror and the Lamp* (New York, 1958).
*Addison, Joseph, *The Works of the Late Right Honorable Joseph Addison, Esq.*, 4 vols. (Birmingham, 1761).
Aitken, G. A., "Swift", in *The Cambridge History of English Literature*, ed. A. W. Ward and A. R. Waller, 15 vols. (Cambridge, 1907-1916, 1927); IX (1912), pp. 91-128.
Allen, Walter, ed., *The Writer on His Art* (New York, 1948).
Allott, Miriam, ed., *Novelists on the Novel* (New York, 1959).
Allport, Gordon W., *Personality* (New York, 1937).
Alonso, Amado, "The Stylistic Interpretation of Literary Texts", *Modern Language Notes*, LVII (1942), pp. 489-496.
Aristotle, *Art of Rhetoric*, tr. J. H. Freese (Loeb Classical Library) (London, 1926).
Arkin, Herbert and Raymond R. Colton, *Tables for Statisticians* (New York, 1950).
Atkins, J. W. H., *Literary Criticism in Antiquity*, 2 vols. (Cambridge, 1934).
Auerbach, Erich, *Mimesis*, tr. Willard Trask (Princeton, 1953).
Aurner, Robert R., "Caxton and the English Sentence", *Wisconsin Studies in Language and Literature*, XVIII (1923), pp. 23-59.
——, "The History of Certain Aspects of the Structure of the English Sentence", *Philological Quarterly*, II (1923), pp. 187-208.
Bain, Alexander, *English Composition and Rhetoric* (London, 1866).
Baker, Robert, *Remarks on the English Language* (London, 1779).
Baker, Sheridan, *The Practical Stylist* (New York, 1962).
Baldwin, Charles Sears, *Medieval Rhetoric and Poetic* (New York, 1928).
Ballard, Philip Boswood, *Thought and Language* (London, 1934).
Barth, Gilbert, *Recherches sur la Fréquence et la Valeur des Parties du Discours en Français, en Anglais et en Espagnol* (Paris, 1961).
Barthes, Roland, *Le Degré Zéro de l'Ecriture* (Paris, 1953).
Bateson, F. W., *English Poetry and the English Language* (Oxford, 1934).
Baugh, Albert C., *History of the English Language*, 2nd ed. (New York, 1957).
Beattie, James, *On Poetry and Music*, 3rd ed. (London, 1789).

* Starred titles indicate texts used for samples.

Beattie, Lester M., *John Arbuthnot: Mathematician and Satirist* (Cambridge, Mass., 1935).
Berwick, Donald M., *The Reputation of Jonathan Swift, 1781-1882* (Philadelphia, 1941).
Bloomfield, Leonard, *Language* (New York, 1933).
——, "Secondary and Tertiary Responses to Language", *Language,* XX (1944), pp. 45-55.
Böckmann, Paul, ed., *Stil- und Formprobleme in der Literatur* (Heidelberg, 1959).
Boder, David P., "The Adjective-Verb Quotient; a Contribution to the Psychology of Language", *The Psychological Record,* III (1940), pp. 309-343.
Bond, H. L., *The Literary Art of Edward Gibbon* (Oxford, 1960).
Booth, Andrew D., L. Brandwood, and J. P. Cleave, *Mechanical Resolution of Linguistic Problems* (London, 1958).
Boswell, James, *The Life of Samuel Johnson,* ed. G. B. Hill, rev. L. F. Powell, 6 vols. (Oxford, 1934-1950).
Brady, Frank, "Prose Style and the 'Whig' Tradition", *Bulletin of the New York Public Library,* LXVI (1962), pp. 455-463.
Bredvold, Louis I., Robert K. Root and George Sherburn, eds., *Eighteenth Century Prose* (New York, 1932).
Brinegar, Claude S., "Mark Twain and the Quintus Curtius Snodgrass Letters", *Journal of the American Statistical Association,* LVIII (1963), pp. 85-96.
Brower, Reuben A., ed., *On Translation* (Cambridge, Mass., 1959).
Brown, Norman O., *Life Against Death* (New York, 1959).
Brownell, William C., *The Genius of Style* (New York, 1924).
Bruneau, Charles, "La Stylistique", *Romance Philology,* V (1951), pp. 1-14.
Bryant, Margaret M. and Janet Rankin Aiken, *The Psychology of English* (New York, 1940).
Buffon, George-Louis Leclerc, Comte de, *Œuvres Philosophiques de Buffon,* ed. Jean Piveteau (Paris, 1954).
Bullitt, John M., *Swift and the Anatomy of Satire* (Cambridge, Mass., 1953).
Burrow, James, *De Usu et Ratione Interpungendi: an Essay on the Use of Pointing* (London, 1771).
Butler, Samuel, *Samuel Butler's Notebooks,* ed. Geoffrey Keynes and Brian Hill (London, 1951).
Campbell, George, *The Philosophy of Rhetoric,* 7th ed. (London, 1823).
Carroll, John B., *The Study of Language* (Cambridge, Mass., 1959).
Cattell, Raymond B., "The Nature and Measurement of Anxiety", *Scientific American,* CCVIII (March, 1963), pp. 96-104.
Cazamian, Louis and Emile Legouis, *A History of English Literature,* tr. W. D. MacInnes and author. Rev. ed. (New York, 1957).
Chandler, Zilpha Emma, *An Analysis of the Stylistic Technique of Addison, Johnson, Hazlitt and Pater* (Iowa City, 1928).
Chaucer, Geoffrey, *The Works of Geoffrey Chaucer,* ed. F. N. Robinson. 2nd ed. (Boston, 1957).

ope, Earl of, *Letters Written by the Late Right Honourable Philip Dormer Stanhope, Earl of Chesterfield, to His Son Philip Stanhope, Esq.* 11th ed. 4 vols. (London, 1800).
Chomsky, Noam, Review of B. F. Skinner's *Verbal Behavior, Language,* XXXV (1959), pp. 26-58.
——, *Syntactic Structures* (The Hague, 1957).
Chrétien, C. Douglas, "A New Statistical Approach to the Study of Language", *Romance Philology,* XVI (1963), pp. 290-301. [Review of G. Herdan, *Language as Choice and Chance.*]
Churchill, Winston Spencer, *Marlborough: His Life and Times,* 6 vols. (New York, 1933-1938).
Cicero, *Brutus,* tr. G. L. Hendrickson; *Orator,* tr. H. M. Hubbell (Loeb Classical Library) (London, 1952).
——, *De Oratore,* tr. H. Rackham, 2 vols. (Loeb Classical Library) (London, 1960).
Coleridge, Samuel Taylor, *Complete Works,* ed. W. G. T. Shedd, 7 vols. (New York, 1884).
——, *Select Poetry and Prose,* ed. Stephen Potter (London, 1933).
Constable, John, *Reflections upon Accuracy of Style* (London, 1731).
Cooper, Lane, ed., *Theories of Style* (New York, 1907).
Crane, Ronald S., ed., *New Essays by Oliver Goldsmith* (Chicago, 1927).
Cressot, Marcel, *Le Style et Ses Techniques* (Paris, 1947).
Croce, Benedetto, *Aesthetic,* tr. D. Ainslie (New York, 1948).
Croll, Morris W., "The Baroque Style in Prose", in *Studies in English Philology, A Miscellany in Honor of Frederick Klaeber,* ed. Kemp Malone and Martin B. Ruud (Minneapolis, 1929), pp. 427-456.
Croxton, Frederick E., *Elementary Statistics* (New York, 1959).
Curle, Richard, *Joseph Conrad: A Study* (London, 1914).
Curme, George O., *English Grammar* (New York, 1947).
——, *Parts of Speech and Accidence* (Boston, 1935).
——, *Syntax* (Boston, 1931).
Davie, Donald, *Articulate Energy* (London, 1955).
——, "Irony and Conciseness in Berkeley and Swift", *Dublin University Magazine* (1952), pp. 20-29.
Davies, Hugh Sykes, "Trollope and His Style", *A Review of English Literature,* I (1961), pp. 73-85.
Davis, Herbert, "The Canon of Swift" in *English Institute Essays, 1942* (New York, 1943), pp. 119-136.
——, "The Conciseness of Swift" in *Essays on the Eighteenth Century Presented to David Nichol Smith,* ed. J. R. Sutherland and F. P. Wilson (Oxford, 1945), pp. 15-32.
——, *Stella* (New York, 1942).
*Defoe, Daniel, *Novels and Selected Writings,* 14 vols. (Oxford, 1926-1927).
[Delany, Patrick], *Observations ... on the Life and Writings of Dr. Jonathan Swift* (London, 1754).
Demetrius on Style, tr. W. Rhys Roberts (Loeb Classical Library) (London, 1960).

Deming, William Edwards, *Some Theory of Sampling* (New York, 1950).
Denniston, J. D., *The Greek Particles*, 2nd ed. (Oxford, 1954).
De Quincey, Thomas, *Collected Writings*, ed. D. Masson, 14 vols. (Edinburgh, 1889-1890).
Diamond, A. S., *The History and Origin of Language* (New York, 1959).
Dobrée, Bonamy, *English Literature in the Early Eighteenth Century, 1700-1740* (Oxford, 1959).
——, *Modern Prose Style* (Oxford, 1934).
——, "Some Aspects of Defoe's Prose" in *Pope and His Contemporaries*, ed. J. L. Clifford and L. A. Landa (Oxford, 1949), pp. 171-184.
*Dryden, John, *Essays*, ed. W. P. Ker, 2 vols. (Oxford, 1900).
Duff, I. F. Grant, "A One-Sided Sketch of Swift", *Psychoanalytic Quarterly*, VI (1937), pp. 238-259.
Durham, Willard Higley, ed., *Critical Essays of the Eighteenth Century, 1700-1725* (New Haven, 1915).
Eddy, W. A., *Gulliver's Travels: A Critical Study* (Princeton, 1923).
Edwards, S. L., ed., *An Anthology of English Prose from Bede to Robert Louis Stevenson* (London, 1917).
Ehrenpreis, Irvin, *The Personality of Jonathan Swift* (London, 1958).
——, *Swift: The Man, His Works and the Age* (London, 1962).
Elderton, W. P., "A Few Statistics on the Length of English Words", *Journal of the Royal Statistical Society*, CXII (1949), pp. 436-443.
Ellegård, Alvar, "Estimating Vocabulary Size", *Word*, XVI (1960), pp. 219-244.
——, *A Statistical Method for Determining Authorship: The Junius Letters, 1769-1772* (Göteborg, 1962).
——, *Who was Junius?* (Stockholm and Uppsala, 1962).
Emerson, Oliver F., *The History of the English Language* (New York, 1894).
Entwistle, W. J., *Aspects of Language* (London, 1953).
Erdman, David V., "Newspaper Sonnets Put to the Concordance Test: Can They Be Attributed to Coleridge?" *Bulletin of the New York Public Library*, LXI (1957), pp. 508-516, 611-620; and LXII (1958), pp. 46-49.
——, "The Signature of Style", *Bulletin of the New York Public Library*, LXIII (1959), pp. 88-109.
Everett, C. W., ed., *Letters of Junius* (London, 1927).
Ewald, William B., Jr., *The Masks of Jonathan Swift* (Oxford, 1954).
Eysenck, H. J., *Sense and Nonsense in Psychology* (Harmondsworth, 1958).
The Federalist, ed. Jacob E. Cooke (Cleveland and New York, 1961).
Felton, Henry, *A Dissertation on Reading the Classics and Forming a Just Style,* 4th ed. (London, 1730).
Ferguson, Charles W., *Say It With Words* (New York, 1959).
Ferguson, Leonard W., "The Evaluative Attitudes of Jonathan Swift", *The Psychological Record,* III (1939), pp. 26-44.
Flaubert, Gustave, *Correspondence: Deuxième Série (1850-1854)* (Paris, 1889).

Flesch, Rudolf, *The Art of Readable Writing* (New York, 1949).

Fogel, Ephim G., "Salmons in Both, or Some Caveats for Canonical Scholars", *Bulletin of the New York Public Library,* LXIII (1959), pp. 223-236, 292-308.

Fort, Joseph-Barthélemy, *Samuel Butler l'Ecrivain: Etude d'un Style* (Bordeaux, 1935).

Francis, W. Nelson, *The Structure of American English* (New York, 1958).

"Freeing the Mind", *Times Literary Supplement* (March-June 1962).

Frei, Henri, *La Grammaire des Fautes* (Paris, 1929).

French, N. R., C. W. Carter, and W. Koenig, "The Words and Sounds of Telephone Conversations", *Bell System Technical Journal,* IX (1930), pp. 290-324.

Fries, Charles C., *American English Grammar* (New York, 1940).

——, *The Structure of English* (New York, 1952).

Frye, Northrop, *Anatomy of Criticism* (Princeton, 1957).

Fucks, William, "On Mathematical Analysis of Style", *Biometrika,* XXXIX (1952), pp. 122-129.

Fulcher, Paul M., ed., *Foundations of English Style* (New York, 1928).

Fussell, Paul, Jr., "Speaker and Style in *A Letter of Advice to a Young Poet* (1721), and the Problem of Attribution", *Review of English Studies,* X (1959), pp. 63-67.

Galton, Arthur, ed., *English Prose, from Maundeville to Thackeray* (London, 1888).

Gansl, Irene, *Vocabulary: Its Measurement and Growth* (New York, 1939).

Gerwig, George William, "On the Decrease of Predication and of Sentence Weight in English Prose", *University of Nebraska Studies,* II (1894), pp. 17-44.

Gibbon, Edward, *The Autobiography of Edward Gibbon,* ed. John Murray (London, 1896).

*——, *The Decline and Fall of the Roman Empire,* ed. J. B. Bury, 7 vols. (London, 1896-1900).

——, *The Letters of Edward Gibbon,* ed. J. E. Norton, 3 vols. (New York, 1956).

——, *The Memoirs of the Life of Edward Gibbon,* ed. G. B. Hill (London, 1900).

Gleason, H. A., Jr., *An Introduction to Descriptive Linguistics,* Rev. ed. (New York, 1961).

Godin, Henri J. G., *Les Ressources Stylistiques du Français Contemporain* (Oxford, 1948).

Goethe, Johann Wolfgang von, *Conversations with Eckermann* (Washington, 1901).

*Goldsmith, Oliver, *Selected Works* (London, 1950).

——, *The Works of Oliver Goldsmith,* ed. Peter Cunningham, 4 vols. (New York, 1881).

Gosse, Edmund, *Sir Thomas Browne* (New York, 1905).

Graves, Robert and Alan Hodge, *The Reader over Your Shoulder* (New York, 1944).

Gray, Thomas, *Correspondence of Thomas Gray*, ed. P. Toynbee and L. Whibley, 3 vols. (Oxford, 1935).

Gray, W. S. and B. E. Leary, *What Makes a Book Readable* (Chicago, 1935).

Greenacre, Phyllis, *Swift and Carroll* (New York, 1955).

Greenberg, Joseph H., *Essays in Linguistics* (Chicago, 1957).

Greene, Donald J., "Is There a 'Tory' Prose Style?" *Bulletin of the New York Public Library*, LXVI (1962), pp. 449-454.

Guiraud, Pierre, *Bibliographie Critique de la Statistique Linguistique* (Utrecht, 1954).

——, *Les Caractères Statistiques du Vocabulaire* (Paris, 1953).

——, *Problèmes et Méthodes de la Statistique Linguistique* (Dordrecht, 1959).

——, *La Stylistique* (Paris, 1954).

——, "Stylistiques", *Neophilologus*, XXXVIII (1954), pp. 1-12.

Hadas, Moses, *Hellenistic Culture* (New York, 1959).

Hale, William Bayard, *The Story of a Style* (New York, 1920).

Harris, Zellig S., "Discourse Analysis", *Language*, XXVIII (1952), pp. 1-30.

——, *Structural Linguistics*, 4th imp. (Chicago, 1960).

Hatzfeld, Helmut, *Bibliografia Critica de la Nueva Estilistica Aplicada a las Literaturas Romanicas* (Madrid, 1955).

——, *A Critical Bibliography of the New Stylistics* (Chapel Hill, N. C., 1953).

——, "Methods of Stylistic Investigation", *Literature and Science: Proceedings of the Sixth Congress of the International Federation of Modern Languages and Literatures* (Oxford, 1955), pp. 44-51.

——, "Stylistic Criticism as Art-Minded Philology", *Yale French Studies*, II (1949), 62-70.

Henle, Paul, ed., *Language, Thought and Culture* (Ann Arbor, Mich., 1958).

Herdan, Gustav, "Chaucer's Authorship of *The Equatorie of the Planetis*", *Language*, XXXII (1956), pp. 254-259.

——, *Language as Choice and Chance* (Groningen, 1956).

——, *Type-Token Mathematics* (The Hague, 1960).

Highet, Gilbert, *Poets in a Landscape* (Harmondsworth, 1959).

Hildreth, Carson, "The Bacon-Shakespeare Controversy; a Contribution", *University of Nebraska Studies*, II (1897), pp. 147-162.

Hockett, Charles F., *A Course in Modern Linguistics* (New York, 1958).

Hodgart, Matthew, "Politics and Prose Style in the Late Eighteenth Century: *The Radicals*", *Bulletin of the New York Public Library*, LXVI (1962), pp. 464-469.

Hoel, Paul G., *Elementary Statistics* (New York, 1960).

Holloway, J., "The Well-Filled Dish: An Analysis of Swift's Satire", *Hudson Review*, IX (1956), pp. 20-37.

Hotchner, A. E., "Hemingway Talks to American Youth", *This Week* (Oct. 18, 1959), pp. 10-11, 24, 26.

Hume, David, *Letters*, ed. J. Y. T. Greig, 2 vols. (Oxford, 1932).

——, *The Philosophical Works of David Hume*, 4 vols. (Boston, 1854).

Hytier, J., "La Méthode de M. L. Spitzer", *Romanic Review*, XLI (1950), pp. 42-59.

Ives, Sumner, *A New Handbook for Writers* (New York, 1960).

Jacobsson, Bengt, *Inversion in English* (Uppsala, 1951).

Jakobson, Roman and Morris Halle, *Fundamentals of Language* (The Hague, 1956).

Jefferson, D. W., "An Approach to Swift", *From Dryden to Johnson* (Harmondsworth, 1957), pp. 230-249.

——, ed., *Eighteenth-Century Prose, 1700-1800* (Harmondsworth, 1956).

[Jeffrey, Francis], Review of Walter Scott's edition of the Works of Swift, *Edinburgh Review*, XXVII (1816), pp. 1-58.

Jespersen, Otto, *A Modern English Grammar on Historical Principles*, 7 vols. (London and Copenhagen, 1949-1954).

Johnson, Burges, *Good Writing* (Syracuse, 1932).

Johnson, Samuel, *A Dictionary of the English Language*, 3rd ed., 2 vols. (London, 1765).

*——, *The History of Rasselas*, ed. R. W. Chapman (Oxford, 1927).

*——, *The Lives of the Poets*, 4 vols. (London, 1781).

*——, *The Lives of the Poets*, ed. G. B. Hill, 3 vols. (Oxford, 1905).

*——, *Prose and Poetry* (London, 1950).

Johnson, S. F., "An Uncollected Early Poem by Coleridge", *Bulletin of the New York Public Library*, LXI (1957), pp. 505-507.

Johnson, W., "A Program of Research", *Psychological Monographs*, LVI (1944), pp. 1-15.

Jones, Richard Foster, *The Seventeenth Century* (Stanford, 1951).

——, *The Triumph of the English Language* (Stanford, 1953).

Jonson, Ben, *Timber or Discoveries*, ed. Ralph S. Walker (Syracuse, 1953).

"Junius" (anon. rev.), *Times Literary Supplement* (March 8, 1928), p. 161.

"*Kai*ropractice", *Time*, LXXXI (March 15, 1963), p. 56.

Kantor, J. R., *An Objective Psychology of Grammar* (Bloomington, Ind., 1936).

Karpman, Ben, "Neurotic Traits of Jonathan Swift . . .", *Psychoanalytic Review*, XXIX (1942), pp. 26-45, 165-184.

Keller, Rudolf, *Die Ellipse in der Neuenglischen Sprache als Syntaktisch-Semantisches Problem* (Winterthur, 1944).

Kenney, William, "Addison, Johnson, and the 'Energetick' Style", *Studia Neophilologica*, XXXIII (1961), pp. 103-114.

Kligman, Elsie, "Contemporary Opinion of Swift", Unpubl. M. A. Essay. (Columbia, 1931).

Knight, G. Wilson, *The Burning Oracle* (London, 1939).

Krapp, George Philip, *The Rise of English Literary Prose* (New York, 1915).

Krishnamurti, S., "Dr. Johnson's Use of Monosyllabic Words", *Journal of the University of Bombay*, XIX (1950), pp. 1-12.

——, "Frequency Distribution of Nouns in Dr. Johnson's Prose Works", *Journal of the University of Bombay*, XX (1951), pp. 1-16.

——, "Vocabulary Tests Applied to (Dr. Johnson's) Authorship of the 'Misargyrus' Papers in the *Adventurer*", *Journal of the University of Bombay*, XXI (1952), pp. 47-62.

Krishnamurti, S., "Vocabulary Tests Applied to the Authorship of the 'New Essays' Attributed to Dr. Johnson", *Journal of the University of Bombay*, XXII (1953), pp. 1-5.

Kroeber, A. L., *Style and Civilizations* (Ithaca, 1957).

Kruisinga, E., *A Handbook of Present-Day English*, Part II, 5th ed., 3 vols. (Groningen, 1931-1932).

Landa, Louis A. and James Edward Tobin, *Jonathan Swift: A List of Critical Studies Published from 1895 to 1945* (New York, 1945).

Lannering, Jan, *Studies in the Prose Style of Addison* (Uppsala, 1951).

Lanson, Gustave, *L'Art de la Prose* (Paris, 1907).

Lascelles, Mary, *Jane Austen and Her Art* (London, 1939).

Leavis, F. R., *The Common Pursuit* (New York, 1952).

Lee, William, *Daniel Defoe: His Life and Recently Discovered Writings*, 3 vols. (London, 1869).

Leonard, Sterling Andrus, *The Doctrine of Correctness in English Usage, 1700-1800* (Madison, Wis., 1929).

Levy, R., "A New Credo of Stylistics", *Symposium*, III (1949), pp. 321-334.

Lewis, Charlton T. and Charles Short, eds., *A New Latin Dictionary* (Harper's Latin Dictionary) (New York, 1907).

Locke, John, *An Essay Concerning Human Understanding*, ed. A. C. Fraser, 2 vols. (Oxford, 1894).

Locke, William N. and A. Donald Booth, eds., *Machine Translation of Languages* (Cambridge, Mass., 1955).

Long, Ralph B., *The Sentence and Its Parts* (Chicago, 1961).

Lord, George de F., "Comments on the Canonical Caveat", *Bulletin of the New York Public Library*, LXIII (1959), pp. 355-366.

——, "Two New Poems by Marvell?" *Bulletin of the New York Public Library*, LXII (1958), pp. 551-570.

Lovejoy, Arthur, *The Great Chain of Being* (Cambridge, Mass., 1948).

Lowth, Robert, *A Short Introduction to English Grammar* (London, 1762).

Lucas, F. L., *Style* (London, 1955).

*Macaulay, Thomas Babington, Lord, *The History of England*, ed. C. H. Firth, 6 vols. (London, 1913-1915).

*——, *Literary and Historical Essays*, 2 vols. (London, 1923).

McDonough, James T., Jr., "Classics and Computers", *Graduate Faculties Newsletter*, March, 1962, pp. 4-5.

Mann, Elizabeth L., "The Problem of Originality in English Literary Criticism, 1750-1800", *Philological Quarterly*, XVIII (1939), pp. 97-118.

Marouzeau, Jules, *Précis de Stylistique Française*, third ed. (Paris, 1950).

——, *Traité de Stylistique Latine* (Paris, 1946).

Martin, Harold C., ed., *Style in Prose Fiction* (New York, 1959).

Mason, William Monck, *The History ... of St. Patrick* (Dublin, 1820).

Maugham, W. Somerset, *The Summing-Up* (New York, 1957).

Mayo, T. F., "The Authorship of the History of John Bull", *PMLA*, XLV (1930), pp. 274-282.

Melmoth, William, *Fitzosborne's Letters on Several Subjects* (Boston, 1815).

——, *Letters on Several Subjects by the Late Sir Thomas Fitzosborne, Bart.* (London, 1748).

Mencken, Henry L., ed., *A New Dictionary of Quotations* (New York, 1946).

Miles, Josephine, *Renaissance, Eighteenth-Century, and Modern Language in English Poetry: a Tabular View* (Berkeley, 1960).

Miller, George A., *Language and Communication* (New York, 1951).

——, E. B. Newman and E. A. Friedman, "Length-Frequency Statistics for Written English", *Information and Control*, I (1958), pp. 370-389.

Miller, Henry Knight, *Essays in Commentary on Fielding's "Miscellanies"* (Princeton, 1961).

Montaigne, Michel de, *Essais*, ed. Albert Thibaudet (Paris, 1946).

Morison, Elting, ed., *American Style: Essays in Value and Performance* (New York, 1958).

Moritz, Robert E., "On the Variation and Functional Relation of Certain Sentence-Constants in Standard Literature", *University of Nebraska Studies*, III (1903), pp. 229-253.

Morley, John, *Burke* (New York, 1879).

Moroney, M. J., *Facts from Figures* (Harmondsworth, 1956).

Morris, Charles, *Signs, Language and Behavior* (New York, 1955).

Morris, Edward P., "A Science of Style", *Transactions and Proceedings of the American Philological Association*, XLVI (1915), pp. 103-118.

Mosteller, Frederick and David L. Wallace, "Inference in an Authorship Problem", *Journal of the American Statistical Association*, LVIII (1963), pp. 275-309.

Muller, Herbert J., *Science and Criticism* (New Haven, 1943).

Murry, John Middleton, *Jonathan Swift* (London, 1954).

——, *The Problem of Style* (London, 1936).

Neumann, J. H., "Eighteenth-Century Linguistic Tastes as Exhibited in Sheridan's Edition of Swift", *American Speech*, XXI (1946), pp. 253-263.

——, "Jonathan Swift and the Vocabulary of English", *Modern Language Quarterly*, IV (1943), pp. 191-204.

Nice, Margaret M., "On the Size of Vocabularies", *American Speech*, II (1926), pp. 1-7.

Ohmann, Richard M., *Shaw: The Style and the Man* (Middletown, Conn., 1962).

Orrery, John, Earl of, *Remarks on the Life and Writings of Dr. Jonathan Swift* (London, 1752).

Orwell, George, *Selected Essays* (Harmondsworth, 1957).

Palmer, H. E., "Word Values", *Psyche*, IX (1928), pp. 13-25.

Pancoast, Henry S., ed., *Standard English Prose*, 2nd ed. (New York, 1905).

Pascal, Blaise, *L'Œuvre de Pascal*, ed. Jacques Chevalier (Paris, 1941).

Pater, Walter, *Appreciations: With an Essay on Style* (London, 1944).
Paulson, Ronald, *Theme and Structure in Swift's "Tale of a Tub"* (New Haven, 1960).
Perrin, Porter G., *Writer's Guide and Index to English*, 3rd ed. (Chicago, 1959).
Piaget, Jean, *The Language and Thought of the Child*, tr. Marjorie Gabain (New York, 1955).
Pike, Kenneth L., *Language* (Glendale, Calif., 1960).
Piozzi, Hester Lynch, *British Synonymy*, 2 vols. (London, 1794).
Plato, *The Republic*, tr. Paul Shorey, 2 vols. (Loeb Classical Library) (London, 1953).
Pons, Emile, Review of Teerink's *The History of John Bull, Revue Anglo-Américaine*, IV (1927), pp. 354-356.
——, *Swift: Les Années de Jeunesse et le "Conte du Tonneau"* (Strasbourg, 1925).
Pope, Alexander, *The Dunciad*, ed. James Sutherland (New York, 1943).
Potts, Abbie Findlay, "Butterflies and Butterfly-Hunters", *Bulletin of the New York Public Library*, LXIII (1959), pp. 148-152.
Pound, Louise, "Romaunt of the Rose; Additional Evidence That It Is Chaucer's", *Modern Language Notes*, XI (1896), pp. 97-102.
Poutsma, H., *A Grammar of Late Modern English*, 5 vols. (Groningen, 1914-1926).
Price, Derek J., ed., *The Equatorie of the Planetis* (Cambridge, 1955).
Price, Martin, *Swift's Rhetorical Art* (New Haven, 1953).
Queneau, Raymond, *Exercises de Style* (Paris, 1947).
Quintana, Ricardo, *The Mind and Art of Jonathan Swift* (New York, 1936).
Quintilian, *Institutio Oratoria*, tr. H. E. Butler, 4 vols. (Loeb Classical Library) (London, 1958).
Read, Herbert, *Collected Essays in Literary Criticism* (London, 1938).
——, *English Prose Style* (Boston, 1955).
——, and Bonamy Dobrée, eds., *The London Book of English Prose*, 2nd ed. (London, 1949).
Rhetorica ad Herennium, tr. Harry Caplan (Loeb Classical Library) (London, 1954).
Richards, I. A., *The Philosophy of Rhetoric* (London, 1936).
Rickert, Edith, *New Methods for the Study of Literature* (Chicago, 1927).
Ridenour, George M., *The Style of Don Juan* (New Haven, 1960).
Riffaterre, Michael, "Criteria for Style Analysis", *Word*, XV (1959), pp. 154-174.
——, "Réponse à M. Leo Spitzer: sur la Méthode Stylistique", *Modern Language Notes*, LXXIII (1958), pp. 474-480.
——, *Le Style des Pléiades de Gobineau* (New York, 1957).
——, "Stylistic Context", *Word*, XVI (1960), pp. 207-218.
Roberts, Paul, *English Sentences: Teacher's Manual* (New York, 1962).
——, "Fries's Group D", *Language*, XXXI (1955), pp. 20-24.
——, *Understanding English* (New York, 1958).
——, *Understanding Grammar* (New York, 1954).

Rockas, Leo, "The Description of Style: Dr. Johnson and His Critics", *Dissertation Abstracts*, XXI (1961), pp. 338-339.

Ross, John F., *Swift and Defoe* (Berkeley and Los Angeles, 1941).

Runion, Howard L., "An Objective Study of the Speech Style of Woodrow Wilson", *Speech Monographs*, III (1936), pp. 75-94.

Saintsbury, George,*Collected Essays and Papers, 1875-1920,* 4 vols. (London, 1923-1924).

——, *A History of English Prose Rhythm* (London, 1912).

Sandys, Sir John Edwin, *A History of Classical Scholarship,* 3 vols. (New York, 1958).

Sanford, Fillmore H., "Speech and Personality", *Psychological Bulletin,* XXXIX (1942), pp. 811-845.

Sapir, Edward, *Language* (New York, 1921).

Saporta, Sol, ed., *Psycholinguistics* (New York, 1961).

Sayce, Richard Anthony, *Style in French Prose* (London, 1953).

Schopenhauer, Arthur, *The Art of Literature,* tr. T. Bailey Saunders (Ann Arbor, Mich., 1960).

"A Science of Literature?" (anon, rev.), *Times Literary Supplement,* Jan. 20, 1961, p. 40.

Scott-Thomas, Lois M., "The Vocabulary of Jonathan Swift", *Dalhousie Review,* XXV (1946), pp. 442-447.

Sebeok, Thomas A., ed., *Style in Language* (Cambridge, Mass., 1960).

Seneca, *Ad Lucilium Epistulae Morales,* tr. Richard M. Gummere, 3 vols. (Loeb Classical Library) (London, 1925).

Shaw, Bernard, *Selected Plays,* 3 vols. (New York, 1948).

Shenstone, William, *The Works in Verse and Prose of William Shenstone, Esq.,* 5th ed., 3 vols. (London, 1777).

Sherbo, Arthur, "A Reply to Professor Fogel", *Bulletin of the New York Public Library,* LXIII (1959), pp. 367-371.

——, "Can *Mother Midnight's Comical Pocket Book* Be Attributed to Christopher Smart?" *Bulletin of the New York Public Library,* LXI (1957), pp. 373-382.

——, "The Uses and Abuses of Internal Evidence", *Bulletin of the New York Public Library,* LXIII (1959), pp. 5-22.

Sherman, L. A., *Analytics of Literature* (Boston, 1893).

——, "On Certain Facts and Principles in the Development of Form in Literature", *University of Nebraska Studies,* I (1892), pp. 337-366.

——, "Some Observations Upon the Sentence Lengths in English Prose", *University of Nebraska Studies,* I (1888), pp. 119-130.

Shipley, Joseph, ed., *Dictionary of World Literature.* New rev. ed. (Paterson, N. J., 1960).

Sidney, Sir Philip, *The Complete Works of Sir Philip Sidney,* ed. A. Feuillerat, 4 vols. (Cambridge, 1923).

Singer, Isidore, ed., *The Jewish Encyclopaedia, 12 vols.* (New York, 1901-1906).

Skinner, B. F., *Verbal Behavior* (New York, 1957).

Sledd, James, *A Short Introduction to English Grammar* (Chicago, 1959).

Smith, Adam, *Lectures on Rhetoric and Belles Lettres,* ed. John M. Lothian (London, 1963).

Söderlind, Johannes, *Verb Syntax in John Dryden's Prose,* 2 vols. (Uppsala, 1951, 1958).
Souter, Alexander, comp., *A Glossary of Later Latin to 600 A.D.* (Oxford, 1949).
The Spectator, ed. G. A. Aitken, 8 vols. (London, n.d.).
Spingarn, J. E., ed., *Critical Essays of the Seventeenth Century,* 3 vols. (Oxford, 1908).
Spitzer, Leo, "Explication de Texte", *Archivum Linguisticum,* III (1951), pp. 1-22.
——, *Linguistics and Literary History* (Princeton, 1948).
——, "Les Théories de la Stylistique", *Le Français Moderne,* XX (1952), pp. 165-168.
Spurgeon, Caroline, *Shakespeare's Imagery* (Cambridge, 1935).
Stanhope, Philip Henry Stanhope, Earl (Lord Mahon), *History of England from the Peace of Utrecht to the Peace of Versailles,* 5th ed., 7 vols. (London, 1858).
Starkman, Miriam Kosh, *Swift's Satire on Learning in "A Tale of a Tub"* (Princeton, 1950).
"The Statistics of Style" (anon. rev. of Ellegård), *Times Literary Supplement* (Jan. 25, 1963), p. 67.
*Steele, Richard, *The Englishman,* ed. R. Blanchard (Oxford, 1955).
*——, *Periodical Journalism, 1714-1716,* ed. R. Blanchard (Oxford, 1959).
Steiner, George, "Half Man, Half Beast" (rev. of John Updike's *The Centaur*), *Reporter,* XXVIII (1963), pp. 52-54.
Stephen, Leslie, *Swift* (London, 1882).
Sterne, Laurence, *Letters of Laurence Sterne* (Oxford, 1935).
Stevenson, Robert Louis, *Essays in the Art of Writing* (London, 1908).
Sturtevant, E. H., *An Introduction to Linguistic Science* (New Haven, 1960).
——, *Linguistic Change* (Chicago, 1961).
Sutherland, James R., *On English Prose* (Toronto, 1957).
——, *The Oxford Book of English Talk* (Oxford, 1953).
——, "Some Aspects of Eighteenth Century Prose", in *Essays on the Eighteenth Century Presented to David Nichol Smith,* ed. James R. Sutherland and F. P. Wilson (Oxford, 1945), pp. 94-110.
Sweet, Henry, *A New English Grammar,* 2 vols. (Oxford, 1891-1898).
Swift, Deane, *An Essay Upon the Life, Writings and Character of Dr. Jonathan Swift* (London, 1755).
Swift, Jonathan, *The Correspondence of Jonathan Swift,* ed. F. E. Ball, 6 vols. (London, 1910-1914).
——, *Drapier's Letters,* ed. Herbert Davis (Oxford, 1935).
——, *An Enquiry Into the Behavior of the Queen's Last Ministry,* ed. Irvin Ehrenpreis (Bloomington, Ind., 1956).
*——, *Gulliver's Travels and Selected Writings,* ed. J. Hayward (London, 1934).
——, *Journal to Stella,* ed. Harold Williams, 2 vols. (Oxford, 1948).
*——, *The Prose Writings of Jonathan Swift,* ed. Herbert Davis. 14 vols. (Oxford, 1939-in progress). [Referred to as *Works*; individual volumes listed below.]

Swift, Jonathan, *A Tale of a Tub*, ed. H. Davis (Oxford, 1939). [Vol. I.]
——, *Bickerstaff Papers*, ed. H. Davis (Oxford, 1940). [Vol. II.]
——, *The Examiner*, ed. H. Davis (Oxford, 1940). [Vol. III.]
——, *A Proposal for Correcting the English Tongue, Polite Conversation, Etc.*, ed. H. Davis and L. Landa (Oxford, 1957). [Vol. IV.]
——, *Miscellaneous and Autobiographical Pieces, Fragments and Marginalia*, ed. H. Davis (Oxford, 1962). [Vol. V.]
——, *Political Tracts, 1711-1713*, ed. H. Davis (Oxford, 1951). [Vol. VI.]
——, *The History of the Four Last Years of the Queen*, ed. H. Davis (Oxford, 1951). [Vol. VII.]
——, *Political Tracts, 1713-1719*, ed. H. Davis and I. Ehrenpreis (Oxford, 1953). [Vol. VIII.]
——, *Irish Tracts, 1720-1723, and Sermons*, ed. H. Davis (Oxford, 1948). [Vol. IX.]
——, *The Drapier's Letters*, ed. H. Davis (Oxford, 1941). [Vol. X.]
——, *Gulliver's Travels*, ed. H. Davis (Oxford, 1941). [Vol. XI.]
——, *Irish Tracts, 1728-1733*, ed. H. Davis (Oxford, 1955). [Vol. XII.]
——, *Directions to Servants and Miscellaneous Pieces*, ed. H. Davis (Oxford, 1959). [Vol. XIII.]
Taine, Hippolyte, *Histoire de la Littérature Anglaise*, 5 vols. (Paris, 1864).
Taube, Mortimer A., *Computers and Common Sense* (New York, 1961).
Taylor, W. D., *Jonathan Swift* (London, 1933).
Teerink, H., ed., *The History of John Bull* (Amsterdam, 1925).
Tempest, Norton R., *The Rhythm of English Prose* (Cambridge, 1930).
Thomson, James Alexander Ker., *Classical Influences on English Prose* (London, 1956).
Thomson, Robert, *The Psychology of Thinking* (Harmondsworth, 1959).
Thorndike, E. L. et al., "An Inventory of Grammatical Constructions, with Measures of Their Importance", *Teachers College Record*, (March, 1927), pp. 580-610.
Thornton, Harry and Agathe, *Time and Style* (London, 1962).
Thrall, William Flint and Addison Hibbard, *A Handbook to Literature*, Rev. and enl. C. Hugh Holman (New York, 1960).
Tillotson, Geoffrey, *Essays in Criticism and Research* (Cambridge, 1942).
Traill, H. D., *Sterne* (London, 1882).
Trevelyan, G. M., *An Autobiography and Other Essays* (London, 1949).
Trollope, Anthony, *An Autobiography* (Berkeley and Los Angeles, 1947).
Tucker, Susie I., *English Examined* (Cambridge, 1961).
Tucker, W. J., "Irish Masters of Prose", *Catholic World*, CXLIV (1937), pp. 712-717.
Ullmann, Stephen, *Language and Style* (Oxford, 1964).
——, *Principles of Semantics*, 2nd ed. (Oxford, 1957).
——, "Psychologie et Stylistique", *Journal de Psychologie*, XLVI (1953), pp. 133-156.
——, *Style in the French Novel* (Cambridge, 1957).
Van Doorn, C., *An Investigation Into the Character of Jonathan Swift* (Amsterdam, 1931).
Vernon, P. E., "The Matching Method Applied to Investigations of Personality", *Psychological Bulletin*, XXXIII (1936), pp. 149-177.

Vinay, J. P. and J. Darbelnet, *Stylistique Comparée du Français et de l'Anglais* (London and Paris, 1958).

Voltaire, *Letters Concerning the English Nation* (London, 1733).

Wagner, R. L., *Supplément Bibliographique à l'Introduction à la Linguistique Française* (Geneva, 1955).

Watkins, W. B. C., *Perilous Balance* (Princeton, 1939).

Webster's New International Dictionary of the English Language, 2nd ed. (Springfield, Mass., 1954).

Webster's Third New International Dictionary (Springfield, Mass., 1961).

Wellek, René and Austin Warren, *Theory of Literature* (New York, 1949).

Whately, Richard, *The Elements of Rhetoric* (London, 1828).

White, Eugene, *Fanny Burney, Novelist* (Hamden, Conn., 1960).

Whitehall, Harold, *Structural Essentials of English* (New York, 1961).

Whitehead, A. N., *The Organisation of Thought* (London, 1917).

Whitridge, Arnold and John Wendell Dodds, *An Oxford Anthology of English Prose* (New York, 1937).

Williams, C. B., "A Note on the Statistical Analysis of Sentence-Length as a Criterion of Literary Style", *Biometrika,* XXXI (1940), pp. 356-361.

Williams, Harold, *Dean Swift's Library* (Cambridge, 1932).

——, *The Text of "Gulliver's Travels"* (Cambridge, 1952).

Williamson, George, *The Senecan Amble* (London, 1951).

Wimsatt, W. K., *The Prose Style of Samuel Johnson* (New Haven, 1941).

Winter, Ralph Dana, "English Function Words and Content Words: A Quantitative Investigation." Unpubl. Ph.D. Diss. Cornell, 1953.

Yule, G. U., "On Sentence Length as a Statistical Characteristic of Style in Prose; with Application to Two Cases of Disputed Authorship", *Biometrika,* XXX (1938), pp. 363-390.

——, *The Statistical Study of Literary Vocabulary* (Cambridge, 1944).

Zickgraf, Gertraut, *Swifts Stilforderungen und Stil* (Marburg, 1940).

Zipf, G. K., *Human Behavior and the Principle of Least Effort* (Cambridge, Mass., 1949).

——, *The Psycho-Biology of Language* (Boston, 1935).

——, *Selected Studies of the Principle of Relative Frequency in Language* (Cambridge, Mass., 1932).

INDEX

310   INDEX

Burke, Kenneth, 79
Burney, Fanny, 57
Bury, J. B., 140 (n.12)
Busemann, F., 198 (n.133), 199
Butler, Samuel (novelist), 29, 65
  (n.108), 84 (n.5), 124
Byron, Lord, 40

*Cambridge History of English Lit-
  erature*, 29
Campbell, George, 84, 123, 126
  (n.13), 271
Carlyle, Thomas, 20 (n.2)
Carroll, John B., 69 (n.126)
Carter, C. W., 156 (n.65)
Cattell, Raymond B., 55 (n.61)
Caxton, William, 62, 125 (n.11)
Chaucer, Geoffrey, 42, 71
Chesterfield, Earl of, 45 (n.21)
Chretien, C. Douglas, 71 (n.134)
Cicero, 46, 86
Ciceronian style; *see* style, types
  and periods
Claudel, Paul, 120 (n.156)
Coleridge, Samuel T., 25, 122, 181
computers: electronic data-proc-
  essing, 72; encoding, 151; IBM
  1620, 207 (n.151); program, 142-
  143; *see also* quantitative proce-
  dure
concordances, 58, 72
connectives, classification, 128-
  129; *see also* style features;
  Swift, style
Conrad, Joseph, 57
constants, linguistic; *see* language
"continuator"; *see* Swift, style
Cooke, Jacob E., 237 (n.1)
copia verborum, 86-87
correctness; *see* Swift, style, reputation
Cressot, Marcel, 65
Croce, Benedetto, 45, 48-49, 51, 66
Croll, Morris W., 63 (n.97)
Curle, Richard, 57 (n.70)
Curll, Edmund, 35
Curme, George O., 122, 129 (n.18),
  151 (n.43), 175 (n.97), 177
Curtis, Lewis P., 243 (n.22)

Dampier, William, 26
D'Avenant, Charles, 22
Davie, Donald, 39
Davis, Herbert, 34, 36, 38-39, 95
  (n.47), 112 (n.127), 238, 239 (n.
  6), 272 (n.2)
Defoe, Daniel, 21 (n.3), 26, 88-91
Delany, Patrick, 22 (n.7)
Demetrius, 47 (n.32)
Deming, William Edwards, 279 (n.
  2)
Denniston, J. D., 123 (n.5), 134 (n.
  38)
De Quincey, Thomas, 26, 59
diction; *see* style, definition
dictionaries: Latin, 42 (nn.11, 12),
  Oxford, 42, 129 (n.19), 151 (n.
  43); *Webster's*, 41, 151 (n.43)
Dobrée, Bonamy, 85 (n.9), 118 (n.
  151)
Dryden, John, 20 (n.2), 26, 31, 38,
  72 (n.141), 88-89

Eddy, W. A., 87 (n.19)
editorial revision, 286
Ehrenpreis, Irvin, 80 (n.14), 135
  (n.41)
Elderton, W. P., 71-72
Eliot, T. S., 171 (n.91)
Ellegård, Alvar, 77 (n.7), 83 (n.20),
  169 (n.86), 237 (n.2), 286, 290
Emerson, Ralph W., 67
Equatorie of the Planetis, 71
etc.; *see* Swift, style, seriation
Euclid, 137
Everett, C. W., 237 (n.2)
Ewald, William B., Jr., 37, 87 (n.
  20), 243 (n.23)
Eysenck, H. J., 81 (n.18)

Faulkner, George, 112 (n.127),
  238-239
Federalist, The, 72, 77 (n.7), 157
  (n.69), 237 (n.1), 286
Fielding, Henry, 21 (n.2), 38
figurative description of style, 27
  (n.25); *see also* style, definition
figures of speech, 45, 85; *see also*
  style, features